# Caribbean Revolutions
# and Revolutionary Theory

# Caribbean Revolutions and Revolutionary Theory

An Assessment of Cuba,
Nicaragua and Grenada

Brian Meeks

**University of the West Indies Press**
Barbados • Jamaica • Trinidad and Tobago

University of the West Indies Press
1A Aqueduct Flats   Mona
Kingston 7   Jamaica

05  04  03  02  01      5  4  3  2  1

CATALOGUING IN PUBLICATION DATA

Meeks, Brian.
   Caribbean revolutions and revolutionary theory : an assessment of Cuba, Nicaragua
and Grenada / Brian Meeks.
   p. cm.
   Originally published: London: Macmillan 1993.
   Includes bibliographical references and index.
   ISBN: 976-640-104-7
   1. Revolutions – Caribbean Area – History – 20th century. 2. Revolutions – Case
studies. 3. Caribbean Area – History – 1945–. 4. Cuba – History – 1959–. 5.
Nicaragua – History – 1979–1990. 6. Grenada – History – 1979–1983. I. Title.
   F2183.M44 2001          972.905/220

Cover design by Errol Stennett

Printed in Jamaica by Stephenson's Lithopress

# Contents

# Preface to the Second Edition

Good books do not need prefaces. I write this, therefore, not as a preface but as a celebration. I celebrate the fact that the author, aside from writing an interesting and relevant account of revolution in three countries, does two things of larger import: he has broken with parochialism and he writes without polemics.

How refreshing it is to read a book which makes a clear break with the stultifying parochialism of so much of the social science writing on and in the West Indies. Meeks does this through enormous thematic breadth, from Cuba to Nicaragua to Grenada. The book is Caribbean-wide in scope thus. It is a lamentable fact that too few social scientists in the West Indies seem to pay any heed to Gordon K. Lewis's admonition cum scolding when he asked rhetorically, 'What does he know about the Caribbean, who only knows about the West Indies?' It is time that the long overdue talk about regionalism, of the need to broaden and deepen our intra-regional associations, be accompanied by the kind of scholarship that advances those worthy goals. The reasons are self-evident.

Because there is no linguistic or cultural 'core' to this complex region, the only truly illuminating approach is the comparative one. Interestingly enough, the record of comparative work has been considerably better in disciplines other than the social sciences. There have been many models to follow. In history, Guyanese Elsa Goveia's monumental study of comparative slave laws and practices or Trinidadian Eric Williams's detailed comparisons of plantations in the English, Spanish and French Caribbean are exemplary cases. In literature, who can ignore that splendid piece of comparative literary criticism, equally good as social science, of Jamaican Gabriel Coulthard, *Race and Colour in Caribbean Literature*?

What is it, then, with the social sciences? The language barrier is certainly one cause. Beyond that, might it be that the demand for causal explanation, as distinct from historical or ethnographic description, with its strict rules of validation, makes social science analysis less amenable to cross-cultural studies? Could it be that the progress towards regional integration has advanced much more in the economic field than it has in the intellectual and academic?

Be the answer as it may, Meeks quite evidently lets none of it deter him. He engages the analysis of revolution with gusto and without the intellectual hubris of the 'End of History' advocates or those who perpetually predict revolution. Meeks does find in Marxist and socialist thought important elements that speak to Man's and Woman's perennial search for justice and ultimate liberation. He accepts this as theoretically useful, not as an article of faith. Similarly, from positivism he adopts the methodology necessary for a cause-and-effect analysis that is empirically grounded. This is necessary because he has chosen the most demanding of all genres: comparative analysis.

Comparison – let it be said up front – involves more than merely juxtaposing case studies for the sake of describing distinctions. It involves the construction of a conceptual framework within which a particular effect – the phenomenon to be explained – can be studied across cases in pursuit of possible similarities, or, indeed, dissimilarities, of causation. There are, of course, various ways to approach this task. The method chosen by Meeks, that of J.S. Mill's Method of Agreement, is not only amply explained in the text, it actually works splendidly in his analysis of the phenomenon of 'revolution' in three different societies. The similarities and dissimilarities between these Caribbean cases are probed, uniformities are noted by Meeks who then lets the unfolding story provide the explanations for each. It is a good approach which combines analytical rigour with ease and clarity of exposition.

It is precisely the theme of revolution that brings us to the second area in which this book breaks with West Indian practice: it is neither polemical in tone nor deterministic in theory. Meeks is neither preaching to the converted nor in pursuit of converts. He has read widely in the rich and variegated vineyard of theories of revolution and, consistent with his evident intellectual independence, he has reaped the best. Meeks uses theory as building blocks to new insights, not as mortar to further seal existing explanatory structures. Quite evidently attracted to Theda Skocpol's state-centric approach to social change and revolution, he is neither intellectually nor ideologically wedded to her interpretations but rather pursues a series of 'post-Skocpol' formulations which he finds useful. The reason for this theoretical flexibility lies in his broader epistemological view. History, says Meeks, is open-ended and consequently one's theoretical approach has to be eclectic. Within a solid post-Marxian framework which highlights the geopolitical realities of asymmetries of development and power, he also keeps a sharp eye on the state and the interests of political elites and their ideologies. Again, ideology is not mechanically or deterministically bound solely to economic interests but can be sustained by other factors, including a variety of beliefs, be they nationalist, religious or more broadly ethnic. There is also a cumulative effect that has to be reckoned with: each revolution influences the next, not mechanically or teleologically but through the interpreting eyes of major protagonists. He returns the revolutionary to the study of revolutions. In short, to Meeks revolutions are like multilevel chess games, 'like life in all its multiple dimensions' with 'incalculable options and choices at any single moment'.

It is wonderful, therefore, that the new edition of this enlightening and path-breaking book is being produced in the region for it is there fundamentally that Meeks's ideas need to be reflected on and discussed. It is in anticipation of that reflection and those discussions that I celebrate this its reappearance.

Anthony P. Maingot
Florida International University

# Acknowledgements

Many persons and institutions helped to bring this idea to fruition. The Association of Commonwealth Universities and the British Council provided a Commonwealth Fellowship which allowed me to spend a memorable, peaceful and productive year at the University of Cambridge. The University of the West Indies gave me leave and the Department of Government provided the support and the space for intellectual growth. The Centre of Latin American Studies at Cambridge helped, somewhat ironically, to steer me away from narrowly anglophone concerns and to recognise that we are only a part of a much wider American project. To all these I owe many thanks.

At the individual level, I wish to thank especially John Dunn, whose critical but positive reading of my first chapter gave me the necessary confidence to press on and finish the entire manuscript; David Lehmann and David Brading, both of the Centre of Latin American Studies at Cambridge who were my hosts and who listened patiently to half-formed ideas at various seminars; my colleagues at the Department of Government, Mona, the most accommodating people I have ever met, and especially Trevor Munroe, Rupert Lewis and Carl Stone, for providing logistical and intellectual support; Alistair Hennessy of the Centre for Caribbean Studies at Warwick University, who thought my manuscript worth publishing and pursued it; and last, but certainly not least, my dear wife Patsy who endured my bouts of silence and absent-mindedness, while I tried to decipher Unger's opacity in the late January chill.

# Introduction:
# Historical conjuncture
# and paradigm change

It has already become almost too trite and obvious to say that while not the end of history,[1] recent international events collectively signify the most important watershed in the postwar world. The pre-Christmas breaching of the Berlin Wall and the November 1990 unification of the German state; the overwhelming trend for plural democracies to break through first in Poland and then more rapidly in the rest of Eastern Europe; and, the break-up of the Soviet Union and the demise of communism[2] all indicate that the order of the European state system which has remained essentially stable for the past four decades, is once again in a state of dissolution. Beyond all this lies the emerging European super state which will be one step closer in 1992 when the European market is unified.

Europe is once again looking inward. While financial pundits discuss the potential markets in the underdeveloped consumer economies of Eastern Europe, primary goods producers in the formerly colonial countries of the African, Caribbean and Pacific (ACP) group battle against the likelihood that the new arrangements will exclude them from their preferential trading position in the European Market. There is increasing debate for and against the creation of a 'white laager', of a united Europe erecting an impenetrable barrier around its borders to prevent immigration from the Third World. The United States, faced with the possibility of a less conspicuous role in European affairs and with a gargantuan budget deficit preventing even the contemplation of a Marshall-type plan, has instead opted for gouging out aid for Eastern Europe from its traditional Third World allocations. The USSR which, for much of the postwar period, appeared to many in the Third World if not a 'natural ally' then a useful foil against the overarching power of the United States, has in the light of overwhelming domestic considerations and changing ideological perspectives, shifted its focus inward and away from the south. In the developing countries the oft-mooted danger of bi-polar triumphalism – the convergence of the north against or without the south – is now expressed as a real danger.

In Europe, at least, despite the resurgence of nationalism and economic difficulties in the East, there is unbounded optimism for a future both more peaceful and potentially more plentiful. From the Third World perspective, there is a deep current of pessimism. If Gerard Chaliand could have written in sober tones more than 15 years ago that 'Third Worldism' – the euphoria

*1*

which emerged out of decolonisation and the revolutionary victories of the fifties and sixties – was a myth,[3] then events of the last decade, with the possible exception of the growing struggle to dismantle apartheid in South Africa, have decisively buried any vision of Third World Utopia.

The project of Third World revolution has witnessed blow after blow against its credibility. The genocidal murders by the Khmer Rouge on the killing fields of Kampuchea in the name of socialism; the brutal militaristic 'Marxism–Leninism' practised by the Mengistu regime in Ethiopia; the bloodletting between rival factions of the Marxist regime in South Yemen; and the almost medieval displays of religious chauvinism in Iran coupled with its sanguinary war with Iraq, have done tremendous if not irrecoverable damage to both revolution and socialism as liberating and humanitarian visions. With this recent background, the violent repression of the pro-democracy demonstrators in Tienanmen Square in 1989 was a predictable if poignant reminder that even the Chinese regime, which many saw two decades ago as following an alternative and better path to socialism, was incapable of tolerating even localised, student-led demonstrations within a supposedly consolidated political system.

In the Caribbean and Latin America, other, if less world–traumatic events have served a similar end. The collapse of the tiny Grenada Revolution with the elimination of one part of the Marxist leadership by the other, reinforced, this time for the Caribbean, the image of the revolution as an unthinking animal, devouring its children. Grenada's significance went far beyond its importance as a micro-state, because it was the first revolution carried out by black English-speakers, with direct lines of communication to the major black and West Indian population centres in North America and Great Britain and because it presented the United States for the first time since the Vietnamese War with an opportunity to reassert its hegemonic tendencies, by invading a state and overthrowing a regime which had already been shattered.[4]

In El Salvador, the guerrilla insurgency which has surprised many by remaining viable and with the ability to launch occasional offensives, has nonetheless in the face of a determined oligarchy backed by the United States, been unable to take power.[5] The result has become an open-ended bloodbath with no immediate end in sight, although the prospects of an outright FMLN victory are increasingly unlikely in the face of the changing political landscape of Eastern Europe and, closer home, the electoral defeat of the Sandinistas in neighbouring Nicaragua.

In Cuba, the inability to generate a process of self-sustained growth, with concomitant economic dependence on the Soviet Union, together with the unwillingness of the leadership to look beyond the centralist and authoritarian framework of the sixties and seventies, has contributed to a regime which is increasingly out of step not only with progressive currents in the rest of Latin America, but with democratic socialist trends in Eastern Europe and in the Soviet Union. Cuba is now less of a vision and a model than it has ever been since the 1959 revolution. The irony of the present moment is captured in the bizarre fact that the Cuban Government prevented the distribution of some Soviet magazines and journals, presumably on the grounds of their counter-revolutionary content.[6] Bureaucracy and orthodoxy seem indeed to have migrated from Moscow to find temporary residence in Havana.

Only in Nicaragua, if in an extremely distorted way, did the possibility of a more democratic, less authoritarian vision of revolution survive. The Nicaraguan economy had been wrecked by war, disinvestment, US sanctions and no doubt a degree of mismanagement, but the revolution survived for many years despite the unremitting pressure from the United States. The defeat of the Sandinistas by the pro-American UNO coalition in the 25 February 1990 election signalled a new stage for that process. Unlike Grenada, where the revolution had been crushed, the FSLN remains the largest single party, has powerful influence in the state, and has emerged, thanks to the very act of conceding defeat, with enhanced prestige and standing within and outside the country. The final act of the revolution has not been written, but even at this stage, the fact of a revolutionary government conceding power on the basis of an electoral defeat in free and fair elections, has established a powerful precedent for an alternative possibility of radical social change coupled to a genuinely democratic political process.

It is not surprising, then, given this bleak landscape, that at the theoretical level, relative if guarded hope in the future of the newly-independent countries in general and the revolutionary states in particular, has descended into despair. Theda Skocpol, for example, perhaps the most significant of the recent theorists on revolution, could remark with some optimism in 1979 that the Chinese road of a mass-mobilising party state represented a less coercive and potentially more democratic path to revolution than the Soviet model.[7] A decade later, however, Skocpol appeared to have shifted emphasis, placing less importance on the likely democratic content of revolutionary regimes and more on their potential as mass mobilisers for war-making purposes. She concludes, writing in 1988, that:

> many social-revolutionary regimes have excelled at channelling enhanced popular participation into protracted international warfare. Because of the ways revolutionary leaders mobilize popular support in the course of struggles for state power, the emerging regimes can tackle mobilization for war better than any other task, including the promotion of national economic development.[8]

While this does not depart *tout court* from her earlier path-breaking study, the emphasis is totally different. Then, Skocpol saw state-building elites as moving in potentially different directions. Now, that optimism is largely absent and replaced by a conclusion which suggests the inevitability of military options. In the Third World and interested academic circles, there is an absence of explanations for and answers to the emerging situation. On the left, hope in the emergent state forms of the sixties and seventies has been shattered by concrete experiences of corruption, mismanagement, authoritarianism and outright defeat.[9] Room for political manoeuvre and flexibility which seemed to be available in the earlier period, has been eroded or eliminated by deteriorating terms of trade and massive and growing debt burdens. Attempts at concerted action have either petered out or yielded little, and neither have the recent US and IMF initiatives to reform the structure of the debt appeared to yield much success.

At the theoretical level, the present period has been characterised as one of 'paradigm change',[10] reflected in Latin America in the failure of dependency theory – the dominant paradigm of the seventies – to provide adequate answers or solutions to the present crisis. But, equally, other 'models' which sought to explain and prescribe, have come to nought. Most notably, 'socialist orientation', or the 'non-capitalist path' which in the mid-seventies influenced a range of left-wing parties and governments, turned out to have been severely flawed. Its very premise, that the balance of forces in the world was shifting decisively in favour of socialism, is seen from the present, ludicrous at best. Given the rapidity with which dominant left positions have lost credibility in recent years, it is perhaps even more appropriate to describe the moment as one of 'paradigm collapse', where no clear alternatives, certainly from the left of the intellectual spectrum, have been able to gain similar status.

There is need for the theoretical re-examination of the directions for Third World development in a context where the postwar European and inter-states system is in a process of reorganisation and in which the newer independent countries of the Third World are in a moment of intense crisis at the political and economic levels and more critically, at the level of ideas. This book is a modest and incremental step in that direction. By tracing the historical narrative through a small cluster of Caribbean countries which have experienced revolutionary upheaval and transformation, the aim is to examine the meaning of revolution and the likelihood of meaningful and substantial change occurring via this route. As John Dunn points out,[11] revolutions raise all the key issues which concern the discipline of politics, so, in a sense, the study of revolution is inevitably a study of politics and of how things change.

This is an admittedly exploratory study to examine whether the concept of revolution remains a useful category to explain political change and whether revolution as myth retains its potential as a liberating vision for intellectuals and countless scores of deprived people in the Third World. The first chapter attempts to trace the history of the concept of revolution and to pick up the various strands of the debate as it developed particularly in the latter part of the twentieth century. The aim is to arrive at an alternative approach to the concept of revolution and an accompanying series of constructs which can then be applied in the second part of the study. In the following chapters, three Caribbean countries which have experienced revolutionary situation and rule will be compared to suggest the usefulness and facility of an alternative approach to the phenomenon. They are Cuba, Grenada and Nicaragua. The justification for these cases and the methodology which will be used in comparing them, will emerge in the first part of the study.

## Notes

1. Francis Fukuyama's controversial neo-Hegelian view that the collapse of communism signals the triumph of the Western 'idea' and the 'end of history', was faced within months of its statement with the hard fact of the Iraqi invasion of Kuwait. This suggests that in the South, at least, the news that history has ended has not yet arrived. See Francis Fukuyama, 'The End of History?', *The National Interest*, Summer 1989.
2. It is interesting to note, in retrospect, how few realistic commentators predicted the collapse of the system in Eastern Europe. Huntington writing in 1984, for example, felt that the likelihood of democracy emerging in Eastern Europe was virtually nil. Although his conditions for such a likelihood – the weakening of the Soviet Union through war, domestic upheaval or economic collapse – was dead on target, he ruled out such an event as highly unlikely. See Samuel P. Huntington, 'Will More Countries Become Democratic?', *Political Science Quarterly*, Vol. 99, no. 2, Summer 1984, p. 217.
3. See Gerard Chaliand, *Revolution in the Third World* (Brighton: Harvester Press, 1977), p. 185.
4. For reasonable accounts of the legal and political arguments surrounding the invasion of Grenada, see William C. Gilmore, *The Grenada Intervention: Analysis and Documentation*, (London, New York: Mansell, 1984) and M. Shahabuddeen, *The Conquest of Grenada: Sovereignty in the Periphery* (Georgetown: University of Guyana, 1986).
5. See for an account of the background and some features of the Salvadorean situation, Walter Lafeber, *Inevitable Revolutions: The United States in Central America* (New York, London: Norton, 1984).
6. Both *Novedades de Moscu* and *Sputnik* were banned on 4 August 1989 on the grounds that they were 'paving the way to undermine Leninism' by the publication of distorted reports about Cuba. See *Latin American Weekly Review*, 17 August 1989.
7. See Theda Skocpol, *States and Social Revolutions* (Cambridge: Cambridge University Press, 1979), pp. 278–9.
8. Theda Skocpol, 'Social Revolutions and Mass Military Mobilization', in

*World Politics*, Vol. XI, no. 2, January 1988, p. 168.

9.  See in particular, Cy Thomas's study, *The Rise of the Authoritarian State in Peripheral Societies* (New York: MR, 1986).

10. See, for example, Magnus Blomstrum and Bjorn Hettne, *Development Theory in Transition* (London: Zed, 1984), p. 2, and David Lehmann, *Democracy and Development in Latin America* (Cambridge: Polity, 1990).

11. See John Dunn, *Modern Revolutions: An Introduction to the Analysis of a Political Phenomenon* (Cambridge: Cambridge University Press, 1989 [1972]), p. xvi.

# CHAPTER 1 | Revolution as theory

Revolutions are the locomotives of history.
Karl Marx

It takes a revolution
To make a solution
Too much confusion
So much frustration
Bob Marley

## *The idea of revolution: main threads in the debate*

The first recorded analysis of revolution as a phenomenon is widely accepted as having been made by Aristotle (384–322 BC), who is also generally accepted as being the first person to seriously attempt to approach the study of politics with scientific rigour.[1] He spoke of *stasis* with *metaboli politeias* or a violent coup with a change of constitution.[2] The term *rivoluzione* first appears in its modern sense in the fourteenth-century Italian city-states to describe the replacement of an oligarchic regime by a democratic one. While, however, accepting the concept of political change, this notion did not conceive of a change in the social order, did not involve the active participation of the lower classes and was most critically seen as a cyclical event, the return as a result of natural movements to an earlier, more peaceful time.[3]

It was the occurrence of the French Revolution of 1789 which gave impetus to a new concept of revolution, which, as David Close suggests, contained two radical assumptions. The first of these was the view that society could be completely overhauled without necessarily referring to the past. Thus, after 1789, 'revolutionaries . . . looked to posterity not to tradition for justification'.[4] The second assumption was the equally radical notion that inequality was not inherent and that there existed such a thing as universal human rights. Thus, emerging out of, and closely connected to the French Revolution and its ideas, the concept of revolution has been intimately tied to the view that mankind could change society, that this change was in the direction of progressive steps toward the improvement of mankind's condition, and that this progression was in the direction of greater equality which was justifiable in natural law.

In his description of the Marquis de Condorcet's *Outline of a Historical Picture of the Human Mind,* John Dunn captures some of the main features of this new outlook. Condorcet, he points out:

> foresaw a future of expanding wealth and increasing economic
> and political equality generated above all by the expansion of
> educational opportunity and by a steady diminution in the hold
> of superstition at all levels of society. He saw existing inequal-
> ity and poverty as a product of the manipulative egoism of elites
> which were prepared to keep the majority in a state of abject
> superstition in order to preserve their own political control.[5]

That the French Revolution had also cemented a view of revolution itself as the vehicle for progress is captured in De Maistre's comment that the counter-revolution would not be the revolution in reverse, but the opposite of revolution.[6]

But it was not until after another European revolutionary impulse that a theory would emerge which would have the greatest impact on revolution both as theory and as a practice. Karl Marx's and Frederick Engels' *Communist Manifesto* was published in 1848, the same year as a series of democratic revolutions rocked the European continent. Building on the notion of history as the progress of humanity, Marx used Hegelian dialectics as the best methodology to explain the inner logic of historical development, while at the same time turning Hegelianism on its head and grounding it in political economy.[7]

For Marx, history moved through a series of stages characterised by modes of production which described a certain relationship of the forces of production (technology and techniques), to the relations of production (classes which emerge within the given mode). According to Marx,

> At a certain stage of their development the material forces of
> production in society come into conflict with the existing rela-
> tions of production, or – what is but a legal expression for the
> same thing – with the property relations with which they had
> been at work before. From forms of development of the forces
> of production these relations turn into their fetters. Then comes
> the period of social revolution.[8]

Marx and Engels identified five stages in the development of human society – communalism, slavery, feudalism, capitalism and socialism. Capitalism, the stage typical of nineteenth-century Europe, would eventually be replaced by socialism, the prelude to class-free or communist society. It is interesting to recall one of Marx's better-known statements on how capitalism would eventually be destroyed as an indicator of the overall logic of his theory. In the *Communist Manifesto* he posits:

> The essential condition for the sway of the bourgeois class is the formation and augmentation of capital; the condition for capital is wage labour. Wage labour rests exclusively on competition between the labourers. The advance of industry, whose voluntary promoter is the bourgeoisie, replaces the isolation of the labourers due to competition, by their revolutionary combination due to association. The development of modern industry, therefore, cuts from under its feet the very foundation on which the bourgeoisie produces and appropriates products. What the bourgeoisie, therefore produces, above all, is its own grave diggers. Its fall and the victory of the proletariat are inevitable.[9]

Four features of the Marxian approach need to be highlighted for our purposes. The first is the continuation and development of the late eighteenth-century concept of progress inherent in the successive and progressive stages of development mentioned above, although it should be noted that Marx acknowledged in the very beginning of the *Manifesto* that class struggle could end either in revolutionary reconstitution or in the 'common ruin of the contending classes'.[10] And both Marx and Engels at various times, most outstandingly in relation to the peculiarities of the Russian situation, saw the possibility of short-cuts or alternative routes to socialism.[11] The second feature, quite obviously a continuation of the positions inherited from the French Revolution, is the view captured sufficiently in the above quotations, that it was the act of revolution itself which would be the means by which systemic change would be accomplished, allowing the transition from one mode of production to another. The third feature, and central issue of a recent and continuing debate, is the emphasis placed on economics as the ultimately determining factor in history. While recent reinterpretations of Marx have tried to adhere to Marxist theory while making out a case for the relative autonomy of the state[12] and for the area of ideas and the cognitive,[13] Engels' letter to Bloch in September 1890 is quite clear in its basic position. Political and juridical forms, theories and ideas, etc., may help determine the form of history, but the ultimately determining factor is the 'production and reproduction of real life'.[14] In other words, it is explicitly stated that it is in those societies where the economic conditions have developed sufficiently that transition from one mode of production to another, via revolution, would be most likely. The final factor for our purposes is the recognition that it is the proletariat, the peculiar social class produced by the economic and social imperatives of developed capitalism, which is the single truly revolutionary class able to grow, consolidate, attain a measure of class consciousness and overthrow capitalism.

Ever since the French Revolution, theorising on the topic of revolution has to a significant degree rotated around the theme of whether revolution represented barbarity, best exemplified in Edmund Burke's study of revolutionary France,[15] or as exemplified in Condorcet's writings and, of course, Marx, whether it signified progress. Since 1848 and the emergence of Marxism, this debate has been altered to rotate around a further pole, as to whether Marxism, the *raison d'être* of many of the contemporary revolutionary movements, was an adequate and sufficient explanation of reality and whether the revolutions of this century with their accompanying Marxist credentials, represented the progressive development described by Marx and Condorcet or what Burke described as the descent into barbarity. From the perspective of the hopeful, of those who saw and continue to see the need to change society for the better, an image of revolution has persisted, which is adequately captured by S. N. Eisenstadt:

> First is the violent change of the existing political regime, its bases of legitimation and its symbols. Second is the displacement of the incumbent elite or ruling class by another. Third are far-reaching changes in all institutional spheres – primarily in economic and class relations – leading to the modernization of most aspects of social life, to economic development and industrialization, and to growing centralization in the political sphere. Fourth is a radical break with the past. . . . Fifth . . ., that they will create or generate a new man.[16]

Revolutionary events of the twentieth century have, however, brought into question most of the tenets of Marxist theory and increasingly undermined the view that it represents progress in any unilinear interpretation of that concept. Among the main historical contradictions, the fact that, generally speaking, revolutions have not taken place in the developed centres of capitalism, is of primary importance. At best, revolutions have taken place in weak secondary capitalist countries with developed industry but backward rural sectors, as in the case of Russia; in formerly colonial primary goods producing states, such as Cuba or Nicaragua; in semi-colonial countries with highly distorted capitalist economies, such as China; or in the least developed countries in the world, as in Ethiopia or Mozambique in southern Africa. Where attempts were made to build socialism in the relatively developed parts of Eastern Europe, this has been the result not of internal revolution, but the existence of a favourable military balance of forces for experimentation due to the presence of the Soviet Red Army after the Second World War.

The second major contradiction, and one which will be looked at in greater depth later on in the study, stems from the first. The main force in the majority of twentieth-century revolutions has not been the proletariat, but the peasantry – perhaps an inevitability in countries where the peasantry constituted the vast majority of the population, but nonetheless one which requires explanation from adherents to the Marxist approach.

Third, Marx saw socialism as an interim measure – the Dictatorship of the Proletariat – which would be followed by the withering away of the state and communist society, thus:

> As soon as there is no longer any social class to be held in subjection, as soon as class rule and the individual struggle for existence based upon our present anarchy in production, with the collisions and excesses arising from these, are removed, nothing more remains to be repressed, and a special repressive force, a state, is no longer necessary . . . . State interference in social relations becomes, in one domain or another, superfluous, and then dies out of itself . . . . The state is not 'abolished'. It dies out.[17]

But socialist states, beginning with the Soviet Union, have consistently been engaged in a process of state-building, and huge authoritarian structures have been established, with various degrees of coercion.[18] More critically, centrally-planned, bureaucratic socialist economies have not been able to solve key economic questions, particularly in the areas of agriculture, high technology and consumer goods production.[19] Finally, the turn of the decade, 1989–1990, witnessed the internal collapse of socialism in Eastern Europe and the end of the Soviet Union itself.

Finally, but not of least importance, unlike Marx's and Engels' mid-nineteenth-century prognostications and Lenin's even more urgent statements on the imminent collapse of imperialism prior to the First World War, capitalism not only survives, but has shown the remarkable capacity not only to overcome serious crises, but to retain its functional viability. And, as the victory of the right in the elections in the German Democratic Republic would suggest, it has retained a certain popularity based on the reality of relative economic success. The remarkable feature of Marxism in the twentieth century is that despite these contra-factual developments, it has, at least until very recently, retained a remarkable degree of popularity as a mode of explanation and a guide to action for numerous movements and millions of people throughout the world.

## *Theories of revolution*

Three waves of theory are generally accepted to have arisen since the eighteenth-century Enlightenment and the French Revolution, and all have clearly been responses to successive revolutionary impulses which have had global significance. The first wave of normative theorists immediately preceded or emerged in the aftermath of the French events and include Burke, Hegel and of most importance, if somewhat later, Marx and Engels.[20] A second wave, largely if not exclusively responding to the Bolshevik Revolution, developed after 1917. Among its most significant representatives are Crane Brinton, George Pettee, and G. LeBon.[21] A third group arose in response to the post-Second World War revolutionary impulses which have largely originated in the Third World, and includes Ted Gurr, Chalmers Johnson, Samuel Huntington, Neil Smelser and Charles Tilly as leading members.[22] Since the mid-seventies, a new and important trend critical of this third wave has developed, including Theda Skocpol, Kay Trimberger and S. N. Eisenstadt.[23]

Jack Goldstone's categorisation is perhaps, more useful for our purposes, as he looks at theoretical developments in the twentieth century, excluding the more normative thrusts of the previous one hundred years. His approach includes Brinton, *et. al.* in the first wave; Gurr, Johnson, Tilly etc. in the second and Skocpol, Trimberger and Eisenstadt in the third.[24] The approach adopted here is a modification of Goldstone's. The first and second waves remain essentially the same. The third wave, however, is a logical sequence of thought, which in terms of temporal sequence, overlaps with the second. Thus it begins with Barrington Moore's *Social Origins of Dictatorship and Democracy,*[25] is followed by Eric Wolf's *Peasant Wars of the Twentieth Century*[26] and is developed to its fullest in Skocpol's *States and Social Revolutions.* An emerging fourth wave, not yet fully developed, appears in embryo in John Dunn's *Modern Revolutions,*[27] is developed by Eisenstadt and is further elaborated in Roberto Mangabeira Unger's *False Necessity.*[28]

## The first wave

The main feature of the first twentieth-century wave of thinking on revolution is the absence, as Goldstone suggests, of any serious theoretical corpus.[29] Thus, perhaps the most important member of this school, Crane Brinton, in his *Anatomy of Revolution,* simplisticly sought to develop the concept as metaphorically a fever. Thus, stages of revolution were identified – the rule of the moderates, the accession of the extremists, the reign of terror and virtue and the return of order or Thermidor which corresponded with the typical curve of a fever, from mild beginnings through crisis and back to normality. Obviously implied is the conservative view that revolution is a sickness and an aberration which needs to be prevented and, if it does break out, to be cured as urgently as possible.[30] Variations on this conservative approach with limited theoretical basis are to be seen in LeBon who adopted *ad hoc* psychological schemata in identifying the causes of revolution in mob psychology, and Sorokin, whose study begins by actually disavowing any pretensions to objectivity and who defines revolution as the repression of basic instinctual needs.

The essentially polemical quality of these works is their major weakness and the reason why little attention is paid to them here. Nevertheless, at least in the Brinton variation, which is developed in a later period by Jaroslav Krejci, his observations of what can be called the routine of revolution – the incompleteness of the revolutionary project and its repeated inability to fulfil its promise and break decisively with the past, need to be thought through and taken seriously. Throughout the literature, this routine of revolution, the recurrence of Thermidor as outcome is either ignored or inadequately addressed.

## The second wave

A second wave of thought can be identified as emerging after the Second World War in response to the far-reaching changes which took place as decolonisation and the national liberation movements gathered momentum in the 1950s, and later as the desegregation and subsequent black power movements took root in the United States. If an immediate impetus is to be sought for this trend, which was largely based in the United States, it is the Cuban Revolution of 1959. In 1960, the Centre of International Studies at Princeton held its Conference on Internal War which stimulated a new round of debate on the question of revolution.[31] Three schools can be identified in an area which has been extensively discussed, but which will be briefly retraced for the sake of clarity.

### *The psychological school*

This school argued that the likelihood of aggression and revolution, which was seen as somewhat of an extension of the former, depended on the state of mind of the masses. The Relative Deprivation variety of this school, led by James Davies, argued with his 'J-curve of rising expectations' that revolution took place after a long period of improved standards of living followed by a short period of regression.[32] The frustration–aggression variety, exemplified by Ted Gurr, in the process of a complex and multi-faceted argument, came to a fairly simple conclusion. He suggested that frustration–aggression occurs when a sufficient number of people become angry, and people become angry when they experience relative deprivation. The degree of frustration caused by different degrees of deprivation may, in turn, lead to different degrees of political violence, ranging from turmoil through conspiracy to internal war. Revolution, interestingly, was not seen as a specific event in its own right, but subsumed under the heading of internal war alongside quite distinct events such as civil war.

## The sociological school

The sociological school is best represented by Chalmers Johnson, who, basing his approach on Talcott Parsons' functionalism, argued that the task of a functioning social system was to maintain a consensus of values among the population. Where such a consensus did not exist there was disharmony or, in other words, the system was dis-synchronised and in disequilibrium. Dis-synchronisation could occur as a result of a combination of reasons including a change in exogenous values and environment, and/or a change in endogenous values and environment. Importantly for Johnson, ruling elites could either re-synchronise the system by carrying out reforms, which would forestall revolution, or face revolutionary upheaval which would lead to a re-synchronisation of the system and the establishment of a new value consensus.

## The political conflict school

This school included Charles Tilly and Samuel Huntington, who, while arriving at somewhat different conclusions, derived their approach from the common plural tradition, which identifies political outcomes as the result of intersecting conflicts between political groups. Normal conflict is escalated during revolutions by the magnitude of resources brought to bear by the competing political interests, to the point where the conflict-resolving re-sources of the system can no longer cope and the political system is split apart. The resultant situation, where more than one pole of power exists, is defined as one of multiple sovereignty and is ultimately resolved in favour of one or the other poles of sovereignty depending again on the magnitude of resources that each group can bring to bear on the situation.

Criticisms of the second wave are replete and in-depth[33] and a detailed repetition of established points is not necessary. As a summary, however, Rod Aya's general description of these critics as being 'volcanic theorists', is a useful beginning, thus:

> the volcanic model pictures the etiology of revolt and revolu-
> tion like this: the onrush of uncontrolled changes in the struc-
> ture of society begets multiplex tensions, which, if unrelieved,
> erupt into mass violence where and when social controls relax
> or weaken. . . . Whereas these discontents mount first in the

hearts and minds of uncoordinated individuals, they find outlet sooner or later in collective behaviour.[34]

Five main criticisms can be identified. The first is the clear failure to differentiate between the complex of institutions and issues specific to the state and those common to the broader society. Thus, both psychological and sociological schools ignore the strength of the state, its cohesiveness, etc., and instead concentrate on the state of mind of individuals and collective groupings in society as necessary and sufficient conditions for revolt. For Skocpol, this was a damning indicator of the flaws in this perspective, most evident in the inability to explain the retention in societies like South Africa of a political system which obviously did not have value consensus, and bred all the conditions for frustration–aggression but continued to hold on to power.[35] Tilly, while not guilty of this error, fell into the opposite trap. For Tilly, the political is collapsed into the social and the social into the political. All is state, and as a result, the clarity which could be afforded from a differentiation between the two is lost.[36]

The second criticism was methodological and struck at the heart of these theories. There was no way to systematically establish the connection between frustration, value dis-synchronisation and revolt. The assumption was that the greater the frustration, deprivation, etc., the greater the revolt would be and, while Gurr, Davies, etc., drew on vast statistical support to prove frustration, deprivation, etc., there was and remains nothing to connect this deprivation with revolt. This, according to Aya, required a 'two-stage leap of faith' for one to accept their conclusions: 'There is, in short, no direct passage from anger to action, save through tautology.'[37]

The third criticism largely originates from the second. Most writers saw revolution as part of a continuum beginning with minor forms of collective violence such as riots, and ending with revolutions. Gurr, we recall, did not even give revolutions special definition, but saw them as just one subcategory of a larger group entitled internal war. This failure meant that the critical factor which made an episode a revolution or not was the degree of violence and not necessarily the extent of structural change in the state and the society, regardless of the actual extent of violence. Thus, Goldstone, criticising Tilly, argued that his methods of study

> would certainly class as situations of multiple sovereignty the periodic wars of succession in the Ottoman and Mogul empires, the English War of the Roses and the American and Nigerian civil wars. None of these situations however, is considered to be a revolution in the sense of the French, Russian, Chinese, or Mexican revolutions. Thus some factor that bridges the gap between mere violence and revolution is required for Tilley's

measures of multiple sovereignty to be useful in explicating the occurrence of revolution rather than mere domestic turmoil.[38]

A fourth criticism, suggested by Goldstone, surrounds the view, best expressed by Chalmers Johnson, that a revolution could be prevented by the actions of the elites. Faced with dis-synchronisation, an 'intransigent' elite would most likely precipitate revolution whereas reforming elites could forestall such an outcome. In fact, Goldstone points out, the elites of both France and Russia and as Skocpol argues, China, were all reforming elites immediately prior to the revolutions in those countries and, as de Tocqueville noted, the French monarch's attempts at reform appeared to speed up, rather than retard the impending revolutionary situation.[39]

A final criticism surrounds the universal absence of explanations for the outcomes of revolutions. Thus, no attempt is made to explain why the French and American revolutions evolved in liberal democratic directions while the Russian, Chinese and Cuban evolved in the direction of one-party, authoritarian socialist states.[40] It was precisely these weaknesses that the third wave, as defined in this study, attempted with significant success, to address.

## The third wave

Barrington Moore's classic work, *Social Origins of Dictatorship and Democracy*, which first appeared in 1966, marked a qualitative advance over the second wave of largely American-based social scientists, and also made important amendments to the classical Marxist approach to explaining revolutions. Moore not only sought to explain the causes of revolutions – the main objective of the second wave – but moved decisively beyond this, in attempting to show how the peculiar juxtaposition of social classes in particular historical circumstances led either to liberal democratic outcomes, to fascism or to communism.

To simplify and in a sense, to mechanise Moore's study, he argued that revolutions took place in contexts where traditional ruling classes were faced with external competition and forced to carry through modernising reforms. If in the face of carrying out these reforms, there existed a relatively strong commercial class or bourgeoisie; if this bourgeoisie was able to form an alliance with a section of the landed upper classes who were already becoming involved in commercial agriculture; and if the peasantry was weak, either because its positions were already being eroded, as in Britain, or because it did not really exist, as in the United States, then the outcome of these modernising attempts was 'bourgeois democracy'.[41]

The second route, identified by Moore as revolution from above, also culminated in capitalism, but its fascist variety. Where there is a weak bourgeoisie, or bourgeois impulse, modernisation occurs as the result of 'dissident elements'[42] in the older and still dominant ruling class who put through changes leading to industrialisation under a semi-parliamentary regime. A relatively weak peasantry was also a necessity for this course to be successful. In the third case, powerful agrarian bureaucracies served to inhibit commercial and industrial impulses. The result was that a huge peasantry remained which provided the main impetus for the destruction of the old order from below – the result being communism.

Moore represented a definite advance over the second wave in that he suggested a critical minimum list of conditions for revolution which appeared far more tangible and subject to scrutiny than the disconnected sociological variables of the previous generation. External pressure and competition led to attempts to modernise; these attempts would have different outcomes depending on the strengths of the national classes and their relationship to each other. Referring, for example, to numerous peasant uprisings which had failed in seventeenth-century France, he distances himself from the 'volcanic' approach:

> By itself, however, popular resentment could not make a revolution. Whether it increased just before the revolution is not absolutely clear; very likely it did. Nevertheless, only when popular grievances could coalesce even briefly with those of more powerful groups would they help to bring the monarchy crashing down amid fire, blood and smoke.[43]

Further differentiating himself from the second wave, Moore tried to explain not just causes but outcomes and the reasons for different types of outcome.

Moore's observations on the role of the peasantry provided a critical departure from the Marxian tradition of analysis. He argued that the revolutionary potential of the peasantry did not vary in relationship to the degree to which it had been proletarianised, but rather, on the degree of paternalism and labour repression which surrounded its relationship to the landowners. The greater the degree of paternalism, he suggested, the less likelihood there would be of revolt and vice versa. This argument was subsequently developed at length by Eric Wolf in his *Peasant Wars of the Twentieth Century*, where he argued that the key issue determining revolutionary potential among the peasantry is what he describes as 'tactical power':

> The poor peasant or the landless labourer who depends on a landlord for the largest part of his livelihood, or the totality of it, has no tactical power: He is completely within the power

> domain of his employer, without sufficient resources of his own
> to serve him as resources in the power struggle.[44]

The rich peasant, for more obvious reasons, is unlikely to embark on the road of rebellion, so it is only the middle peasant, or a peasant outside immediate landlord control, who will be likely to be engaged in rebellion.

While critical of aspects of Marxist analysis, Moore operates within its basic parameters. Thus, revolutionary struggles and outcomes occur essentially as clashes between economic classes for reasons which are largely economic. While the state is recognised as a player in the process of change, it is not given a degree of autonomy in its own right, as Skocpol's subsequent criticisms elegantly argued. And importantly, Moore remains within the mainstream Marxist (and pre-Marxist) view that revolution represents a logical and progressive stage in historical development. This comes out most clearly in his 'control' study of India – a country which had not experienced a revolution of modernisation. The failure for such a revolution to take place had placed India in a sort of historical dead-end of development, leading Moore to conclude:

> As I have reluctantly come to read this evidence, the costs of
> moderation have been at least as atrocious as those of revolu-
> tion, perhaps a great deal more.[45]

The bulk of criticism of Moore's work has, unfortunately, concentrated on whether his characterisation of individual revolutions could be justified, or whether his outcomes, e.g. the American Civil War as an example of a bourgeois revolution, were too highly selective to be useful.[46] The most important line of criticism has come from Theda Skocpol and, since her critique of Moore was a prelude to her own path-breaking approach, this is a good point to look at Skocpol's state-oriented and structuralist approach to understanding revolutions.

### Skocpol's state-centred approach as landmark: the critique of Moore

Skocpol's approach really began with an extensive critique of Moore's analysis, in which she argues that Moore's emphasis on the economic – what she described as a 'kind of Marxist approach' – as opposed to the earlier approaches which relied almost exclusively on ideas and values, was a far more fruitful endeavour. Despite this, his analysis failed in four main areas. She suggested that Moore's use of the concept 'bourgeois impulse' as a key variable and explanatory phenomenon, was difficult to tie down and his failure to do this weakened his findings significantly. In Japan, for example, where Moore argued that a 'moderate' bourgeois impulse facilitated a fascist outcome, i.e. revolution from above, Skocpol posits that the evidence could not support such a conclusion. Rather, industrialisation was initiated by bureaucrats, who

> created whole industries administratively without drawing much
> on the capital, the personnel or the political support of the old
> commercial strata.[47]

In her second criticism, Skocpol again attacked Moore's over-reliance on economic determinants as critical variables in his explanatory frame. Central to Moore's analysis had been the view that the character of agrarian commercialisation of the propertied upper classes played a prominent role in the final social and political outcome. If it was market-oriented, as in England, the outcome was likely to be liberal democracy; if labour-repressive, then possibly fascism or communism. Skocpol again argued that the evidence could not support such a conclusion. Both in Prussia and Japan, market relations had undergone significant development, negating the dichotomy, while in England, the market-oriented commercial landlords relied just as much on the state and political mechanisms to extract a surplus as the other supposedly labour-repressive examples suggested. If the differences were not to be found in this economic factor, then they should be sought for in how the political mechanisms of the state were organised and who controlled those mechanisms.[48]

The third criticism logically flowed from the first two and was also presented as part of an alternative approach. Surveying Marxist-oriented literature on the state, she argued that while the trend is to place more and more emphasis on the relative autonomy of capitalist state structures, nowhere, including in Moore's writings, is it admitted that the state might act against dominant elites, or to create a new mode of production, without reference to the dominant economic sectors:

> Through all of the debates about the political role of dominant
> class personnel, Marxist theory has remained frozen within the
> assumption that 'in the last instance' political structures and
> struggles are determined by the economic.[49]

Having asserted and then applied her state-centred approach of examining social change, Skocpol's final criticism was then directed at the absence in Moore's work of what she referred to as an 'intersocietal approach'. In Moore's approach, the motor of change was the ubiquitous 'commercial impulse', which appeared as a fairly constant variable, unchanged over time or space. By moving away from an approach which saw different outcomes determined largely on the basis of whether this impulse existed internally, to one which recognised that changes were largely initiated and shaped by the pressures exerted on states within a system of competitive states, entirely new perspectives appeared. Thus, one had to place great importance on the influence which early modernising states (Great Britain) had on the options for later modernisers (Germany, Japan). Further,

> National Economic Modernization (as the early modernizers knew it) cannot be assumed. Its rate and indeed the very possibility of its occurrence, are determined by international political–economic conditions. Revolutions from above or below are not only (or perhaps even primarily) responses to intrasocietal developments. Possibilities for continued industrialization and/or democratization in the wake of 'bourgeois revolutions' are in part determined by international relationships and conditions, as are needs and opportunities for 'fascist' military aggression.[50]

These two essential criticisms – the independence of the state and state elites from dominant classes and the importance of an intersocietal approach – are taken to a conclusion in Skocpol's later work on states and social revolutions.

### States and social revolutions
Skocpol's *States and Social Revolutions* is an examination of relatively rare social phenomena – social revolutions – which she describes as

> rapid, basic transformations of a society's state and class structures; and they are accompanied and in part carried through by class-based revolts from below. Social revolutions are set apart from other sorts of conflicts and transformative processes above all by the combination of two coincidences: the coincidence of societal structural change with class upheaval; and the coincidence of political with social transformation.[51]

Such a definition is useful, as it avoids typical second-wave errors. It excludes rebellions, which may involve class upheaval but do not lead to structural change; coups, which involve changes in the state but not in class and social structures; and changes of the Japanese 'Meiji' and Prussian types which are transformative but do not include significant class-based activity from below.

The approach taken is what she describes as a 'non-voluntarist, structural, perspective' in which she begins by asserting her critique of the purposive view of revolution, which, on the one hand, sees the party, personalities, ideologies, etc., as critical or, on the other, the removal of consensus from below as the necessary ingredient to initiate revolution. On the contrary, she asserts that:

> historically, no successful social revolution has ever been 'made'
> by a mass-mobilizing, avowedly revolutionary movement.[52]

Rather, revolutionary situations emerge out of crises within states which are initiated as a result of the intense competition they face as nation-states within a system of competing nation-states. Skocpol's elaboration of the role of the state in this context is helpful:

> The state, in short, is fundamentally Janus-faced, with an intrinsically dual-anchorage in class-divided socioeconomic structures and an international system of states. If our aim is to understand the breakdown and building-up of state organizations in revolutions, we must look not only at the activities of social groups. We must also focus on the points of intersection between international conditions and pressures, on the one hand, and class-structured economies and politically organized interests on the other hand. State executives and their followers will be found maneuvering to extract resources and build administrative and coercive organizations precisely at this intersection. Here, consequently, is the place to look for the political contradictions that help launch social revolutions. Here, also, will be found the forces that shape the rebuilding of state organizations within social-revolutionary crises.[53]

Applying this framework to her three examples of France, Russia and China, the essential thesis is that social revolutions have occurred only in agrarian-bureaucratic states. In these societies, a traditional, more or less centralised bureaucracy exists in cooperation with powerful landowners on the basis of the exploitation of peasants in largely agrarian economies. Faced with external pressures to the state from other states in the European states system (France, Russia) or, in China's case, from encroaching European states, these societies eventually end up in crisis. In its attempts to modernise and compete, the bureaucracy is forced to extract greater surpluses from the landowners and the peasantry. The various responses of these two elements, in the given structural and temporal circumstances, dictate the possibility of social revolution and influence the potential outcomes of these processes. Like Moore and Wolf, Skocpol places great importance on the intensity of peasant rebellion as a key factor in determining outcome and, similarly, the degree of intensity is dependent on the degree of autonomy or independence from the landowners which the peasantry possesses. This independence existed in both the French and Russian cases and, while it did not initially exist in China, it was forged in the long revolutionary struggle. In East Prussia, where close supervision and lack of autonomy were the main features and in England where traditional peasant holdings had been broken up, class-based upheaval, and thus, social revolutions, could not take place.

The strength of Skocpol's approach, like that of Moore's, lies in the fact that she goes beyond the determination of revolutions to look at revolutionary outcomes and important to this is her concept of 'world time':

> One possibility is that actors in later revolutions may be influenced by developments in earlier ones; for example the Chinese communists became conscious emulators of the Bolsheviks and received, for a time, direct advice and aid from the Russian revolutionary regime. Another possibility is that crucial world-historically significant breakthroughs – such as the industrial revolution or the innovation of the Leninist form of party organization – may intervene between the occurrence of one broadly similar revolution and another. As a result new opportunities or necessities are created for the development of the latter revolution that were not open to, or pressed upon, the former, because it occurred at an earlier phase of modern world history.[54]

This aspect of the analysis is very central to its consistency and, controversial, as will be developed later. Although the French revolution had centralising tendencies, it could not develop into a centrally-planned industrial economy because large-scale industrialisation was not yet on the historical agenda. By the time of the Russian revolution, however, 'world time' had placed large-scale industry and accompanying central planning as real possibilities in Russia's industrial heartland and even later in China's northeast, thus dictating the final outcome in the former and influencing the initial direction of events in the latter.

Finally, Skocpol argues that the way revolutionary (and potentially state-building) elites develop relations with the actual peasant revolutionary forces during the course of the revolutionary struggle is critical to its eventual outcome. In Russia, the peasant rebellion took place quite independently of the urban movement which actually seized state power, so there was always an element of disconnection and suspicion between the two. Subsequently, Russia's vulnerable position in the European states system after the war meant that for the country to compete and survive it had to engage in a rapid process of industrialisation, which meant extracting a greater surplus from a sullen and hostile peasantry. Thus the nature of alliances at the start of the revolution and international pressures forced Russia in the direction of a consolidating dictatorial party state.

In China, the Communist Party came to power strongly tied to the peasantry as a result of the prolonged struggle against the KMT and the Japanese and, therefore, while engaged in a parallel process of industrialisation, was compelled to balance this with equalitarian policies of rural development:

> In China, . . . the peasantry could not make its own revolution, and the organized revolutionaries could not come to power directly within the cities and towns. The communists and peasants necessarily allied to complete the revolution. In consequence, special possibilities were created for the revolutionaries once in state power to use participatory mobilization in the further transformation of the economy and society, and for peasant activities and welfare to become a fundamental part of national development in China.[55]

The strengths of Skocpol's work are to a significant degree self-evident and appear prominently in her critique of Moore. By focusing on the state as the central unit of analysis, she distances herself from the second wave, from Moore and, indeed, from the body of Marxist literature. After Skocpol, state-building functions are to be seen not as unimportant, as in the case of much second-wave theorising, not ultimately determined by the activities of economic classes, but as independent activities with their own dynamic of development. The cause of state-building is thus reified and placed on an independent pedestal from that of economic accumulation with plausible conclusions when applied to specific revolutionary outcomes – not least of all, the underlying similarity of state-building functions common to all revolutionary elites, despite ideological garb. Successful too, is her location of these states as part of a world of relatively autonomous and relatively dependent, but constantly competitive nation-states. This constant competition – generated by bureaucratic, military and technological advances in individual states – as the initiator of crisis, seems to be a more fruitful avenue of explanation than the internally-determined (and difficult to quantify) commercial impulse which is at the heart of Moore's explicandum.

But it is in the area of her greatest strength that the analysis is also subject to a potentially debilitating weakness. By relying exclusively on structural determinations as the key factors in deciding revolutions and outcomes, Skocpol loses focus on the human, the role of personality and of the accidental as elements, if not always determinants in history. This is most obvious when questions are raised as to what would have happened in specific revolutionary situations if highly important leaders had died or not been present at critical junctures. Thus, how can one not account for Lenin's presence as an independent factor in the Bolshevik revolution, or his absence for that matter after 1923? Similar examples would be Fidel Castro in the Cuban Revolution or the Ayatollah Khomeini in Iran. Similarly, important junctures, such as Stalin's triumph over Bukharin and the subsequent decision to collectivise the Russian peasantry, with all its brutal (yet also, state-building) consequences, appear too pre-determined by structure and moment in Skocpol's work to conform with reality.[56] Rather, John Dunn seems closer to the mark when he proposes a relatively more significant role for human intervention in history:

> There is very little about the military or political activities of state agents which can be clearly understood except through the categories of human intention and action. The military, diplomatic, economic, welfare and repressive ventures of states (the range of characteristics which make and keep a state a state) are all complicated – if often poorly integrated – human performances. . . . The causal importance of imitation, obduracy and intellectual invention in the history of twentieth century revolution is very hard to overestimate.[57]

Indeed, it is in her discussion of 'world time' that Skocpol is most aware of this weakness and yet arrives at a less than satisfactory conclusion. Thus the invention of the Leninist party is identified as one possible change in world time which has a decisive effect on subsequent revolutions. Yet the Leninist party is not an abstract phenomenon, but the end-product of a process of intellectual and ideological development which took place among a group of revolutionaries in a particular country in response to particular conditions. The fact that Bolshevism won out over Menshevism was as much the result of accident as it was of human struggle, it was certainly not an artificially created object of 'world time' which then affected later events.

However, with this as its most notable weakness, we can conclude that Skocpol's approach represented a clear advance over the important work done by Moore and is sufficiently important for us to speak about the pre-Skocpol theorising on revolutions and the post-Skocpol era, in which the role of the state as independent actor must take centre-stage.

Despite this landmark character, however, there is a nagging feature running through all work on revolution, which is its inconclusive character, the tendency toward partial solutions, the multiplicity of theories and the elements of truth to be found in even relatively weak frameworks. Taylor correctly argues, for example, that while Skocpol's analysis is obviously important, she is unable to prove that non-structural variables are unimportant, and therefore that the weaker theories did not contribute to an understanding of the process of revolution.[58] The underlying assumption of most social science work on revolution (as of most social science work) is that if common features could be found, common causal statements could be developed. However, Dunn at least has questioned whether this is possible and posited that the only uniformities in revolutions were the characteristics that defined them as revolutions; the causes were unique in each case.[59] If this were the case, then causal theory is impossible or inevitably tautological and ideological, leading to Taylor's somewhat pessimistic conclusions that the 'third-Wave' theories of revolution

> did make a contribution to the understanding of revolution, albeit in the form of ideological explanations of an ideologically defined phenomenon, and that they did have some potential as general theories, albeit with the proviso that counter-examples reflected the need to improve theories rather than reject them.[60]

Thus, even with Skocpol's conclusions, Taylor's comments reflected a genuine concern that while making advances and solving new issues, theories of revolution were still far from adequate. New directions seemed appropriate.

## Post-Skocpol: towards a fourth wave

Since *States and Social Revolutions,* three trends, none of them necessarily devoted to the study of revolution *per se,* but which, in attempting to solve some of the broader questions of change, address this central issue, have emerged. The first is the World Systems approach, which is most identified with Wallerstein, Hopkins, Arrighi and others and which has rapidly gained popularity since the 1974 publication of the first volume of Wallerstein's *The Modern World System.* The second, which we can call 'Skocpol further modified', attempts to apply Skocpol's approach to a broader range of countries, using various modifications including aspects of World Systems theory. The third, for which the title 'Open-ended history' is as appropriate as any, approaches revolution as an element in systemic change and therefore tries to work not only in, but around revolution as the fundamental issue requiring explanation in historical development. Dunn, Eisenstadt and Unger are among the main exponents of a coalescing trend which is perhaps the most original, and has the potential, in building on the existing theory, to yield the most fruitful results.

### *World systems as an explanation of revolution*

The World Systems approach is the most important trend in the transition away from dependency theory, which, as an explanation for underdevelopment in the Third World, if less of a solution,[61] attained almost paradigmatic status in the 1970s. Unlike dependency theory, which generally distinguished between a central and peripheral capitalism, Immanuel Wallerstein identified a world system, which, beginning in the sixteenth century, has come to encompass the entire globe.

There is in this framework, one capitalist world system which is to be distinguished from world empires like the Roman Empire. In this world system, one can distinguish between core states at the centre, semi-peripheral states in the middle and peripheral states at the rim, with different levels of appropriation and different production functions appropriate to each sphere. Production in this framework is organised in a series of commodity chains,[62] which extend from the periphery to the core. Outside the world system is an external arena consisting of areas which have not yet been incorporated, but as suggested, the process of inclusion is now more or less complete.

States in the world system, far from being given the high degree of autonomy accorded them in Skocpol's analysis, are relegated to having largely economic dimensions. States are essentially points on the commodity chain at which the national bourgeoisie seeks to appropriate or 'cream off' some of the surplus created on the way to the core. In Wallerstein's words,

> Almost all commodity chains will cross state boundaries at some point, and many (even most) will cross them at many points. At each point that there is a labourer, there is a state pressure on the labourer's income. At each point that there is an 'exchange' of product there is a state pressure on the 'price'.[63]

In terms of an understanding of revolution, Wallerstein's argument is in keeping with his view of a single world system. If there is only one capitalist world system which is still intact, then 'revolutions' can, at best, be the expression of tension within that system, with the ultimate effect being the creation of new or differently organised national points for the appropriation of part of the surplus from the commodity chain. This is why:

> The change from 'capitalist state' to 'socialist state', for many who think in these terms, has not had the transforming effects on world history – the reconstituting of trajectories of growth – that they had believed it would have.[64]

Is, therefore, the project of socialism an illusive goal that has existed along with the equally illusory image of progress as a world-historic necessity since at least the eighteenth century? Wallerstein thinks not, and concludes that, socialism is on the agenda but as a world change – not in individual states, as this is impossible with the overall system remaining intact. Secondly, Marx's analysis of the eventual demise of capitalism remains correct, but the conditions for its eventuality have just not yet matured:

The three central structural secular trends of capitalism – mechanization, commodification and contractualization – are at best only partially realized as of 1980 in the world-economy as a whole. And even if we were to take (illegitimately) only the most 'advanced' states as our units of analysis, it would not be the case even then that these states are more than 'halfway' in an approach toward the asymptote on some appropriate scale of measurement. As for the centralization of the world-economy as a whole, it has been proceeding steadily, but when all is said and done, slowly.[65]

It is the complete development and centralisation of the world economy which will fulfil the Marxist conditions for the maturation of capitalism (a process which Wallerstein suggests may be as far as 150 or more years distant) and thus lay the conditions for revolution on a world scale. In the meantime, 'antisystemic movements' continue to grow on both national and international bases as the political expression of the formation of a 'world proletariat'[66] – the social and political basis for worldwide, antisystemic revolution.

While early comments by Wallerstein appeared far more rigid, stagist and deterministic, more recent statements show a greater degree of flexibility in possible outcome, although the central framework remains.[67] In *Antisystemic Movements* for example, he argues that there have been two rehearsals for worldwide revolution – 1848, when there were Europe-wide revolts and 1968, when the anti-war, black power, French and Mexican revolts and other significant rebellions took place throughout the world. Both ended in failure, but can be seen as dress rehearsals for more significant events. The first was the rehearsal for the 1917 Russian Revolution, while the second may be the dress rehearsal for a more significant worldwide upheaval. Importantly, however, Wallerstein proposes that there are multiple options as to what might happen in the future. Counter-revolution might succeed, the world might disintegrate in a nuclear holocaust, or 'it could be reconstructed in the ways in which people hoped in 1848, 1968'.[68]

From a Third World perspective Wallerstein's approach is very important, in that in the tradition of dependency theory, it frontally addresses the blockages, the failure to transform and the debilitating crises which characterised much of 'the periphery' in the last quarter of the twentieth century. Far greater success is gained on the economic side of this analysis, where important features of the present stage are recognised. The axial division of labour with a disproportionate appropriation of the surplus through the mechanism of the transnational corporation, fundamentally altering the already-distorted economies; the simultaneous growth of the centralisation of capital in the core and the decentralisation of industry to cheap labour *loci* in the periphery; the important transformation of communication net-works as powerful economic and ideological tools for the maintenance (and possible destabilisation ) of the system and the use of multilateral financial instruments as means of political control,[69] reflect important features in the present stage of relations between Third World countries and the First World, even if the dreary conclusion for the periphery is that there is little hope for short-term change, outside of occurrence of worldwide revolution.

It is in his overtly political analysis that the weaknesses become more apparent. Some of the more glaring contradictions are, not surprisingly, raised by Theda Skocpol. Thus, in the first part of his still-incomplete opus *The Modern World System,* which looks at the European world economy in the sixteenth century, Wallerstein tried to equate strong states with those that were at the core of the system in its embryonic stages. England and Holland were, therefore, early core states, but, Skocpol effectively points out that neither England nor Holland could have been considered as 'strong states', while Sweden, one of the most powerful absolutist states of the era was located in the periphery and France, which in the early stages was considered a semi-peripheral state had a much stronger state apparatus than that of either England or the Netherlands.[70] If, therefore, the facts contra-dicted Wallerstein's perspective, and strength-of-state did not correspond to position in the world system, the whole notion of the state being subordinate to economic determination had to be rethought. An alternative explicandum, Skocpol suggests, would have to recognise that capitalism develops as a result of the interplay between economic patterns of production and ex-change with peculiar configurations of state institutions, modified by the relationships between states, without the economic being reduced to the political or vice versa. In the hothouse situation of Western Europe, then, any state which as a result of the development of strategic advances in commerce and technology (including military technology), gained a signifi-cant advantage over its competitors, would set in motion a train of events aimed at 'catching up', which would lead to the spread of capitalism (unevenly) across the continent:

> once capitalist relations of production and accumulation were
> firmly established in England, the dynamics of the European
> states system ensured that capitalist relations would spread both
> across Europe and over the entire globe through state initiatives
> by competing powers and through military conquests, as well
> as through market expansion.[71]

This is a far more useful explanation because it effectively answers the question as to why England was both an early and central (core, in Wallerstein's frame) capitalist country and a relatively weak state. Geopolitical reasons – specifically England's relatively protected position as an island nation – meant that a strong bureaucratic/military apparatus including a standing army was not necessary and this in turn meant that commercial developments were able to take place without the restrictions imposed by the strong monarchy in France and without the concurrent protection given to the peasantry against encroachments by commercial interests. Thus, peculiarities of geography and state gave capitalism breathing room to develop and it spread rapidly in a context of intense state competition.

World Systems analysis, as its strongpoint, does describe real economic and social trends which lead away from state sovereignty and autonomy, but appears to be unable to explain the role and character of the state both at the embryonic stages of capitalism, much less the continued growth and resilience of nationalism, authoritarianism and 'stateness'[72] in the contemporary period. Therefore, while it is true to say that there are powerful trends of an inter-state kind which tend to reduce the manoeuvrability and viability of individual, particularly small nation-states, Skocpol's notion of the state as a relatively autonomous (if beleaguered) institution in a system of competitive nation-states, still seems to be a more fruitful avenue of analysis than one which reduces state structures to economic interests.

## *Skocpol further modified*

A number of 'bridging' comments have, in a sense, set the stage for some new departures from Skocpol's rich analysis with, in some cases, surprisingly important results. Elbaki Hermassi argued, for example, that there was a need to differentiate between early and late, and centre and peripheral revolutions.[73] The latter point was of particular importance because many earlier studies had concentrated on the 'Great Revolutions' – the French, Russian, Chinese, etc., – without paying particular attention to the newly-emergent processes in smaller countries. Hermassi also criticised the fact that most studies of revolutionary outcomes tended to examine the short run instead of an examination of how the process developed in the long term, a point echoed by Eric Hobsbawm.[74]

The result has been that much of the post-Skocpol work has tended to concentrate less on Great Revolutions and instead has advanced smaller and more recent Third World examples, with the obvious question brought to the fore as to why these revolutions have been less than successful. John Walton, for example, using Skocpol's framework, has attempted with mixed success to look at a group of revolts in Colombia, Kenya and the Philippines which did not culminate in revolutionary victory. More important are some of the conclusions he arrives at. Walton successfully amends the peasant revolt thesis developed by Moore, Wolf and Skocpol, by recognising the increasing role of the urban sector in specific situations and the interlinkage of the urban and rural. Instead of an exclusively peasant or proletarian approach, he argues:

> these two classes act within a revolutionary field including others (e.g. rural wage workers, artisans, shopkeepers) and their relative contributions vary across time and space. The sense in which any of these classes is 'crucial' appears largely rhetorical. What is needed here is a theory that can direct inquiry toward an explanation of the differential role of classes under specified circumstances, rather than partial theories that place their bets on false or incomplete alternatives.[75]

Walton also tries to incorporate World Systems analysis with Tilly's political conflict perspective and Skocpol's approach, but this seems to have been overly eclectic and ambitious, in that unless significant modifications are made, all these approaches include features which make them, to one degree or another, incompatible with each other. Skocpol's state-centred approach cannot be integrated into Wallerstein's economically deterministic perspective without damage to overall coherence. It should be mentioned that Walton does note that:

> The world system is less a place to start than a set of potent influences whose character is determined through interaction at the national and regional level.[76]

This statement itself proves our point, that in order to incorporate the world system, Walton is forced to modify it, so in the end he is no longer able to speak about the same system as that defined by Wallerstein.

### Goldfrank and permissive world context

In 'Theories of Revolution and Revolution Without Theory', Goldfrank begins with similar objectives to those of Walton, but is more successful. In looking at the causes of the Mexican Revolution, he operates generally within Skocpol's framework, but introduces two important new elements. The first, the reintroduction of ideology, is raised as an issue but not sufficiently elaborated in the body of the discussion. However, it is important to note that he begins by saying that he:

> takes seriously the projects of all the participants, neither reducing ideology to opportunistic sophistry, nor accepting the claims of the powerful at face value, nor endowing the oppressed with virtues they were prevented from developing.[77]

Far more important are his boldly proposed four 'necessary and sufficient' conditions for revolution. Among them are to be found positions which clearly build on Skocpol's framework. Thus, condition 2 is a severe political crisis paralysing the administrative and coercive capacities of the state, and 3 is widespread rural rebellion, modulated in the Moore/Wolf/ Skocpol tradition by the peculiar class/spatial relationships of peasants and agricultural workers in rural Mexico. But his real advance is in his first point, where he identifies, as a necessary and sufficient condition, the existence of a tolerant, or permissive world context.[78]

In a situation where relatively small and weak countries are confronted by powerful neighbouring states with hegemonic tendencies, then successful revolution is unlikely unless such a permissive world context exists. He identifies three conditions as favouring such a situation. Firstly, if the major power is engaged in war, or preoccupied with serious internal difficulties; secondly, when major powers balance each other out, especially when this balance is antagonistic; and third, if rebel movements receive greater outside support than their ruling opponents; then in all these cases, the likelihood of successful revolution is enhanced.[79]

This approach is applied to Mexico with considerable success. It was the changing balance of power in the region, with the United States rising and European powers declining, together with the convulsions of the First World War which (a) prevented Diaz gaining assistance from his European allies and (b) given the large debt owed by Mexico to the United States, led to the Americans putting pressure on his government. At a later stage, it was a combination of internal political distraction in the United States and that country's involvement in the closing stages of the war in Europe which gave the revolutionary movement room to manoeuvre between 1912 and 1914, and finally it was the great depression and the internally-centred distraction which that entailed, which gave Cardenas an opening to carry through many of the national and social goals of the revolution which had remained on paper for almost twenty years after its beginnings.[80]

Goldfrank raises the question of ideology but does not answer it satisfactorily. Thus, in proposing reasons why the revolution did not go further to the left, he says:

> (This) is in part explained by the fact that the constitutionalists made promises to the masses, but unlike the Russian or Chinese communists, did not develop or practice an ideology requiring cadre self-discipline and urging mass participation.[81]

Skocpol's answer to this, of course, would emphasise the way in which power was taken and the relationship of the rebellious peasantry to the dissident elites as among the major determinants of the new regime, or she might have avoided introducing ideology by referring to her 'world time' variable. Goldfrank hints at an ideological alternative but does not present a viable argument for its reintroduction as a useful variable. This is done in a later article by Farideh Farhi, who, in making this and other comments, significantly advances Skocpol's framework, but inadvertently raises questions about its very foundation.

### Farhi: uneven development, the urban factor and ideology

Despite Walton's and Goldfrank's useful interventions, it is Farhi who in her analysis of the Nicaraguan and Iranian revolutions makes the most important advances, particularly for the investigation of small, Third World states. Building her discussion on Skocpol's general assertion of state autonomy and international states pressure, she also adopts Goldfrank's concept of a permissive world context.[82] However, she argues that the Skocpolian notion of international state competition, particularly that of military pressure as the key trigger to revolutionary crisis, is inadequate when applied to small, peripheral states. She acknowledges the importance of international competition, but proposes that greater attention must be paid to the uneven development of capitalism on a world scale, which engenders contradictions and ultimately crisis, as the state tries to satisfy both national interests and the imperatives of accumulation from overseas. This is further enhanced, she suggests, in states like pre-revolutionary Iran and Nicaragua whose formation was directly linked to foreign intervention.[83] Here Farhi makes an important link which successfully adopts the descriptive elements inherent in World Systems theory and the concept of uneven development, without abandoning a state-centred approach to the understanding of revolutionary crisis.

Farhi also effectively modifies the view of a state/propertied class split as the necessary prelude to revolution in her concentration on the peculiarities of peripheral societies, where the weakness of 'polar classes' opens the way for the rise to prominence in politics of intermediate strata.[84] It is as a result of the rifts between prominent intermediate classes and the state, generated perhaps by the exclusion of sections from involvement in the state apparatus, coupled with the existence of a permissive world context, that revolutionary situations arose in her two cases.

Two further important amendments are made by Farhi to Skocpol's framework. Whereas in the latter's three case-studies, the peasantry, where it possessed solidarity and autonomy, provided the main source for revolutionary activity, Farhi is forced to grapple with the fact that in both Nicaragua and Iran, the revolutions were largely urban-based. She argues that the structure of large, peripheral urban communities creates immense grievances which tend to be directed to the state for solutions. When the state loses its ability to fulfil its clientelistic relationships with these strata, then alternative bonds are forged with other social groupings, such as the Shi'a clerics in Iran or the Catholic 'base communities' in Nicaragua. Then, in the face of a weakening of the state, a concerted, powerful attack by the lower classes, united in solidary, autonomous, cross-class groupings is possible.

Finally, Farhi extends Goldfrank's reintroduction of ideology in a more thorough presentation, to make the most distinct departure from Skocpol. The latter, of course, specifically excluded ideology as an element in determination, although in later work on the Iranian Revolution, she admits the importance of Islam.[85] Farhi readily agrees that the intentionalist view of revolution – that processes are self-consciously guided by ideas and that rebellious masses respond directly to the ideologies of their leaders – is wrong. However, ideology as an important factor, intercedes at two levels. As worldview, ideology (through the channel of religion) not only helped to explain an individual's condition on a day-to-day basis but, in the course of upheaval 'religious concepts and symbols acquired new meaning in opposition to the dictates of foreign-dominated repressive states'.[86] And, at the level of culture, in peripheral states with weak bourgeois classes, there may be very limited incorporation of the lower classes into the dominant value system. Where this is so,

> the subordinate classes' reaction to domination can take the form of completely distinct value systems that not only reject the prevalent inequalities but also differentiate them from other classes by rejecting everything with which the dominant class is identified.[87]

Thus, by strengthening and consolidating lower-class consciousness and sense of shared community, culture immeasurably contributes to revolutionary potential and if, as with Shi'ism in Iran, it becomes fused with nationalism, it can have a direct effect on the shape and form of the state which emerges in the revolutionary outcome.

Farhi can then be seen as the most thorough application of Skocpol to a peripheral context, but simultaneously has moderated almost to a point of unrecognisability many of Skocpol's main conclusions. Does this, in fact, negate Skocpol's work? Farhi herself suggests that this is not the case and that there remain critical generalisations in the original framework which remain useful:

> We can learn from them because they direct our attention to certain relationships, possibilities and conjunctures that may be conducive to social change in a revolutionary form. But these generalisations are not – and Skocpol agrees – 'causes' in the sense of high-level generalizations that explain law-like and invariant connections. . . .[88]

These must be viewed in the context of a changing world-historical context which, in turn, alters and changes the structures which 'condition, limit and enable actors whose particular actions constitute human history'.[89]

Therefore, questions fundamental to this project are raised again. Are there any laws governing revolution? Is the study of revolution a continuing unravelling of new causes, new sufficient conditions, new amendments? Is it possible to establish a theory of revolution? These questions were raised by the final set of theorists in our fourth wave, in an approach which is still in the process of formation.

## *Open-ended history: an emerging paradigm?*

Threads of an alternative approach are captured in bits and pieces in a number of sources. Chaliand's comments in *Revolution in the Third World* asked why four of the most important revolutions of this century had taken place in sinised Asia. The answer, he felt, was partly to be found in the spatial distance of these states from Europe and the ancient traditions of a strong national state which existed. These are factors well explored in the course of our examination, but his further suggestions are novel and interesting. Thus China, Vietnam and North Korea all possessed:

> an indelible national consciousness on the part of populations more homogeneous than elsewhere; in most cases Confucianism as a secular morality singularly attuned to interests of state; and dense populations. Once these societies, with their robust traditions still intact, figured out how to adopt whatever contemporary efforts of the Western World struck them as useful, they went ahead without fear of losing identity.[90]

If Chaliand is right (and the experience of the non-revolutionary sinised Asian states of Japan, Taiwan, South Korea and Singapore would seem to support this)[91] then revolution may be a facilitator to rapid change, the 'going ahead' of which Chaliand speaks and not, in the Marxist sense, the necessary motor or midwife of history. In other words, the historic texture of a society, not divorced from its position in a states system or the existence or non-existence of a revolutionary situation, may be the missing object of analysis which would facilitate a better understanding both of revolutionary situations and outcomes.

With this theme in mind, we can go back briefly to our earlier observation on the disappointing routine of revolution, the failure to achieve its expectations, which Wallerstein tries to leap over with the acrobatic conclusion that the revolution is yet to come. Chaliand presents this dreary routine in his stark but accurate comments on the bureaucratisation of revolution in the Third World:

> In those countries where a national and social revolution has taken place, bureaucracy is the central issue. The poorer and

more backward the society, the more all-powerful its bureaucracy turns out to be. Authority can be brutal in societies that have never known bourgeois democracy and its liberalism. (When it comes to freedoms, the bourgeois democratic revolution has so far produced the least despotic societies.) Besides, there is the inevitable delegation of power, which occurs all by itself in a very short time, once the burst of early organisational enthusiasm which got things started has died down.[92]

In Dunn's words, revolutions

offer themselves and their own societies . . . above all an image of power, control, certainty and purpose in a world in which impotence, incomprehension and the terror of sheer meaninglessness are permanent threats.[93]

But, he goes on to assert, supporting Chaliand's point:

Revolution is in many ways a feeble remedy for their ills – and it is no remedy at all for many of them. Also it is a remedy the distribution of which is much affected by factors which are extremely arbitrary from the point of view of the suffering society. But weak though it may be as a remedy, and capricious though the conditions of its supply are likely to remain, it is still today, for those states and societies that cannot go on in the old way, often the only remedy there is.[94]

Some progress in understanding this routine of revolution has been made in studies specifically addressed to the phenomenon as well as a far more ambitious attempt to revise both Marxist and non-Marxist understandings of how societies change.

## *Eisenstadt: revolution without pre-determination*

In *Revolution and the Transformation of Societies,* S. N. Eisenstadt makes some headway in an alternative direction by first emphasising the element of cultural context as a critical variable. He makes the distinction between 'segregative' and 'coalescent' change. Segregative (non-revolutionary) change takes place as uncoordinated changes in the various institutional and cultural aspects of society over time. Coalescent (revolutionary) change occurs where cultural, religious and political demands intersect to create far-reaching changes in politics and economics. The tendency towards coalescence exists where there is

a high level of tension between the transcendental and mundane orders, a relatively strong this-worldly orientation for the resolution of this tension, and/or a high level of commitment to these orders, which are not taken as given.[95]

Thus, traditional, patrimonial empires lacked this transcendental–mundane tension and therefore, could not generate a movement for a total restructuring of the mundane order on transcendentally 'ideal' lines.

Important too, is Eisenstadt's analysis of revolutionary outcomes. He argues that where the revolutionary elite had solid ties to other elites, the outcomes tended to be less coercive, but where these ties did not exist, where the elites were isolated, the tendency was to a greater degree of coerciveness. Eisenstadt's analysis is not presented here as a superior way to approach the specific study of revolution, as opposed to the body of work initiated by Skocpol. Rather, it provides an appropriate coda and reminder – already qualified by Farhi – that the 'cognitive' sphere of ideas and culture does have a far more central role than Skocpol's original analysis allows. But more, it is in his evaluation of the way societies change and the role of revolution as only one aspect of change, that Eisenstadt is important. He notes that

> while social conflict, heterodoxy, rebellion, change and transformation are inherent in human societies, the specific constellation of elements subsumed in the image of the true revolution is not the only national way of 'real' change – in both traditional and modern settings – but rather, just one of several possible ways.[96]

Here Eisenstadt makes a notable break with the pre-determined view of revolution and posits the concept of the 'open-end-edness' of history, in which the specific intersection of elites and collectivities may give rise to innovations and mutations of which the coalescent (revolutionary) variety is but one – albeit one with a greater impact than segregative change on subsequent society.[97] Roberto Mangabeira Unger further develops this novel and important line of thought.

## *Unger and the negation of determined history*

Unger's centrepiece study, *False Necessity,* is part of a broader work, aimed ambitiously at establishing a radical alternative programme for social reconstruction, counter-posed to liberalism, Marxism and social democracy. He begins his project with a critique of both 'deep structure' theories and positivist social science. Deep structure theories, of which Marxism is the most coherent variety, but which also include 'modernisation' and other liberal approaches, sought to establish general laws of social movement based on routines of practical conflict which propose only a finite number of possible outcomes. Unger disagrees with this and suggests that

> there does not seem to be a finite list of possible types of organization or a small number of possible trajectories of social evolution. . . . the alleged law-like tendencies or determining constraints fail to explain the actual identity and sequence of frameworks for social life.[98]

Positivist social science, on the other hand, failed to see the possibility of change inherent in even highly stable societies, but instead looked at social life as 'an interminable series of episodes of interest accommodation and problem solving.'[99] By concentrating almost exclusively on the existing features of a social context, positivism failed to see the existing and potentially radical elements which might contribute to its demise.

Neither deep structure theory nor positivism, he suggests, can explain the reform cycles which are characteristic of both Western democracies and communist societies. Unger's description of the sameness of these cycles, despite the supposed existence of a revolution in one set of contexts, is noteworthy:

> Again and again, we find that partisan conflicts and attitudes about the uses of governmental power with respect to major issues, such as the direction of economic policy, move among a small number of familiar options. Thus, national governments in the industrial West oscillate between bouts of halfhearted redistribution and attempts to rekindle economic growth by concessions to big business and organized labour. Similarly, communist regimes regularly alternate between periods of economic centralism and decentralization, each swing of the pendulum complete with a detailed set of well-tried techniques and recurrent difficulties. Each traditional option is generally conceded to be a second-best solution by all the major contenders in the dispute. Why should policy keep returning to proposals that inspire so little hope?[100]

His answer is that there is hope, but, to begin with, social theorists must break out of the constraints of both deep structural and positivist approaches and adopt an 'anti-necessitarian' approach, which neither treats social reality as inevitable nor determined by a pre-ordained agenda of possible change. Thus, departing from a view similar to Eisenstadt's on the open-ended character of history, Unger's central object of analysis is a 'Formative Context' which, roughly speaking, is an existing social and political reality in a given state at a given point in time. A formative context is a coalescence of institutions, values and structures which define a society and which 'shapes a complex texture of practical and argumentative routines that gain, by their continuance, an aura of naturalness and necessity'.[101]

Formative contexts are self-reinforcing structures with the various institutional and ideational elements acting in concert to reinforce the whole, but at the same time, formative structures are pregnant with change:

> Events or activities take place all the time which may either remain within a formative context, disrupt it, or supply a functional equivalent for an element of the structure leaving the context intact.[102]

Thus for Unger, as with Eisenstadt, substantial change in society may take place via revolution or via other routes:

> formative contexts can be changed piece by piece. They need not be dealt with on a take-it-or-leave-it basis and replaced as indivisible units in the fashion of modes of production in Marxist theory. Such partial substitutions amount to revolutionary reforms as opposed to either reformist tinkering within a formative context (e.g. one more move in a well established reform cycle) or the revolutionary substitution of an entire social framework (a limiting case never more than approximated by any real world situation).[103]

History then, is not determined purely by the practical constraints of organisational or economic necessity, but through a complex process of trial and error:

> At successive points in the history of these institutional arrangements, solutions containing the elements of alternative institutional schemes were proposed or tried out. The deviations emerged repeatedly; each step toward the consolidation of a dominant style of economic or governmental organization created new opportunities to break away from it. There is no end in sight to the rearrangements nor . . . can there be. One of the most important reasons for this continual recurrence of alternatives is that no set of institutional practices or conceptions of social life ever wins a complete victory.[104]

Other aspects of Unger's framework need to be mentioned to appreciate the whole. Looking at the dimension of the formative context of Western industrial society which is concerned with economic organisation, he examines why petty commodity production lost out to large-scale industrial production in the nineteenth century. Petty commodity production, he argues, is not inherently less efficient than large-scale industry and this can be seen in the fact that today the industrial vanguard, where rapid adaptation to technology and markets is required, is developed around relatively small-scale production. Further, it has the greater potential to empower people – a central task of Unger's project – because of the shorter lines of communication which can facilitate democracy and flexibility of response at the factory-floor level. In the nineteenth century, however, large-scale production, with its inherent features of inflexibility and hierarchy, meshed in with dimensions of technique and governmental organisation which were equally supportive of authority and rigidity of structure. The intersecting elements gelled to constitute a formative context within which petty commodity production still existed, but only at the rear – and as suggested, the vanguard of the economy.[105] With new technology and techniques developing shorter lines of communication between managers and shop-floor workers and new political institutional and ideational arrangements, i.e. the basic elements of a new formative context, petty commodity production may well re-emerge as the dominant form in a formative context with far greater potential for empowerment. Indeed, at the centre of Unger's project is not only an attempt to understand change *per se,* but to propose the possible avenues and ways to advance empowerment which is captured in his construct of Negative Capability.

Unger identifies different formative contexts by the extent to which they are 'entrenched' or 'disentrenched', i.e. the degree to which a formative context is open to challenge and change, on the one hand, and, on the other, the extent to which social station influences an individual's life-chances. The extent to which a hardened 'grid of social division and ranking'[106] exists and the extent to which the society is open to constant experimentation and renovation would indicate the extent to which empowerment and by extension, negative capability existed.[107] Thus, for example, the emergent Western capitalist states were more open to experimentation and less hierarchical than their feudal predecessors while retaining critical features which were authoritarian, inflexible and class-based. To this extent, they were partially disentrenched.

Negative capability is, therefore, the aim of Unger's social project. Revolutionary change may advance negative capability or may retard it. Incremental change may do the same thing. Many possibilities are open with the main constraint coming from what he calls the idea of 'sequential effects'. Elements within a formative context are unequally vulnerable to change and each context affords different social groups unequal opportunities. These sequential influences, while never determining outcomes, nevertheless enhance the possibility of change following certain lines rather than others. It is therefore the texture and character of formative contexts and the actual struggles for change which develop within them which influence and suggest the form of the new formative contexts which eventually emerge with all the obvious implications of haphazardness and uncertainty.

With this schema, Unger proposes a programme towards the building of a disentrenched society, which cannot be discussed in detail here, but includes among its elements: the reification of petty commodity production as the leading organisational form accompanied by a plural democracy without the constraints of entrenched property relations; a democratically controlled rotating capital fund; and a cultural revolution.[108]

## Conclusion

In conclusion, it should be noted that Unger's analysis is not being presented as an alternative explanation of revolutions. The argument presented here is that Theda Skocpol's analysis and the important amendments in the line of thought directly descended from it, provide an acceptable if continually unfolding framework to approach the subject. What Skocpol did was to make the decisive break with an economy-centred approach to the determination of revolution. What Eisenstadt and Unger after him do, is to carry this schism to its logical conclusion.

Unger places revolution on a broader canvas of social change, which, if it does not explain the course of the phenomenon, suggests an answer to the recurring questions about the inadequacy of theories of revolution as well as the inadequate answers provided by revolutions themselves. By demythologising the concept of revolution and breaking with the law-given and deterministic structures of Marxist historicism without necessarily abandoning Marx's insights on class conflict, Unger suggests a more flexible, multi-layered and cumulative approach to change, with surprising results. Revolution is seen as no longer an inevitability for progress nor an inevitable descent into barbarity, but rather, as a window which may look out in many possible directions, including one opening towards greater disentrenchment. If 'existing socialism' is to be assessed not on an historically determined view of its necessity, but as a formative context with a given degree of disentrenchment which is subject to change in many possible directions, then a less obfuscated view of recent events in Eastern Europe, for example, may be possible.

Further, by identifying negative capability as a possible, if not predetermined, objective, Unger has reified the ethical question as a legitimate goal of social science. While absent in much recent theorising on the subject, concepts approaching negative capability – Arendt's freedom or Marx's communist society – have been at the centre of revolutionary thought and the practical slogans of mobilised and revolutionary people since the French Revolution. But it is precisely here, on the practical ground, that Unger's work is weakest. While he admits that the theory of context-making consists of a series of loosely-connected suggestions, it cries out for concrete references and application. Very little appears on the Third World, certainly nothing approaching the richness of Wallerstein's work on the subject. He does, however, suggest that, because mass mobilisation is a necessity for survival in the Third World, these countries may be able to leapfrog Western democracies on the road to disentrenchment:

> (these countries) may be able to escape governmental and social oppression only by catapulting beyond the social democratic heritage to a style of democratic politics and of economic organization that more successfully effaces the contrast between structure-preserving routine and structure-transforming context.[109]

One of the tasks of future studies would therefore seem to be to use Unger's approach to examine Third World countries with the rich insights on the economic constraints to change which dependency, World Systems and other approaches have developed, without the historically deterministic elements.

If our critical discussion of theories of revolution can then be taken as a point of departure, we can suggest that the study of revolution – particularly but not exclusively in the Third World – might benefit from a type of analysis which

(a)  abandons the notion of history as pre-determined and inevitable.

(b)  recognises that formative social contexts are determined in the course of fierce struggles for resources on economic, technical, political and ideological plains with no absolute ordering of their importance except in the context of sequential historical effects.

(c)  recognises, however, the special significance of the state and the elites directly concerned with its construction, functioning and management as a central object of revolutionary analysis in its own right, not simply a superstructure of the society.

(d)  appreciates at the same time the relatively independent role of ideology, culture and other cognitive factors as influences and shapers of revolutionary situations and outcomes.

(e)  gives great significance to the pressures placed on individual states by the military and economic stresses of operating within a highly competitive international states system which is characterised by uneven economic development. This pressure is often the immediate trigger which eventually leads to a revolutionary situation and in the post-revolutionary context places severe constraints on the potential for consolidation and social change by the new regime. These constraints, however, are neither absolute nor pre-determined by the existence of an economically-driven, all-encompassing world system, although tendencies toward political, economic and ideological hegemony are constantly at work.

(f)     within the context of state competition, recognises that for small and subordinate states, particularly when geographically close to states with hegemonic tendencies, the existence of a permissive world context is likely to be – even where the other favourable conditions exist – the necessary element for revolution to take place.

(g)     finally, recognises that context change is possible via revolution, once the structural conditions in the given situation are fulfilled, or via non-revolutionary avenues, and that the object of analysis is not only the question of state-building nor the elite state-builders themselves, but the degree of negative capability, of disentrenchment or the degree to which the new society is moving away from one based on hierarchy and towards one based on a continuous freedom to experiment and to change.

With this general framework, the task of the remainder of this study will be to examine, in a purely experimental way, aspects of revolutionary development in three Caribbean and Central American contexts. An obvious question to ask at this stage, would be, why such a small sample and from only one part of the world? The answer is fairly simple. Firstly, my own familiarity with the Grenadian Revolutionary experience provided a ready-made launching-pad of experience and examples which has been complemented by a more or less close scrutiny of the other cases over the past decade. Convenience is therefore an important reason, but the second and more significant, is that the Caribbean and Central American region has, over the last thirty years been a virtual laboratory of different revolutionary experiences. The brief four-and-a-half year experience on the tiny island of Grenada, by its very ability to survive for as long as it did, raises important questions about the international context, as its collapse appears to confirm conclusions about the dismal routine of revolutions. The Cuban Revolution of course, is the outstanding example of a small state attempting to build socialism and is naturally, of central interest as a relatively consolidated process, with its combination of authoritarian structures and popular mobilisation. The Nicaraguan revolution is different and of significance not only because of its relatively pluralist and democratic framework, but because in the 25 February 1990 elections it has set an historical precedent of a revolutionary regime conceding power in free and fair elections.

The aim then is, following Skocpol, to use J. S. Mill's comparative approach based on his 'method of agreement' and 'method of difference'[110] to establish whether there are common causal factors to account for the making of these revolutions and their outcomes. Rather than repeating long-winded histories which in most cases have been explored at length, we will be examining certain basic themes which as we have suggested, are likely to have been causally relevant.

Thus, in comparing outcomes, we will be focusing on the uneven development of states in the international system of states, the pressures which this creates on ruling elites at particular junctures and most importantly, on the existence of a permissive world context. At the level of the state we will be looking at the nature of the class alliance at the helm of state affairs and the existence of a dynamic of conflicts and contradictions between it and other statal and non-statal elites at the 'top'. Third, we will be looking at the mass base of the revolution, to establish whether those from 'below' were rural or urban, a combination of both and, of course, their relative roles in the revolutionary upheaval and effect on the outcome. Fourth, we will be paying particular attention to the elite insurgents, the character of their relationship with the mass base and their ideological and organisational predilections. The notion of 'cumulative and available ideological context' will be introduced in the course of the discussion to explain the outlook of the elites and the impact which this might have on the emergent regime. Finally, we will be examining how all of these factors come together to make revolutionary upheavals and produce different revolutionary outcomes, each with its own potential for survival, for empowerment, or in Unger's words, advancing negative capability. If nothing else is accomplished, then, a typology of revolutions, based in the final analysis on their potential for empowerment, will be a modest, but hopefully significant contribution to the continuing study of the revolutionary dilemma.

## Notes

1. See P. A. Howell, 'The Greek Experience and Aristotle's Analysis of Revolution', in David Close and Carl Bridge (eds), *Revolution: A History of the Idea* (London: Croom Helm, 1985), p. 15.
2. See David Close, 'The Meaning of Revolution', in Close and Bridge (eds), 1985, p. 4.
3. See Close and Bridge (eds), 1985, pp. 4–5.
4. Close and Bridge (eds), 1985, p. 8.
5. John Dunn, *Modern Revolutions: An Introduction to the Analysis of a Political Phenomenon*, Second edn (Cambridge: Cambridge University Press, 1989), p. 6.
6. See reference to this in Hannah Arendt, *On Revolution* (London: Faber and Faber, 1963), p. 8. Arendt herself, in making a good case for the historical significance of the American Revolution, develops a slightly different perspective than those mentioned above on the meaning of revolution, while retaining the central element of progress. Arendt suggests that the great task of revolution has been the introduction of freedom, which she defines as not essentially the negative or passive rights of life, liberty and property, but 'participation in public affairs or admission to the public realm'. Ibid., p. 25.

7.  See for a discussion of the transition from Hegelianism to Marxism, F. Engels, 'Ludwig Feuerbach and the End of Classical German Philosophy', in Lewis S. Feuer (ed.), *Marx and Engels: Basic Writings on Politics and Philosophy* (London: Fontana, 1969), pp. 236–83.
8.  Karl Marx, excerpt from 'A Contribution to the Critique of Political Economy', in Feuer (ed.), 1969, pp. 84–5.
9.  K. Marx and F. Engels, *The Communist Manifesto*, in Feuer (ed.), 1969, p. 61.
10. Feuer, (ed.), 1969, p. 49.
11. See for example, Marx's 'Letter to Vera Ivanovna Zasulich in Geneva, March 1881', in *Marx, Engels: Selected Correspondence*, Third edn (Progress, 1975), p. 319.
12. See, for example, Louis Althusser, *For Marx* (New York: Vintage, 1970) and Nicos Poulantzas, *Political Power and Social Classes* (London: New Left Books, 1973).
13. See, for example, Antonio Gramsci, *Selections From the Prison Notebooks* (New York: International, 1971).
14. 'Engels to Joseph Bloch in Konigsberg', 21–2 September 1890 in Marx, Engels, 1975, pp. 394–5.
15. See Carl Bridge, 'Burke and the Conservative Tradition', in Close and Bridge (eds), 1985.
16. S. N. Eisenstadt, *Revolution and the Transformation of Societies* (New York: Free Press, 1978), p. 3.
17. F. Engels, 'Socialism: Utopian and Scientific', in Feuer (ed.), 1969, p. 147.
18. See, for example, Theda Skocpol, *States and Social Revolutions: A Comparative Analysis of France, Russia and China* (Cambridge: Cambridge University Press, 1979; Roy Medvedev, *Let History Judge: The Origins and Consequences of Stalinism* (London: Spokesman Books for the Bertrand Russell Peace Foundation, 1976); Gerard Chaliand, *Revolution in the Third World: Myths and Prospects* (Brighton: Harvester Press, Hassocks, 1977).
19. See, for example, John Dunn, *The Politics of Socialism: An Essay in Political Theory* (Cambridge: Cambridge University Press, 1984).
20. See A. S. Cohan, *Theories of Revolution* (London: Nelson, 1975) and Stan Taylor, *Social Science and Revolutions* (London: Macmillan, 1984).
21. Crane Brinton, *The Anatomy of Revolution* [1938] (London: Jonathan Cape, 1953). George Pettee, *The Process of Revolution* (New York: Harper and Brothers, 1938) and G. Lebon, *The Psychology of Revolution* (New York: Putnam, 1913). Jaroslav Krejci, writing at a much later date, is quite clearly a throwback to this earlier group. See *Great Revolutions Compared: The Search for a Theory* (Brighton: Wheatsheaf, 1983).
22. See Ted Gurr, *Why Men Rebel* (Princeton: Princeton University Press, 1971); Chalmers Johnson, *Revolutionary Change* (University of London, 1968); Neil Smelser, *Theory of Collective Behaviour* (London: Routledge and Kegan Paul, 1961); Charles Tilly, *From Mobilization to Revolution* (London: Addison–Wesley, 1978), among other works.
23. Theda Skocpol, *States and Social Revolution* (Cambridge: Cambridge University Press, 1979), Ellen Kay Trimberger, *Revolution from Above: Military Bureaucrats and Development in Japan, Turkey, Egypt and Peru* (Transaction, 1978) and S. N. Eisenstadt, *Revolution and the Transformation of Societies* (New York: The Free Press, 1978).
24. See Jack Goldstone, 'Theories of Revolution: The Third Generation', in *World Politics*, no. 32, 1979.

25.  Barrington Moore, *Social Origins of Dictatorship and Democracy*, First edition 1966 (Harmondsworth: Penguin, 1987).
26.  Eric Wolf, *Peasant Wars of the Twentieth Century* (London: Faber and Faber, 1971).
27.  John Dunn, 1989.
28.  Roberto M. Unger, *False Necessity: Anti-Necessitarian Theory in the Service of Radical Democracy* (Cambridge: Cambridge University Press, 1987).
29.  Goldstone, 1979, p. 427.
30.  See also for a succinct criticism of Brinton's position, Rod Aya, 'Theories of Revolution Reconsidered', *Theory and Society*, Vol. 8, no. 1, July 1979.
31.  See David Horowitz, *The Rise and Fall of Project Camelot* (Cambridge, Mass., 1974).
32.  See James Davies, 'The J-Curve of Rising and Declining Satisfactions as a Cause of Some Great Revolutions and a Contained Rebellion', in *Violence in America*, Hugh D. Graham and Ted Gurr, (eds) (New York: Signet, 1969), pp. 671–709.
33.  See Taylor, 1984, Cohan 1975, Skocpol, 1979, Barbara Salert, *Revolutions and Revolutionaries: Four Theories* (New York: Elsevier, 1976), Aya, 1979 and Goldstone, 1979 among the more important.
34.  Rod Aya, 1979, p. 51
35.  See Skocpol, 1979, p. 16. Skocpol's book first appeared in 1979, after the Soweto uprising had been crushed, an event which illustrated both the absence of value consensus between the black and white populations and also the ability of a powerful South African state without serious fissions to rule effectively in the absence of consensus.
36.  Ibid., p. 26
37.  Aya, 1979, p. 67.
38.  Goldstone, 1979, p. 432.
39.  Ibid., p. 433.
40.  Ibid., p. 434.
41.  Moore, 1987, p. xii.
42.  Ibid.
43.  Ibid., p. 70.
44.  Eric Wolf, 1971, p. 290. See also Jeffry Paige, *Agrarian Revolution: Social Movements and Export Agriculture in the Underdeveloped World* (New York: Free Press, 1975), who differs substantially with Wolf on the role of the poor peasantry.
45.  Moore, 1987, p. 505.
46.  See Taylor, 1984, p. 31.
47.  Theda Skocpol, 'A Critical Review of Barrington Moore's Social Origins of Dictatorship and Democracy', in *Politics and Society*, Fall, 1973, p. 14.
48.  See Skocpol, 1973, pp. 14–16.
49.  Ibid., p. 18.
50.  Ibid., p. 32.
51.  Skocpol, 1979, p. 4.
52.  Ibid., p. 17.
53.  Ibid., p. 32.
54.  Ibid., pp. 23–4.
55.  Ibid., pp. 279–80.
56.  See, for example, Skocpol, 1979 for her discussion of the Stalin–Bukharin struggle on pp. 223–5.
57.  Dunn, 1989, p. xxii.

58.  See Taylor, 1984, p. 150.
59.  Ibid., p. 153.
60.  Ibid., p. 158.
61.  See for example, Gabriel Palma, 'Dependency: A Formal Theory of Under-development or a Methodology for the Understanding of Concrete Situations of Underdevelopment?', in *World Development*, Vol. 6, nos 7 and 8.
62.  See Immanuel Wallerstein, 'World Networks and the Politics of the World Economy', in *The Politics of The World Economy* (Cambridge: Cambridge University Press, 1984), p. 4.
63.  Ibid., p. 4.
64.  Immanuel Wallerstein, Terrence Hopkins and Giovanni Arrighi, *Antisystemic Movements* (London: Verso, 1989), p. 40.
65.  Immanuel Wallerstein, 'Nationalism and the World Transition to Socialism' in Wallerstein, 1984, p. 127.
66.  Ibid., p. 128.
67.  We have referred to Wallerstein as the main exponent of World Systems theory, although it should be noted that his positions and those of Gunder Frank tend to err on the side of determinism while those of Samir Amin and Giovanni Arrighi, other supporters of this perspective, do so to a lesser degree. See Magnus Blomstrum and Bjorn Hettne, *Development Theory in Transition* (London: Zed, 1984), p. 184.
68.  Wallerstein, 1989, p. 115.
69.  Ibid., p. 50.
70.  See Theda Skocpol, 'Wallerstein's World Capitalist System: A Theoretical and Historical Critique', *American Journal of Sociology*, Vol. 82, no. 5, March 1977, p. 1084.
71.  Ibid., p. 1087.
72.  See, for example, Clive Y. Thomas, *The Rise of the Authoritarian State in Peripheral Societies* (New York and London: MR, 1984).
73.  See Elbaki Hermassi, 'Toward a Comparative Study of Revolutions', *Comparative Studies in Society and History*, Vol. 18, no. 2, April 1976, pp. 218–22.
74.  Ibid., p. 216 and Eric Hobsbawm, 'From Social History to the History of Society', *Daedalus*, Vol. 100, no. 1, Winter 1971.
75.  John Walton, *Reluctant Rebels: Comparative Studies of Revolution and Underdevelopment* (New York: Columbia University Press, 1984), p. 16.
76.  Ibid., p. 203.
77.  Walter Goldfrank, 'Theories of Revolution and Revolution Without Theory', *Theory and Society*, Vol. 7, nos 1 and 2, 1979, p. 138.
78.  Ibid., p. 148.
79.  Ibid., p. 149.
80.  Ibid., pp. 149–50.
81.  Ibid., p. 160.
82.  See Farideh Farhi, 'State Disintegration and Urban-based Revolutionary Crisis, A Comparative Analysis of Iran and Nicaragua', *Comparative Political Studies*, Vol. 21, no. 2, July 1988, p. 241.
83.  Ibid., p. 236.
84.  See Farhi, 1988, p. 236 who relies on Gramsci's comments in *Selections From Political Writings, 1910–1920* (New York: International; London: Lawrence and Wishart, 1977).
85.  See Theda Skocpol, 'Rentier State and Shi'a Islam in the Iranian Revolution', *Theory and Society*, Vol. 11, May 1988, pp. 265–304.

86. Farhi, 1988, p. 249.
87. Ibid., p. 250.
88. Ibid., p. 253.
89. Ibid., p. 253.
90. Chaliand, 1977. p. 168.
91. See Berger and Hsiao.
92. Chaliand, 1977, p. 190.
93. Dunn, 1989, p. 256.
94. Ibid., p. 257.
95. S. N. Eisenstadt, 1978, p. 101.
96. Ibid., pp. 9–10.
97. See Eisenstadt, 1988, p. 337 for his conclusions on this notion of open-endedness.
98. Roberto Mangabeira Unger, *False Necessity: Anti-Necessitarian Theory in the Service of Radical Democracy*, (Cambridge: Cambridge University Press, 1987), p. 15.
99. Unger, 1987, p. 16.
100. Ibid., p. 5.
101. Ibid., p. 58.
102. Ibid., p. 65.
103. Ibid., p. 64.
104. Ibid., p. 221.
105. See ibid., pp. 183–7.
106. Ibid., p. 279.
107. Unger, 1987, p. 279, defines negative capability in this way: 'Thus, we may use the poet's turn of phrase to label the empowerment that arises from the denial of whatever in our contexts delivers us over to a fixed scheme of division and hierarchy and to an enforced choice between routine and rebellion.'
108. Ibid., Ch. 5, 'The Programme of Empowered Democracy: The Remaking of Institutional Arrangements', pp. 341–595.
109. Ibid., p. 28.
110. This is how Skocpol, 1979, p. 36, describes her methodological approach:
    Logically speaking, how does comparative historical analysis work? Basically, one tries to establish valid associations of potential causes with the given phenomenon one is trying to explain. There are two main ways to proceed. First, one can try to establish that several cases having in common the phenomenon one is trying to explain also have in common a set of causal factors, although they vary in other ways that might have been causally relevant. This approach is what Mill called the 'Method of Agreement.' Second, one can contrast the cases in which the phenomenon to be explained and the hypothesized causes are present to other cases in which the phenomenon and the causes are both absent, but which are otherwise, as similar as possible to the positive cases. This procedure Mill labelled the 'Method of Difference'.

| CHAPTER 2 | Cuba: State-building, mass mobilisation and limited disentrenchment |

For, after all, it is the July 26th Movement and it alone that has struggled throughout the country and continues to do so. It is the militants of the movement and nobody else who have brought the revolt from the rugged mountains of Oriente all the way to the western provinces; . . . you must understand once and for all that the July 26th militants have not given up and will never give up guiding and leading the people . . .

Fidel Castro

Now is as difficult a time as any in the past thirty years in which to make a worthwhile comment on the future of the Cuban Revolution. In the wake of the recent upheavals in Eastern Europe, the common view, most vociferously expressed in the Cuban exile community in the United States, is that the 'domino theory' has been reversed and that Cuba will be the next communist domino to go.[1] Cooler heads, however, recognise that the Cuban situation is substantially different from that which existed until recently in much of Eastern Europe, not least of all being the fact that the former is an indigenous process arising out of Cuban history and not an imposition by the Red Army in the closing stages of the Second World War.[2] The view expressed here is that while the present period of economic stagnation and international shifts away from 'socialism' represents the greatest crisis Fidel Castro and his regime has ever had to face, the reverse domino theory is deterministic, fails to appreciate the fact that the Cuban revolution has never relied singularly on economic prosperity and popular support for its survival, and fails to comprehend the factors which lead to social revolution, many of which are not necessarily present in Cuba today.

The Cuban state system which has developed since 1959 can best be described as a mass-mobilising, authoritarian political system, its main success having been state-building. The ruling elites who took power then have been able, against all odds, to move Cuba from being a subservient, client state of the United States with an extremely limited foreign policy, to a relatively strong, if still dependent state with its distinct profile in international affairs. Cuba is now a definite, if circumscribed, competitor in the

48

system of nation-states; but in order to achieve this, the state-building elites, in the course of a long, arduous and continuing struggle with the United States, were compelled to enlist the support of broad sections of the population, via methods of mass mobilisation and with a wide range of social benefits. Simultaneously, the military and hegemonic pressures from the United States, the exigencies of survival in a climate of blockade and threats of invasion and the consequences of close relations with the Soviet Union, itself a highly centralised state, combined with the peculiar articulation of social forces at the time of the seizure of power and the ideological predilections of the leaders, emerging out of a possible and cumulative ideological context, to create a highly authoritarian political structure, overwhelmingly dependent on the charismatic leadership of Fidel Castro. The emergence of 'institutionalisation' in the mid-seventies initially amended without substantially changing the authoritarian character of the regime and in the most recent period, centralist tendencies, never far below the surface, have returned as the visible and dominant feature in response to a rapidly changing international landscape.

Three issues seem generally appropriate to this project. The first is to examine why there was a successful revolution in 1959 and to describe the political thrust of the forces which emerged at the helm of that process. The second is to try to sketch how the nature of the revolutionary victory and the new social forces contributed to the character and trajectory of the post-revolutionary state system and thirdly, to establish what this can tell us about the viability of the revolutionary regime and its likelihood of surviving this period of intense difficulty.

## *The making of the 1959 revolution*

An obvious and vital factor which is seldom approached frontally in the literature, is the recollection that there was a revolutionary upsurge in 1933–34 which failed.[3] While noting John Dunn's reservations that 'The inevitability of particular revolutions is strikingly easier to perceive in retrospect than it is to predict in advance',[4] we need to compare the events of 1933 with those of 1959 in order to get some bearing on the reasons for the latter's success. Among the first things to note, is the economic differences between 1933 and the period 1953–59.

Throughout this century, the Cuban economy, almost totally reliant on trade,[5] has also been dependent on sugar exports for its survival. In the period 1902–6, of total Cuban exports of $89 million, $52 million were earned by sugar. In 1952–6, of $623 million exports, sugar earned $508 million. This dependency was exacerbated by the fact that up to 1960, most of the sugar went to one market – the United States. Cuba's trade-dependency on the United States varied from a high in 1902–6 when the US accounted for 82 per cent of Cuban exports, through several fluctuations, and accounted for 66 per cent in 1952–6.[6] With extreme dependence on trade, on one crop and one market, Cuba had always suffered severely from fluctuations in the US economy. Downturns in the economy had taken place in 1907–8 and following the 'Dance of the Millions'[7] in 1921, but the most severe was in 1927–28 when the international sugar market broke down. Real national per capita income in constant pesos, fell from 188 in 1927 to 109 in 1933. The index of daily wages in Havana, which was at 100 in 1921–22, had fallen by a third in 1931. The sugar harvest of 1932 was the lowest since 1915, with an annual sugar price of less than a cent per pound.[8]

While it is true, as Seers argues, that there was chronic stagnation in the Cuban economy from 1923 to 1958 due in part to sugar monoculture and the open nature of the economy,[9] the 1950s in other respects did not resemble the early thirties. Real per capita income had grown constantly from 1953 until 1957 and although it fell in 1958, its level of 142 pesos was, with the exception of the previous two years, the highest since the war. Income levels alone can, of course, be deceptive. High levels of unemployment were sustained throughout the 1950s, the high figure of 16 per cent for the period 1956–57 being the lowest for the middle of the decade.[10] However, in the critical wages sector, employed workers still managed to secure a sizeable part of the national income. Although wages as a percentage of domestic national income had fallen immediately after Fulgencio Batista's coup in 1952, it had managed to recapture some ground by 1958 and its level of 62.3 per cent in that year was still far above the 55.3 per cent of 1945.[11] The fact that labour under Batista was not doing badly was partly a result of his conscious policy of wooing the trade union movement and partly due to the initial successes of his broader economic strategy. As Dominguez suggests:

> The policy of labour protection and high wages throughout the 1940's discouraged private foreign investment; when policies were less clearly pro-labour and wages were rising less rapidly during Batista's second administration, it increased again and, consequently, the economy in the late 1940's and 1950's began again to grow. Labour's share fell, increasing profits, but without leading to a decline in real wages. No one lost. It was not surprising then, that Cuban labour supported Batista until the very end.[12]

This evident economic difference and its impact on wage workers, strikingly demarcates 1933 from 1953–59. In 1933 it was the 12 August strike of transport workers, eventually developing into a general strike, which is acknowledged to have been a critical moment in the departure of

Machado. The notes of Ruby Phillips, wife of the *New York Times* correspondent are useful, in that, not only do they outline the importance of the strike, but also suggest the absence of leadership – critical in 1933:

> A marvellous thing, a whole nation folds its arms and quits work. I don't know exactly what they can accomplish . . . they intend either to starve themselves to death or to force the US to take pity on them and intervene . . . there is no leadership . . . it is entirely spontaneous – a nation without a leader acting in perfect accord, . . .[13]

The situation on 9 April 1958, with the 26 July movement already a highly effective guerrilla force in Oriente province, with a structure of underground cells in Havana, was completely different:

> When 9 April came, there was a good deal of confused violence but most shops were open, as were most factories and the harbour. Neither the CTC nor the communists took any notice of the 26 July's calls and the transport system therefore worked normally. Some electric companies were sabotaged, some buses overturned, two big shops were attacked, but the Havana electricity supply was left alone, though that had been supposed to signal the beginning of the strike.[14]

This failure was partly due to the lack of influence in the trade union movement of 26 July and this in itself hints at the possible class-orientation of its leaders,[15] but the more important suggestion, as the statistics seem to indicate, is that there was not sufficient economic deterioration and therefore, popular support in the trade unions for a general strike. This conclusion of lack of active political support 'below' can be extended to much of rural *campesino* Cuba, where, as Dominguez suggests, with the exception of the clearly aggrieved squatters of Oriente province, earlier land reform had meant that there was very little basis for support of insurrection:

> When Fidel Castro's insurrection came, it had settled in the only part of Cuba where latifundia and land-tenure insecurity were still issues, and where pre-revolutionary agrarian legislation had had little protective effect. Its survival in the Sierra Maestra would have been unlikely without peasant support. Providentially for Castro, this was the only area of Cuba where he could have found insecure peasants facing hostile landowners and government.[16]

This is not to say that there were not grievances, and in some cases deep ones, among the popular classes. Black Cubans had after all, revolted in 1912 and significant discrimination – most notoriously, a colour bar at the best beaches around Havana – continued to be practised against this third of the Cuban population.[17] But ironically both Batista, who was a mulatto, and indeed Machado before him, were considered as protectors of negroes and inequality was therefore not automatically focused on them.[18] If economic disaster and working-class revolt are not common factors of both processes and if, indeed, the revolutionary upsurge which failed was the one in which the popular classes played a more active role, then we need to look elsewhere for explanations for the failure in the earlier period and the success in 1959.

The proposal we shall advance is that since uprising from below is not a common feature in both events, it is obviously not an absolute prerequisite for revolution. What is common to both, and therefore seems to be a necessary feature, is a rupture between fractions of the state elites. In the Cuban case this took the form of younger middle-class aspirant state elites, who became aggrieved because their natural passage into the highest echelons of the state was blocked by an older, aggressive and monopolistic fraction. The open struggle to break this monopoly in a specific international and temporal context, the emergence of peculiar leaders with specific and cumulative ideological opportunities intertwined with the luck of the moment, all helped to determine the final outcome.

The dominant and autonomous role of the middle classes in the state structure of peripheral societies has already been suggested by Farhi in the first chapter, although the specifics of the Cuban case need to be pursued. The second independence war of 1895–98 had led to devastating consequences for Cuba. Over 300 000 people died, or well over a tenth of the total population.[19] Apart from the obvious consequences for the mass of the people, one of the repercussions was that a Cuban big landowning class as a viable social grouping, had been destroyed. In 1899, for example, there were only 200 sugar mills worth reviving compared with 1100 in 1894.[20] After the American intervention in 1898, but more so after the Platt Amendment[21] to the Cuban Constitution of 1901, US investment and business had come to dominate the Cuban economy. In 1927, over 62.5 per cent of total sugar production took place in US-owned mills.[22] After the termination of the Platt Amendment in 1934, this situation changed, with Cubans playing a bigger role in the economy, but it is still fair to say that in the 1950s, with the critical decisions about the economy in American hands, with commerce in Havana in the hands of Chinese and Spaniards, that the sphere of activity open to young educated Cubans was more often than not the state.

However, it was a state which had a very limited ambit for its operation. If the Platt Amendment restricted Cuban sovereignty on paper, the United States showed that they were willing to back it up in practice, intervening with troops twice, in 1906–8 and again in 1912. In the absence of real sovereignty, then, and with the economy largely out of their hands,[23] office-holding became for office-holders inevitably a means to accumulate profit and thus an end in itself. As Hennessy suggests, this

> perpetuated the Spanish legacy that public office should be made a source of private profits. Politics thus became the key to social advancement and so little more than a squabble between factions for the ownership of the government.[24]

For the young Cuban middle classes in the years after independence, there must have been an acute awareness that the state, employing some 186 000 people, or 11 per cent of the population, and allocating to them 80 per cent of its revenues in 1950,[25] was their natural avenue of operation. Any attempt to close off that avenue could be expected to meet resistance in a system where other avenues of advancement were generally not open.

In the years before Gerardo Machado's accession to power in 1925, particularly the relatively stable period between 1913 and 1920 when Menocal was president, the system seemed to have worked in its peculiarly Cuban and dependent way. There remained a sharp distinction between economic growth and political life, with economic prosperity not so much the result of government policy as a response to US investment and the buoyant nature of the US economy. Office-holders used their positions of power to enrich themselves through control of the national lottery, corrupt public works programmes or other forms of graft.[26] Elections were, quite naturally, hotly contested and inevitably fraudulent, with constant appeals to Washington to intervene, which the US did, acting as final arbiter sometimes on the side of the incumbents and at others on the side of the opposition.[27] Actual US military intervention, or the threat of it, served to 'pluralise' the system. More pointedly, it allowed for a circulation of elites which precluded any single set of incumbents from dominating.

All this changed with Machado. He took office in 1925 on the liberal ticket, but an agreement with the other parties to cooperate with him, soon brought any pretence of political competition to an end. Within three years he had called a constitutional convention, abolished the vice-presidency and extended his term from the day his first administration was supposed to end in May 1929 until May 1935.[28] In his first three years in power, Machado repeatedly demonstrated his aggressive and ruthless character in his destruction of the anarchist movement and his brutal persecution of trade unionists and members of the nascent communist party. The term 'being thrown to the sharks' was given a literal interpretation by Machado, whose henchmen tied weights to trade unionists and other members of the opposition and dumped them in the shark-infested seas around Havana.[29]

By aggressively attacking the labour movement, Machado was able to postpone rebellion from below, but it was his monopolistic tendencies in the state, creating a fissure at the level of state-building elites between the 'ins' and the 'outs' which led to crisis and a revolutionary situation. Thus, Thomas notes that Machado's illegal decision to extend his power in 1928 had 'in effect forced many people not automatically opposed to (him) into active opposition'[30] and his feeding of four students to the sharks for allegedly being communists on the eve of his declaration had helped to change the class composition of his enemies, who were 'thereafter middle class, professional men, together with (in many instances) their sons, students anyway . . .'.[31]

Machado's rapid accumulation of power needs to be seen in the context of a deteriorating economic situation in which the traditional methods of corruption were inadequate to relieve the politicians' growing debts. Thus,

> Senators found it impossible not to accept the distribution of lottery collectorships with the right to sell 30% or 50% above the market price. The President and his friends absorbed a graft equivalent to a fifth of the national product or $M10 a year. Most politicians, like most Cubans , had over-extended themselves in the boom years; prices were now falling, and so those who could, grasped at corruption in order to help themselves, even if they had previously not stooped so low.[32]

This in itself, though, is insufficient to explain the phenomenon. Machado came to power in the context in which a left-wing and radically nationalist movement was growing in response to the deteriorating economy and external revolutionary events such as the Mexican and Bolshevik revolutions. His attempts to smash these movements and to keep Cuba open for business, clearly endeared him to the US. On his visit to Washington in 1927 he was warmly praised by President Coolidge, and fêted by big business. A representative of J. P. Morgan's, the financial conglomerate, expressed the hope that Cubans would find a way of keeping Machado in power indefinitely.[33] It was not until the middle of 1929, deep into his second illegal term, that elements in the State Department began to argue against Machado and not until Roosevelt's election in March 1933 that the balance in the US began to tip decisively against him.[34]

The parallel with Batista's *coup d'état* of 1952 is striking. Under the presidencies of Grau (1944–48) and Prio (1948–52) corruption, always a constant in Cuban politics, had grown dramatically. In addition, violence, based on quasi-political gangs which had arisen in the Machado era and much of which had its origins in the University of Havana, had intensified. In the 1952 Presidential elections, many young middle-class persons (including, most notably, Fidel Castro), placed their hopes for an end to violence, corruption and greater access to the state apparatus in the Ortoxodo party led by Roberto Agramonte. Dominguez is correct in asserting that in the 1950s, the most potent ideological factor in Cuba, best exemplified in the young middle-class supporters of the Ortoxodos, was not nationalism, but issues of legitimacy and the question of corruption.[35]

Batista's coup of 10 March forestalled the possibility of an Ortoxodo win in the elections and a subsequent circulation of state-building elites. This was compounded by fraudulent elections in 1954 and 1958, which, as in the case of Machado's extension of power in 1928, served to deepen the fissures at the top and align increasingly large elements of the excluded middle against him. In a growing economy, corruption also grew. In addition to the traditional use of the lottery to disburse patronage as well as for personal enrichment, Batista gave out sinecures to loyal supporters in the civil service and offered subsidies to enterprises or directly to workers in exchange for political support.[36] More critically, corruption under Batista extended into the military, his base of support, where Batista supporters were promoted over professional officers, creating dissatisfaction, lowering morale and further complicating the question of circulation in that fraction of the middle class presumably most loyal to the regime.[37] This factor would, of course, contribute significantly to his eventual overthrow. Clues as to the conditions which allowed Batista to carry through a successful coup and return to prominence, are more difficult to identify than the overt case of economic contraction which preceded and intensified during Machado's tenure. One strong possibility was that the Batistiano officers in the army who remained in place and retained their privileges from the period of his first regime in the forties, feared that a new government, particularly if it was Ortoxodo, might move against them. One established fraction in the middle then, sought to preserve its position in the state against potential competitors. However, as with Machado, the international situation, in particular the attitude of the United States, was of paramount importance. This period was at the heart of the Cold War and Batista realised that this situation 'gave him new opportunities for ingratiation with the US'.[38] As with Machado, any regime, no matter how distasteful it might otherwise be, was preferable to one which included communists or leaned to the left.

Two individuals in twentieth-century Cuba before 1959 stopped the flawed but accepted system of legitimation which allowed for a circulation of elites and for new elements to share in the fruits of office. On both occasions, not as a result of uprising from below, but as the consequence of middle-class rebellion, fissures were created at the top which precipitated revolutionary situations. A closer look has therefore to be taken at the specific character of the middle-class elites to begin to understand why revolution was successful in one instance, but not in another.

## Revolutionary elites

Much attention is placed in the vast literature on the Cuban Revolution, on the role of the so called 'subjective factor'. The independent intervention of Fidel Castro and a small band of brave *guerrilleros* is often, and with some justification, viewed as the critical element which led to success in 1959. Wolf, for example, argues that in a political situation which was finely balanced, in which Batista had developed a symbiotic relationship with different groups in the society, only the injection of a new force from outside could provide the push to break the deadlock of existing political forces.[39] This is, at best, only partly correct. Although Fidel Castro is an exceptional leader and human being and has been a remarkably lucky person, he was not outside, but very much a part of, Cuban society and traditions. Secondly, his success, remarkable as it was as a demonstration of human perseverance and will, could not have been attained without a favourable or permissive international context. Finally, the very nature of the victory, virtually given to the people instead of taken by them, helped to configure the possible, though not determinate direction which post-revolutionary Cuba would take.

Faced with blockages to their accession to state power and privileges, young middle-class elites revolted in 1933 and 1952. What is most remarkable about them is not the differences in their ideological outlook and strategies, which one would expect with a gap of twenty years, but the remarkable similarities. In 1931, in the face of Machadista incursions, a middle-class opposition secret society called the ABC and headed by young professionals was founded. Its members were

> serious idealists, interested in the regeneration of Cuban life
> ... in Cuba itself their relations were restricted to the students. Their seventeen original points proposed elimination of *latifundias,* restriction on the acquisition of land by US companies, producers' co-operatives, nationalization of the public services, preference for Cubans in business appointments, and new men, new ideas, political liberty, social justice and recovery of the land.[40]

ABC was not the only middle-class group opposed to Batista. There were others to the left based in and around the University of Havana, inspired by Mella, the student leader who was a founding member of the Cuban Communist Party in 1923, but who had been assassinated in 1929. ABC, however, came from that same middle-class mainstream of which Castro was to be a part. All the early statements of Castro and the 26 July Movement emphasised, as a first priority, a return to honest and legitimate government and only secondly, a moderate nationalism. In Castro's most famous pre-revolutionary speech, *History will Absolve Me,* Dominguez notes that:

> The main theme . . . goes to the core of the problem of political legitimacy in the 1950s: the Batista government had come to power unconstitutionally by force; the constitutional organs had been either scuttled or ignored; corruption, torture, repression and officially sanctioned murder had replaced the rule of law. Nationalism played a very limited role in Castro's defense.[41]

ABC, 26 July and student organisations of both periods were also united in their favoured tactic against the dictatorships, in that all were, initially at least, concerned with armed violence to either weaken or overthrow the regime. However, in this also lies a critical distinction. Whereas ABC's terrorism was less aimed at overthrowing the Machado regime by force than to make Cuba ungovernable so that the US would intervene,[42] the 26 July Movement, initially moderate on nationalism, nevertheless envisaged a revolution without US intervention.

Two trends seem to have predominated among Cuban middle-class state-building elites and their ideologists since the nineteenth century and can be seen in this divergence between ABC and 26 July. Liss identifies a distinction at the colonial university of Havana between those *pensadores* who envisioned a completely autonomous Cuba, freed by revolutionary means and those who, conceding Spanish hegemony, also proposed independence, but in a peaceful way, retaining ties to Spain.[43] Both trends existed in 1933 as they obviously did in 1953, but new conditions allowed the autonomous trend to gain ascendancy and lead the movement to victory. To understand how this happened, however, we need, first of all, to look at how Fidel Castro, the middle-class representative of the autonomous trend in the 1950s, developed ideologically and as a leader *par excellence.*

One of the central controversies of the Cuban Revolution surrounds the question as to when did Fidel Castro adopt communist ideological positions. Much of this debate has become sterile, if indeed it ever had great significance, particularly that surrounding the 'betrayal of the revolution' thesis.[44] Location of Castro's ideological position is important, though, if it can support our assertion that he was and remains, a fairly consistent representative of a state-building middle-class fraction and that there has not so much been a shift in ideology as an adaptation of ideology to suit the exigencies of an older, state-building project.

On 16 January 1959, two weeks after taking power, Castro denied at the grave of the dead Ortoxodo leader Chibás that he was a communist, a statement he was to repeat often in the following weeks.[45] Yet just two years later, on the eve of the US-supported Bay of Pigs invasion at a mass meeting to rally support after the bombing of Havana, he declared the socialist character of the revolution and on 2 December that same year, he announced that he had been a Marxist convert for many years.[46] Many scholars have sought to establish what precisely is the truth. Thus, Thomas felt that Fidel in 1959 was not a communist, but was a radical nationalist and playing with a number of strategies;[47] Bonsal suggests that it was the abrogation of the sugar treaty by the US which forced Fidel to move to communism;[48] Szulc accepts the official Cuban position that Castro was a long-time supporter of Marxism from his university days and carefully refrained from exposing his true position.[49] While there may be some truth in all of these statements, Domínguez appears to come closest to an understanding of reality when he argues that from the taking of power through to the nationalisation and then socialisation of the economy, the revolutionary leadership acted autonomously:

> they were not compelled to socialize, although they responded to and articulated pressures from below. Rather, they fashioned the future of Cuba by anticipating probable consequences. Nationalization, but with enterprise left in private hands, had been possible in the spring of 1959; it was no longer politically or ideologically sufficient by the fall of 1960: political and economic power had to be concentrated in the hands of the revolutionary government.[50]

What then was the cumulative ideological context – the accumulation of ideas and available options which guided this relatively autonomous elite? It can be argued that it was an ideology, almost a mythology, to fulfil an historical mission – a task given to the 'generation of the centennial'[51] to build an independent Cuban state. The peculiarity of Cuban colonialism had meant that for over two centuries before sugar became absolute king, an independent Cuban creole society was able to develop with limited outside interference to a far greater degree than anywhere else in the Caribbean.[52] A feeling developed, reflected in the long independence tradition at the University of Havana, that Cuba could go it alone. This tradition was best exemplified in José Martí, who was not himself a product of the University but whose influence on Cuba and on Castro in particular, is supreme. Martí placed himself firmly in the camp of the radical nationalists who retained deep reservations and hostility to the United States, distinguished between false and genuine independence for Cuba, saw this independence as linked to a broader Latin American project and perceived the need for social reform, including an end to racial inequality as a necessary part of the independence movement. At the same time, Martí was opposed to socialism and could be considered far more a disciple of Rousseau than of Marx.[53] Anti-Americanism of course, intensified as a central factor in Cuban politics after the US intervention in 1898, after the Platt Amendment and throughout the period of direct US interference before 1934. After the abrogation of the Platt Amendment and with the greater Cuban ownership of the economy, anti-Americanism continued more as an intellectual than a popular phenomenon.[54] This is an important point, because it was precisely the intellectuals or a fraction of them, who were trying to capture the state.

Other influences also weighed on Fidel and his followers. From Tony Guiteras, the radical student-leader of the anti-Machado period, Castro and his generation gained an appreciation of the efficacy of armed struggle and from Eddy Chibás, first leader of the Ortoxodos, who had committed suicide while broadcasting on the radio, a concept of honesty and the need for morality in Cuban politics.[55] To these can be added the formative context of Castro's own experience. His early years at the prestigious Belen catholic school, where Chibás had preceded him years before, had no doubt schooled him to be a leader and honed the expectations that one day he would become one. This is supported by Thomas who suggests that the 'Jesuits were training him to be the white hope of the right'.[56] His experience as a member of one of the ubiquitous armed gangs at the University of Havana[57] would certainly have enforced the notion of armed struggle as a preferable option, as might his observations of, and minor participation in revolutionary upheaval in Colombia in 1948.[58] Other Latin American events also helped to accumulate collective experience and remould the state-building perspective. Thus, the CIA's action in overthrowing the radical Arbenz government in Guatemala in 1954 at which Castro's most important lieutenant, Che Guevara, was a witness, would no doubt have strengthened the view that basic reforms without a revolutionising of the state, would antagonise the US, while not providing Cuba with the wherewithal to protect itself.[59]

Castro, then, was the inheritor of a radical nationalist and state-building tradition of *Cubanismo*,[60] which pre-dated Marxism. While this cannot decisively exclude his assertion that he had been a Marxist for many years, the continuity of his statements and those of 26 July with the traditions inherited from Martí, Guiteras and Chibás, the consistency of his state-building project and his subordination of ideology at critical moments to the priorities of the Cuban state, which we shall discuss later in the post revolutionary period, all support such a conclusion.

It would, however, be remiss to suggest that a fissure at the top – a structural factor – carried through by a fragment of the middle class possessed with a clear state-building ideology, is a sufficient condition to explain revolutionary success. Any such presentation would have to be criticised for being sterile and failing to grasp the role of the individual and of chance in historical determination. It is almost banal, but still important to recall Fidel Castro's qualities as a rare individual. Embracing to some degree the audacity of Guiteras, the integrity of Chibás and if not Martí's intellectualism then his intellect, he is a person with inherent leadership qualities and, equally important if also dangerous from any democratic perspective, with an almost messianic sense of his own importance and place in Cuban and world history; well-read, with an uncanny ability to recall even small details; a man who is personally brave and in the Sierra campaign repeatedly put himself at the head of his troops, he also possessed the *caudillo*'s sense of welfare and personal concern for those loyal to him.[61] The reverse of this was also true. Castro was and is a ruthless opponent when faced with any threat to his personal power or to the power of his regime.[62] When these qualities are combined in someone who is undoubtedly one of the great public speakers of the twentieth century, with the ability to mesmerise small as well as large groups, it is not difficult to understand the fact that

> A month after Batista's flight, Castro had established a personal hold over the Cuban masses such as no Latin American leader had ever had. . . . Already he was the champion to whom multitudes desired to surrender their will, confident that he would not betray such expectations.[63]

Could the Cuban Revolution have been made without Fidel Castro? The question, of course, begs itself, but it seems improbable to conclude that the structural situation alone can account for its success. Among his immediate lieutenants was his brother Raul Castro, who, with a completely different personality has never been able to attain the comparative confidence of the people. Frank Pais, a possible contender, though young, was shot by police. Che Guevara was Argentinian, and while widely appreciated, his nationality and nomadic temperament weighed against him during his brief sojourn, as a possible substitute. Camillo Cienfuegos, who died too early in the day for a full assessment, while appreciated for his military prowess, was never more than a lieutenant and did not possess the intellectual training for the job. Juan Almeida had similar problems but also suffered from the additional stigma that he was black and unlikely to be accepted by the Cuban middle classes, who, up to 1959, were the natural constituency of 26 July. Castro was the only person capable of providing unquestioned leadership and it is even more remarkable that while many others perished, it was he who survived the army massacres after the failed Moncada attack in 1953, the debacle after the landing of the Granma in Santiago and the dangerous campaign in the Sierra Maestra. More critically, it was equally fortunate that he chose to land in Oriente, the cradle of Cuban radicalism, where he could link up with and gain tactical support from a deeply dissatisfied squatter peasantry, which possessed tactical mobility because of its distance from the administrative centres and its location in difficult terrain. It is impossible to understand the victory of the Cuban revolution without mentioning the role of personality and of fortuitous events as it is equally difficult to do anything more than mention them as part of the necessary tapestry of history.

## *Permissive world context*

Located amid the dissatisfied peasantry in the Sierra Maestra; consolidating support in the already disgruntled middle classes of Havana and Santiago; possessing a leader with remarkable skills and fortitude. Is this enough to explain the victory? One critical factor marks off 1959 from 1933 and that is the existence of a permissive world context.

The United States approach to its hegemonic relationship with Cuba changed during the course of the twentieth century. In the first quarter of the century when the Platt regime was in full operation, US intervention was overt, US ambassadors were in fact proconsuls and armed intervention was openly pursued as the effective way to implement Washington's policy. But throughout the 1920s, attitudes in Cuba and in the United States began to change. Even before 1933, Machado had sought a termination of the Platt Amendment and President Roosevelt at his inauguration speech in 1933 had mentioned the beginning of a 'good neighbour policy' towards Latin America.[64] However, in the revolutionary struggle of 1933, Sumner Welles, the Roosevelt appointee, acting ironically as the last proconsul, forced Machado out of office, but even more critically prevented the government of Grau San Martín, with his radical deputy Tony Guiteras, from taking office by withholding recognition.[65] In 1933, with its absolute dependence on the US sugar quota, with no other state willing or able to fill the role of the United States, there appeared to be, and were in fact, no options to that of acquiescing in US hegemony. It is no wonder then that ABC violence sought only to encourage the Americans to intervene and that Grau had to quickly concede to Welles and demit office.

By the late 1950s the situation was substantially different from what it had been even in the earlier part of the decade. Extreme Cold War McCarthyite positions were on the decline in the US. Eisenhower, mistakenly perceived by some because of his military background as a cold warrior, was relatively moderate, had in fact been elected on a platform of ending the Korean War and was reluctant to extend further conflict in Asia.[66] Despite the continued presence of cold warriors John Foster Dulles at the State Department and his brother Allen at the CIA, in 1959 the United States establishment was not totally opposed to a neutralist government even in Cuba.

> Conservatives in the State Department, in business and in other
> government agencies were less well placed in 1959 than in

> 1954. Among many North American government employees,
> . . . there was a strong desire to help a reforming government in
> Cuba.[67]

In Latin America itself, Vice-President Nixon had been jeered and attacked on his Spring 1958 visit to the continent; in the same year the Venezuelan dictator Pérez Jiménez was overthrown and the reformer Frondizi was successful at the polls in Argentina. Further, the upcoming (1960) US presidential election was quite probably a restraining factor, as the already cautious Eisenhower did not wish to preside over a debacle in Cuba which would adversely affect the electoral opportunities of his Republican successor.[68] More critically, if quite understandably, apart from Nixon who had serious reservations,[69] there was no general consensus that Castro was, or would become communist. This grid of circumstances, both national and international, thus constituted the essential features of a permissive world context, captured in the memoirs of Philip Bonsal, the last US ambassador to Cuba, who asserts that in 1959 a US intervention 'was inconceivable in the context of the existing public opinion in Cuba, the United States and Latin America'.[70] One other factor rounds off the new international context: the existence of a highly competitive and relatively powerful state willing and able to substitute for the US sugar quota and provide strategic support to Cuba and this, of course, was the Soviet Union.

So if we temporarily locate ourselves around the year 1957, we can suggest a Cuban society in which there was a sharp differentiation between state-builders, drawn from different fractions of the middle class and Cuban business which was either foreign or in its national dimensions, looking to the US for solutions, or concerned mainly with a stable business climate. The Roman Catholic Church – an important player in national affairs in other Latin American countries – was too weak to form an alternative base either for support or resistance to the regime.[71] In the face of an aggressive and monopolistic fraction of the middle class, responding to the rules of accumulation in the Cuban state which closed off the avenue for the circulation of elites, and with the tacit if not active approval of the US, a section of those elites rebelled. The new factors which make this situation different from 1933 were firstly, the existence of a permissive world context, which meant that the options available to state-building elites were temporarily not limited by the traditional constraints of US hegemony. A second difference was the partly fortuitous location of this elite far from the centre of power where it was able to gradually stimulate the destruction of the already fractured state until, with the minimum of effort, the whole apparatus crumbled. But this factor of minimum effort also points to an important difference from 1933: that there was no widespread uprising from below. The uprising of April 1958 had failed. There was obviously widespread sympathy for Fidel and 26 July, but sympathy and revolutionary support are two different things.

Cuba in this sense is almost the polar opposite to Skocpol's Chinese situation, where a protracted anti-Japanese war mingled with a peasant rebellion, with the peasantry and the revolutionary elites sharing equal responsibility for the final outcome. Fidel Castro and 26 July owed debts to the Cuban peasantry, but on a far different scale than those owed by the communist party to the Chinese peasantry in 1949. In a sense, the tiny vanguard which numbered no more than 300 men in mid-1958, six months before victory and 3000 men at the end of the year,[72] had given the revolution to Cuba, or marched into a *fait accompli* situation in which the state had imploded, in which there were very few structures or institutions to compete with the new state-builders and in which potential opposition was paralysed by its traditional reliance on the United States for solutions. To some extent then, Castro was right to conclude as he did from his base in the Sierra Maestra in 1957 that

> it is the July 26th Movement and it alone that has struggled actively throughout the country and continues to do so. It is the militants of the movement and nobody else who have brought the revolt from the rugged mountains of Oriente all the way to the western provinces.[73]

Starting off with a relatively moderate programme, these elites, in the course of paying their few debts to the Oriente peasantry in the land reform, and in the course of trying to build an independent Cuban state 90 miles from the United States, were forced to go beyond the reformist programme, to seek new internal alliances and to seek new external patrons to substitute for the US. The nature of the state, however, its potential for further democracy and for negative capability, was highly influenced by the articulation of forces at the time of the seizure of power, the huge gap between leaders and led which was an inevitable product of the way power was taken and the peculiar qualities of the premier and powerful state-builder Fidel Castro. This already deeply-entrenched structure would be further moulded by the pressures of the international states system to produce a contemporary state with a high degree of authoritarianism and limited disentrenchment.

## *Mass mobilisation with limited disentrenchment*

Writing in 1964, O'Connor argued that, instead of the policy of outlawing any opposition, Fidel Castro had the alternative of retaining power by allowing the opposition to function as legitimate interest groups and by employing a policy of divide and conquer, preventing any majority coalition from developing.[74] Indeed, the revolutionary moment with the dissolution of the old state, provided many possibilities, and an option in which opposition parties would have been allowed to organise within the context of a revolutionary constitution cannot be dismissed out of hand. This, however, has not happened. Although the Cuban government has 'opened up' during periods of relaxation of tensions with the US, each important juncture in the revolutionary calendar has ultimately served to consolidate central authority, eliminate competitive poles of power, restrict and channel debate and place restraints on genuine experimentation. If Unger's 'negative capability' is used to describe an ideal pole of democratic possibility and social and economic flexibility, then the emergent Cuban state can be said to have provided important social benefits for its people and brought them into national life through a process of mass mobilisation, but this has been done at the expense of democracy and disentrenchment. However, the very act of revolution and popular mobilisation, constrained though it has been by statist tendencies, has provided openings for popular initiative and cultural regeneration as Cubans assert their independence.

While powerful forces emanated from the way the revolution was made, and international pressure and available ideological context, combined with Fidel Castro's own personality, to impel the Cuban Revolution along the line of least resistance towards authoritarianism, we shall suggest that this was not inevitable. Different crises in the recent past might have been seized as appropriate springboards to depart on radically different and potentially more liberating programmes. Even today, in a period of its most profound crisis, options might still be available for the advancement of democracy and the attainment of greater economic independence. We shall propose that, while objective economic factors constrain small states from achieving economic independence, weaknesses in the economy are at least partly due to the authoritarian and centralist character of the society.

When Fidel Castro entered Havana on 8 January 1959 after a triumphal five-day procession through the backbone of Cuba, church bells tolled, factory whistles blew and ships' sirens sounded. It was like the Second Coming, seemingly confirmed when, later that night while addressing a massive crowd at Camp Colombia – recently Batista's military headquarters – a white dove suddenly landed on his shoulders. This powerful piece of symbolism, according to Szulc, 'touched off an explosion of "FIDEL! ... FIDEL! ... FIDEL!"'.[75] Castro had captured the imagination and along with it the loyalty of the Cuban people and now held them in his grip. However, in January while this was the reality, the actual appearance of the government, with the Supreme Court judge Manuel Urrutia as President, was middle-class and moderate. Within two years, this would change drastically. As Domínguez describes it:

The government assumed control of newspapers, magazines, journals, publishing houses, radio, and television. It exercised a monopoly over political socialization in the schools. All became organs of the government and the communist party. The ban on competitive political activity was enforced; by the end of 1960, all political opposition to the government and its policies had become illegal. In 1974 Fidel Castro could report with pleasure that 'the opportunities to carry out opposition against the government are minimal.'. . . The collective ownership of the means of production and the elimination of effective political criticism on a national scale clearly left enormous power in the government's hands.[76]

Whether or not an authoritarian government was inevitable, there were powerful factors forcing the revolution in that direction, some of which have already been mentioned. Thus, the way power was taken, with limited participation from below, thrust the revolutionary leadership and Fidel Castro in particular, into a paternalistic relationship with the rest of the population. This was further enhanced by the absence of a credible opposition, the weakness of institutions such as the church[77] and the migration to Miami of large numbers of skilled Cubans – not all of them by any means counter-revolutionary – who chose the traditional and secure exit route for all Cuban opposition.[78] Cultural currents in Cuba seemed to have also played an independent role in the deification of Castro. Few commentators acknowledge the importance of the Afro–Cuban religion Santería as a political element in the revolution, but if as some argue, it is a more popular religion than Roman Catholicism, then its role may indeed be more significant. Landau argues that for the Santeros, Fidel is Obatala, a messenger deity who was destined to be sent to save the island:

> The messenger would have unusual, almost superhuman qualities. He would possess the strength and stamina of the horse, the determination and presence of a stallion. The figure would be a spellbinding orator who could lead Cuba from its demoralized, discombobulated state into unity, power, greatness on the world stage. *Obatala* would redeem the island's people, save its soul and dignity, forge the populace into a mighty engine of moral force.[79]

While African cultural currents contributed to a cult of leader worship, Azicri is also right to conclude that so too did the Spanish colonial years, which were

> an exercise in authoritarian rule and abuse of power. They left ingrained in the collective psyche a desideratum for caudillo

worship that undermined representative democratic government.[80]

No doubt Castro himself fitted this role perfectly. The effective *caudillo,*
who would later be dubbed *El Caballo* – the horse – by ,the populace,
brooked no opposition. Numerous cases can be mentioned to illustrate the
point. Before 1959, Fidel manoeuvred effectively to neutralise alternative
poles of leadership from the urban arm of 26 July, from the revolutionary
Student Directorate and from the traditional parties.[81] The alliance with the
'old communists' in the PSP can also be seen as an example of Castro's
unrelenting drive to accumulate and secure power. When as Szulc argues,
he realised that the urban 26 July had failed in April 1958 to carry through
a successful general strike and that his movement had insufficient cadres to
wield power effectively, he sought an alliance with the 17 000-man strong
and ideologically trained PSP.[82] This provided the movement with valuable
administrators and disciplined production-based cadres, and helped to smooth
over the initial and vital links with the Soviet Union. However, when in
1962 and later in the 1968 'microfaction' crisis, elements from the old PSP
led by Anibal Escalante sought, obviously with a great degree of self-
interest, to promote their own former party members over the Fidelistas,
Castro was ruthless in denouncing, and in the latter incident sentencing to
long prison terms, the major offenders.[83] A similar motivation may have
been behind the 1989 drugs scandal which led to the execution of highly-
decorated General Arnaldo Ochoa Sanchez and three other officials and the
imprisonment of ten others for periods of from ten to thirty years. The
Cuban government argued that they had been illegally involved in smug-
gling drugs from Colombia to the US, but the subsequent wide-ranging
purges in the Ministry of the Interior and Castro's own statements that the
Ministry had bought arms and 'there was an attempt to put it on par with the
armed forces',[84] suggests that there may have been a plot afoot. If this is the
case, then this is a typical Castroite manoeuvre to eliminate potential
enemies at an early stage.[85]

Unquestionably, the very act of carrying out a revolutionary state-building project on the doorsteps of the United States required, at least initially,
a significant degree of central military as well as economic control. The
need to have a credible and coordinated defence of the country and its
leaders was self-evident after the attempted invasion at the Bay of Pigs in
1961 and the numerous acts of destabilisation and assassination of leaders
attempted by the US in the 1960s.[86] Less obvious as a centralising factor was
the impact of the US-imposed trade embargo of 1960.

> The most significant long-term effect . . . was the need to place
> ever more power in the hands of the government. The fear of
> sabotage required political loyalty in the management of enter-

prise. The need to 'cannibalize' some industries to provide spare parts for others required centralized management of entire sectors of the economy. The need to mobilize people to work where they were needed so that the country could become economically self-sufficient placed the entire economy and society on a quasi-war status.[87]

Other factors made their independent contribution. Cuba's adoption of socialism and its close relationship with the Soviet Union – an inevitability once the US embargo had been established – increased bureaucracy and rigidity as the Soviets sought to establish matching institutions and planning methods to fit into their highly-centralised system.[88] Marxism–Leninism as an ideology can also be cited as an independent variable. While it is our view that national, state-building concepts remain at the heart of the revolutionary project, democratic centralism, a key component of Leninism, requiring absolute fealty to decisions and to higher organs, provided the perfect cover for the elimination of opposition[89] and the consolidation of the centre and leader.

In the face of these real and compelling forces, was there ever a feasible alternative to a highly-centralised, monopolistic leadership? This question can best be addressed by looking at the wide-ranging negative effects which domination of the society by one party and one person have had on the revolution. In René Dumont's study *Is Cuba Socialist?*, the early consequences of monolithic power on the economy are clearly outlined. The inability effectively to criticise decisions from the top meant that mistakes, such as the overemphasis on diversification in the early period, were only corrected long after the damage had been wrought. Even then, there was the tendency to swing from one extreme to the other – in this case, to absolute monoculture – as a solution.[90] Extreme centralisation also meant the growth of a complex and burdensome bureaucracy, which retarded the implementation of decisions and impaired the functioning of the economy; in 1970 Dumont pointed out that it required the cooperation of thirteen government bureaus in order to export one case of tomatoes.[91] Most important though, were his criticisms of the ubiquitous presence of Fidel Castro's influence in all aspects of the economy. While Castro did have a good understanding of Cuban agriculture, his lack of specific technical knowledge meant that his decisions were often wrong, but his overarching power meant that no one could disagree without damaging consequences.

The man who opposes Castro's ideas is quickly rejected, and as a result, when Castro sets forth a mistaken proposition nobody dares oppose him if he wants to hold on to his job, as is usually the case. His entourage seems to be cowed by a mixture of fear and admiration.[92]

Some writers have suggested that a similar case can be made out for the cultural sphere, where, increasingly after Castro's famous 1961 statement that 'within the revolution complete freedom; against the revolution, none',[93] genuine freedom to criticise and experiment rapidly deteriorated. This led to the suggestion that the revolution, certainly in the literary sphere, has produced little of lasting importance and that the great works and individuals of Cuban literature were produced under the *ancien régime*.[94] But this position is mistaken. Despite real constraints, exemplified in Castro's statement and the censorship and blacklisting of the sixties, the act of revolution, the release from US hegemony and the blockade which blunted the availability of popular North American culture, have served to open up a wellspring of creativity. This is best exemplified in the cinema where the Cuban Institute of Cinematographic Art and Industry (ICAIC), starting from nothing in 1959, has built up a solid national film industry.

Between 1959 and 1987, Cuba made 164 feature-length films, 1026 shorts and 1370 newsreels. Of the 120–30 films released in Cuba in 1987, more than 7 per cent were Cuban films, but they attracted 20 per cent of the market share.[95] The early film industry supported the revolution, but its experimentalism soon brought it into conflict with the political leadership, with the banning of the film *P.M.* six weeks after the Bay of Pigs invasion in 1961, for its images 'negative to the ideals of the revolution'. Yet, reflecting the ambiguity in the relationship between central political authority and the cultural sphere, ICAIC continued to serve as a wall of defence against sectarianism and 'provided an umbrella organisation for artists in other disciplines whose experimentation was frowned upon.'[96] In other areas, early 'cultural terrorism' such as the prohibition of Beatles music as degenerate Western culture, has been forced to give way in recent years to a tolerance if not approval of governmental criticism. Exponents of the 20-year-old *Nueva Trova* or New Song Movement like Pablo Milanés and Silvio Rodríguez have been particularly biting. In the summer of 1988, the popular song was 'Ese Hombre Esta Loco' (This Man Is Crazy) – a sarcastic criticism of Fidel and some of his schemes.[97]

The most important single example, though, of the distortions caused by inordinate control at the top, was the damaging events following the 1968 'Revolutionary Offensive' and the decision to produce a ten-million-ton sugar crop in 1970. In 1968, with a faltering economy and the recognition that the economic strategies of the first decade had failed, the government embarked on the 'Revolutionary Offensive' in which the last remaining bastions of private property in small trading and service sectors were socialised.[98] The sudden removal of an important link in the distribution of goods and services which the state could not replace, aggravated shortages already made severe after a decade of embargo and upheaval. More damaging, though, was the highly autonomous, if typical, decision to produce ten million tons of sugar in 1970 and so leapfrog the problems of the past with a massive injection of capital earned from the increased production. The eventual production of some eight-and-a-half million tons, while the largest in Cuba's history, led to even further distortions, with industrial, agricultural, and forestry products showing their worst-ever production figures in that year.[99]

The crisis of production of 1970 was a direct result of the autonomous and autocratic character of the Cuban leadership. At the same time, however, it generated a degree of popular discontent and disenchantment which provided a potential opening in the process for advancement in an alternative direction. Throughout the course of the 1960s, effective grievance procedures had been undermined in the trade union movement, while at the same time, the militarisation of production for the sugar harvest and the worsening economic situation had increased working-class grievances.[100] It was not completely surprising therefore, that after the failed harvest there was a *de facto* strike throughout Cuba. In August and September of 1970, 20 per cent of the workforce were absent on any given day; in August in Oriente province, 52 per cent of the agricultural workers were absent.[101] Growing dissatisfaction with the regime was clearly a motivational factor when Castro offered to resign following the failed sugar harvest, and it was equally predictable that this resignation would be rejected; however, in the months and years following this clear signal of the limits of revolutionary power, the regime was forced to respond by institutionalising the Communist Party, strengthening trade unions and other mass organisations and eventually, in 1976, establishing a new constitution with single-party elections under a system called *poder popular*.[102] The impact of the measures has, from the perspective of democracy, been disappointing. The fact that National Assembly members are elected indirectly; that some can be appointed without going through the electoral procedure; that the Communist Party actually controls the election arrangements; all support the conclusion that while the measures are an important mechanism to facilitate the circulation of elites below the top, 'in effect, membership is an appointment that reflects decisions by the national leadership'.[103] Based on his comparative studies of the 1976 and 1980 National Assemblies, Domínguez concluded that some things had changed. Thus, Fidel Castro, instead of intervening in every aspect of the debate, often came in only to solve disputes, but when he did, his decision was never questioned. Some debate was possible and indeed encouraged, if it took place among the most senior members of the Assembly. If junior members intervened, they were chided. The need for delegates to contact their constituents at the municipal level and the increasing access to the mass media to complain about non-policy matters were democratic, but criticism stopped short at the level of the top leadership and was never accepted over policy matters. Domínguez described this limited system of democracy, coupled with the incorporation of the mass of the people – if in a subordinate position, into political life – with some accuracy, as a 'consultative oligarchy'.[104]

## *The Cuban achievement*

If our proposal is correct, that the elites who marched into power in 1959 were essentially state-builders imbued with an ideology which saw the emergence of an independent Cuba closely linked to a reformist project, then the revolution must be judged on this basis and not primarily on economic terms or on abstract notions of socialism. From this perspective, many of its achievements are remarkable. In health, the system of social medicine, consolidated by 1973, has provided free and high-quality health care for the entire population.[105] Cuba, by its own definition, has become a 'medical power'. Whereas in 1959 there were some 6300 doctors (half of whom left after the revolution), in the first 25 years, 16 000 had been trained and from 1983 to the year 2000, a total of 50 000 new doctors was projected.[106] The accomplishment in the educational sphere is even better. Building on the basis of the pathbreaking literacy campaign of the early years, the country was able to make considerable progress toward giving the entire population at least a sixth-grade education in 1974. In 1983, Cuba could boast that its population of teachers was 11 times greater than it had been in the late fifties in higher education; a student population 14 times greater than before the revolution was equally impressive.[107] In the area of race relations, a constant sore point in pre-revolutionary Cuba, a more mixed picture presents itself. The ending of legal race discrimination, the opening in 1959 of beaches and clubs to all, support the view that the main gains for black Cubans were made in the early years. Since then, however, in keeping with the monolithic character of government power, any attempt to discuss race or organise around issues of racial discrimination has been rebuffed on the grounds that the revolution has solved the race problem. Nevertheless, it can be said that black Cubans, generally at the bottom of the society, have benefited from the general reforms and as such probably form a solid bedrock of support for the revolution.[108] If anything, this has probably been enhanced since 1975 when blacks played an inordinate role in the Angolan intervention, with a commensurate rise in prestige on their return to Cuba.

In the broader economy, however, the picture is far less successful. Brundenius, writing in the early eighties, suggested that Cuba had been able to achieve growth with equity.[109] Open unemployment as a percentage of the labour force had fallen from 11.8 per cent in 1958 to 3.4 per cent in 1981; although the dramatic initial redistribution of income following the land and urban reforms had been redressed somewhat with the subsequent moral incentives policies, Cuba compared favourably with other Latin American countries when looking at the share of total income of the poorest 40 per cent of the population. In the twenty years from 1960 to 1980, Brazil's poorest actually declined from earning 11.5 per cent to 9.9 per cent of total income, while in Cuba for roughly the same period, the share of the poorest increased from 6.5 per cent to 24.8 per cent.[110] Further, Brundenius points to important structural changes in the economy, including increased capital accumulation, a diversification away from sugar monoculture towards other forms of agriculture, manufacturing and, most significantly, the growth of a capital goods industry. Writing in 1983, he then concluded that all this had been done while maintaining respectable rates of growth. Thus, although growth rates had been below expectations in the 1976–80 plan due to the fall in sugar prices, the massive growth of 16.9 per cent in 1981 alone, would allow the economy to achieve its targets for the second plan.[111]

In retrospect, this conclusion was far too optimistic and failed sufficiently to address the underlying structural weaknesses of the economy. While it is true that there has been some diversification away from sugar, the fundamental reality is that the occurrence of booms and crises is still, as throughout the century, determined by the fluctuations in the price of sugar and other international indicators. As Brundenius recognised, growth and slump in the seventies were intimately linked to the rising price of sugar, but he failed to mention that the remarkable boom in 1981, a key factor in his growth projection, was possible at least in part because of the unexpected boost in sugar prices in 1979–80.[112] In this sense, structures had not changed; rather, the typical boom leg of the ten-year price cycle had arrived ahead of schedule. This is best illustrated by the poor performance of the Cuban economy in the second half of the decade. The average annual growth rate of 7.3 per cent for the period 1981–85, which had been the highest under the revolution, had declined to 4.6 per cent in 1985, 1.2 per cent in 1986 and to −3.8 per cent in 1987. In 1988 it increased to 2.3 per cent, but this was still far below the levels of the earlier period.[113] Due to this domestic deterioration and a poor foreign trade performance (exports in 1986 were expected to increase by 3.5 per cent but declined by 11 per cent), there has been a massive increase in the hard currency debt, which in 1988 amounted to twice what it was in 1984.[114] While, as will be further suggested, internal policies were at least partially responsible for these declines, the falling price of sugar and of oil, which Cuba re-exports to earn foreign exchange, and the unavailability of new hard currency loans were all important factors, and underline the continuing structural fragility of the economy.

The most important weakness, however, was manifestly its reliance on, and vulnerability to the Soviet economy.[115] From 1960 to 1979, total cumulative Soviet aid to Cuba amounted to US$16.7 billion; in 1979 alone Soviet aid amounted to US$8.5 million daily.[116] In 1989, 87 per cent of Cuban trade was with the Soviet bloc, of which 72 per cent was directly with the Soviet Union. In the plan period 1981–85, this trade produced a deficit of US$4 billion, a figure which was expected to be repeated for the 1986–89 period.[117] It is this Soviet aid and trade which has always underwritten Cuban independence from the United States at the same time as it has defined the limits of that independence. At least once before, in 1967–68, Soviet dissatisfaction with Cuban national and international policies had led to a curtailment of oil and other supplies. The subsequent acquiescence of Castro in the Soviet invasion of Czechoslovakia, followed by a resumption of supplies, is regarded, with justification, as a belated acceptance of the latent hegemonic power which the Soviet Union possesses.[118] Brundenius also recognises, but fails to elaborate on, the state's weaknesses in the production and delivery of a wide range of goods and services. While the ration system has ensured a basic supply of foods, it has led to a lack of selection and quality and has inadvertently contributed to its own perpetuation. Low prices and easy availability 'reduce the motivation to work harder, so that production declines, scarcity persists and rationing continues'.[119] The government's harassment and discouraging of the farmers' markets in the early eighties which had contributed to the availability of a more varied diet, certainly aggravated the problem of supply and quite probably increased underlying currents of dissatisfaction. More substantially, after the introduction of the 'Rectification Process' in 1986, Cuba has moved away from decentralisation and the use of market mechanisms towards a more austere course, in order to rescue the revolution from what was considered a path leading back to capitalism. The previous emphasis on material incentives, together with market-oriented policies like the farmers' markets and the buying and selling of private houses, had led to speculation, corruption and crime, it was argued. The aim of rectification was to reassert central control, reaffirm the Guevarist principle of moral incentives, fight crime and corruption, increase labour productivity and place new restrictions on private farming, trading and service activities.[120] While it is probably too early to judge the efficacy of the rectification policies, Mesa-Lago, writing in 1988, is on firm ground when he suggests that initially, at least, they have been more negative than positive. Among the main points to support this are: a) increased shortages of agricultural produce, suggesting that the private farmers' markets were far more efficient than their successors – the production cooperatives – in supplying foodstuffs; b) the elimination of small businesses has meant increasing scarcity in a range of services which the state has been unable to fill; c) restrictions on private housing construction and the inefficiencies of the reborn micro-brigades has led to a decline in housing construction; d) labour absenteeism has increased while labour productivity has declined (the average decline in labour productivity for 1986–87 was between 2.6 and 8 per cent, while the planned target was 2 per cent growth).[121] The paradox of the present moment in Cuba is that the government, having satisfied many of the basic needs, is calling for greater sacrifices at a time when the people more than ever want consumer goods and the economy is least able to provide them. Once before, in 1980, a period of relaxation in tensions with the US had led to increased contacts between exiles and their families; the ensuing exodus from the port of Mariel of over 125 000 persons was, at least in part, an indication of the increasing unhappiness with the seemingly never-ending spartan quality of Cuban life.[122] The comments of a European diplomat quoted in 1988, are not far from the truth:

> Cubans now want not only free health care but . . . they want to have a more refined diet, they want to have access to consumer goods, they want to travel. . . .[123]

It is the continuation of these structural weaknesses in the Cuban economy, reflecting its fragility and continued dependency, which is at the heart of the present crisis, cumulatively the gravest it has had to face since the early days of the revolution. In early 1988, addressing the National Assembly, Castro called for more belt-tightening throughout that year, 1989 and 1990. Mentioning the low growth rates for the economy in the late eighties, he predicted equally low growth for the following years. The reasons given for this was the fall in the price of oil which Cuba re-exports from the Soviet Union on the open market; the fall in the value of the dollar, to which Cuban export prices are tagged; and the adverse impact of droughts on sugar.[124] Almost at the same time as these downward trends in the economy began to be felt, a different kind of crisis took hold as the Soviet Union under Gorbachev deepened its policies of *perestroika* and *glasnost*. Central to the notion of *perestroika* is the view that the Soviet Union's low growth rate in the eighties was due largely to its huge defence budget, excessive expenditures on client states and internal production inefficiencies due to overcentralisation. Coupled with this is a new foreign policy orientation, based on a reevaluation of Marxism–Leninism, which no longer regards the United States as an adversary but an essential partner in an interdependent world. This has at least three potentially damaging consequences for Cuba.

The first is a direct effect: if the Soviet Union, no longer interested in Cuba in a post-Cold War world, decides to cut back on the extent of aid which it gives to the island and downgrades its importance as an ally. The second, less direct, effect is the extent to which the Soviet Confederation, by demonstration or through pressure, might try to influence the policies of Cuba which, at the present moment, are moving in a diametrically opposite direction to its own. The third, again a demonstration effect, is the extent to which the accompanying policies of *glasnost* or openness might serve to undermine the closed and centralist features of Cuban society, with damaging repercussions for the political leadership. So it is not surprising that repeatedly, as he did in August 1988, Castro has rejected Gorbachev's policies, arguing that 'Our methods cannot be similar. It would be erroneous to copy other countries'.[125] The economic impact of *perestroika* seemed at first to be postponed, when in May, 1989, Cuba and the Soviet Union signed a 25-year Friendship and Cooperation Treaty, but the rapid changes in Eastern Europe have hastened the crisis situation. In January 1990, the government had to impose even more stringent curbs on food consumption and increase prices of basic foodstuffs. The daily bread ration of Cubans outside Havana fell by 20 per cent; the price of unrationed bread in Havana went up by 30 per cent, as did the price of eggs by 50 per cent.[126] The measures were necessary, due to what at first appeared to be an administrative delay in the shipment of grain from the USSR. The truth was, however, that Soviet ships, which had traditionally shipped Cuban food at subsidised prices, were now, under *perestroika*, compelled to make a profit and therefore unwilling to continue this practice. A similar adoption of a hardnosed approach to trading with Cuba was evident in other shipping arrangements with East Germany and Poland.[127]

Cuba stands at the crossroads of a profound crisis underlined by the fragility of its economy. However, economic wellbeing has never been the only, or at all times the most important goal of the revolution. Alongside the very tangible economic and social benefits, Castro has presented, almost as a fulfilment of the *Santería* prophecy, an image of a highly unified, loyal and peaceful state projecting itself under his leadership, coherently into the world for the greater glory of its people. The success on this front is as yet unsullied. Cuban mass organisations incorporate the vast majority of the population. In. the early eighties, 81 per cent of the women were in the women's federation, the FMC; 80 per cent of the adult population was represented in the Committees for the Defence of the Revolution (CDRs); 1.5 million persons are incorporated into the Territorial Troop Militia, created in 1980 as the first line of defence for the country.[128]

On the international front, Domínguez, Karol and others defined the relationship with the Soviet Union as hegemonic:[129] if so, it was a peculiar form of hegemony which allowed Cuba to resist the United States and, then, project itself in the world. While initial Cuban policy in Latin America supported revolutionary movements, it was always, in keeping with its primary objective of state-building, willing to subordinate revolutionary principle in favour of good relations with states which in turn, maintained amicable relations with it. This 'Rule of Precedence'[130] is best illustrated in the case of Mexico, which has always recognised Cuba and is therefore virtually unique in Latin America to have avoided Cuban criticism. It is remarkable that this small Caribbean country of some ten million people, just recently the gambling den and whorehouse of the US, is now one of the major aid donors in the world. In 1985 some 15 000 Cuban civilians were posted overseas in thirty countries in areas ranging from health and education through forestry, sports, construction and chemicals.[131] The more variegated success in diplomacy has in the past led to leadership of the Non-Aligned Movement, although Cuban support for the invasion of Afghanistan in 1979 seriously damaged its non-aligned credentials.[132] More recently, even as the economic crisis has intensified, Cuba has gradually regained its standing in Latin America, crowning it with the December 1989 election to the UN Security Council with the full backing of the Caribbean and Latin America.[133] At the pinnacle, if also the most controversial achievement, has been the Cuban military engagements overseas, particularly in Angola and Ethiopia. In 1975 Cuban forces intervened in Angola at the request of the new MPLA government and successfully halted a South African invasion and attempt to oust the regime. Again in 1987, Cuban troops, of whom some 200 000 had by then served in Angola, intercepted and decisively defeated a South African thrust into Southern Angola at Cuito Cuanavale.[134] This defeat almost certainly brought the South Africans to the negotiating table, an event which led to the independence in 1990 of Namibia. While US sources portrayed Cuban military activity as simply an extension of the Soviet Union's, Dominguez's balanced account asserts that in Angola in 1975 the Cubans acted independently and brought the Soviets in, whereas in Ethiopia a few years later, it was the reverse.[135]

## *Whither the revolution?*

If we are to abandon the notion of revolution as an orderly, deterministic progression, and to see it, rather as a response to structural circumstances in a given international, temporal and ideological moment, which may proceed in different directions, then the following very tentative suggestions might be made about Cuba. The worsening internationally-determined economic crisis, sharpening ideological differences with the Soviet Confederation and the epochal moves away from communism in Eastern Europe, all serve to increase pressure on the already fragile and delicately balanced Cuban economy and society. Large cross-sections of the population already chafing under three decades of austerity must be approaching the point of total cynicism when asked to make further sacrifices for the revolution. When coupled with increasing US pressure, a hostile and politically powerful exile population in Miami, disgruntled servicemen returning from Angola[136] and increased Cuban isolation following the February defeat of the

Sandinista government in Nicaragua, a scenario of imminent revolutionary crisis seems fairly obvious.

This, however, is not the case. While cuts in Soviet aid have been occurring and will continue, an abandonment by the Soviets is, as Gunn suggests, less likely. Among the salient points are the following. a) While Cuba's exports to Eastern Europe are of a high quality and based on international prices, poor quality manufactured goods from the East would have difficulty competing on the open market. Thus Eastern Europe definitely needs Cuba. b) The cost of replacing Cuban sugar – some 35 per cent of Eastern Europe's consumption – is high, because it is both cheaper than locally-produced beet sugar and does not require hard currency. c) Most of Cuba's trade is with the Soviet Confederation, which of all the Eastern European countries needs Cuba for the intelligence window which it provides on the United States – a need that still exists, as intelligence requirements shift from military to commercial priorities. d) Finally, due to the poor quality of Soviet goods, some estimates suggest that the real subsidy to the Cuban economy, normally estimated at some US$4–5 billion per year, may be half that figure, reducing by an equal proportion the impact of a cut in the subsidy.[137] Further to this, the Cuban government has not been marking time, but is moving to diversify its trade relations and has broadened ties with China and particularly, Latin America, where trade with Cuba increased from US$359 million in 1985 to US$1.33 billion in 1988.[138] Other important initiatives in developing the tourist industry and in increasing Cuban medical equipment and pharmaceutical exports, are also well advanced. Cuba's SUMA32 (AIDS) detection vaccine is already in large-scale production for export to a number of countries.

More specifically, if one examines the factors which accelerate regime crises, it is clear that important features are not present in the Cuban situation. It should be remembered that although there was an economic downturn in 1958, Batista fell in a period of overall economic prosperity and there was no widespread revolt from below. In 1933, there was revolt from below, but the revolution was unsuccessful. If we are to be consistent, a similar methodology must be applied to the present regime. At minimum, an incipient crisis, or the basis for one, needs to be identified between the elites at the top. It may or may not arise out of an economic crisis, but usually occurs when a timely circulation of elites in the topmost echelons of the state is frustrated. The Cuban state and its premier state-builder, Fidel Castro, sought to develop from the 1976 constitution and *poder popular*, a partial system of circulation in which middle-level cadres could be criticised and even replaced, without similar policies being applied to the top leaders. If one interpretation of the Ochoa events is correct, then this was seen as inadequate, and a subordinate section of the ruling elites apparently sought to advance their position in the state by moving against the major source of blockage in the form of Fidel and the old revolutionaries at the top. This was unsuccessful, and Ochoa paid the price which unsuccessful conspirators often pay. However, quite inadvertently, the executions, imprisonments and purges may have opened the door for increased circulation and temporarily, at least, forestalled further fracturing at the top. With a more secure structure, Castro in the recent period has been willing and able further to increase the channels below the top leadership for discussion and circulation through initiatives like the recent proposal for secret balloting in elections to local positions in the Communist Party.[139] At the same time, the crushing of an autonomous pole of power in the Ministry of the Interior has severely reduced the room for manoeuvre of any potential opposition. Fidel Castro, the wily tactician, recognises more than anyone else that without a tactically secure zone for disenchanted state-building elites to retreat into, without, in other words, a Sierra Maestra, then it is infinitely more difficult for coherent opposition to develop. Crisis below may occur but, without a fissure at the top, it is unlikely to succeed.

One should also carefully examine the view that with economic stagnation, shortages and price increases, upheaval down below is inevitable. The image and enhanced sense of identity of revolutionary Cuba, the national effort which has dovetailed into Afro-Cuban *Santería* mythology, possesses a powerful dynamic of its own. Any external pressure against Cuba such as the 1989 attack by the US Coast Guard against a Cuban vessel which refused to be searched in international waters, is likely to lead, as that incident did, to a closing of ranks, not a revolutionary crisis.[140]

In the short term, the absence of a pole for the opposition to organise around, the likelihood of continued, if reduced, Soviet assistance and the limited, though definite circulation of elites, together with the loose conglomeration of factors which can be grouped under the heading national pride, suggests that Cuba, even in a period of economic decline, can sustain an authoritarian, revolutionary state-building project. With totally new developments, such as drastic Soviet cuts,[141] or Fidel Castro's demise, new conclusions may have to be drawn; or the present crisis and the injection of popular discontent into the equation might provide an opening, as it might have done in 1970, for entirely new, and perhaps more liberating directions.

# Notes

1. See for example, Susan Kaufman Purcell in the *New York Times,* 10 January 1990, 'Is Cuba the Next Domino?' where she calls for help for the Cuban people from abroad, so that the 'anti communist momentum will jump the Atlantic and end 31 years of communist rule in Cuba'.

2. See Damian Fernandez, *Miami Herald,* 3 December 1989, 'Domino Fails to Explain Cuban Case', in which he recognises that discontent and economic

decline are not enough to bring down the Cuban regime and that repression is not the only thing which holds it together.

3.  Earlier studies have tended to be of the historical type, such as Hugh Thomas's encylopaedic *Cuba, or the Pursuit of Freedom*; have tried to justify the victory on Marxist economic grounds, such as James O'Connor's *On Cuban Political Economy*; have been of the reflective 'Cuba Hand' variety, such as Philip Bonsal's *Cuba, Castro and the United States*; have embodied the betrayal thesis, e.g. Theodore Draper's *Castro's Revolution, Myths and Realities*; or have been critiques of the early years, such as K. S. Karol's *Guerrillas in Power* and Rene Dumont's *Is Cuba Socialist?* Little direct comparison of 1933 and 1959 appears, with the most important contribution, although as part of a far more ambitious study of Cuba, to be found in Jorge Domínguez, *Cuba: Order and Revolution*.

4.  John Dunn, *Modern Revolutions: An Introduction to the Analysis of a Political Phenomenon*, 2nd edn (Cambridge: Cambridge University Press, 1989), p. 201.

5.  Cuba's trade vulnerability (exports plus imports as a percentage of estimated national income) varied between 1903 and 1929 from a low of 72 to a high of 108 per cent. See Jorge Domínguez, *Cuba: Order and Revolution*, (Cambridge, Mass. and London: The Belknap Press of Harvard University Press), p. 24.

6.  See for sugar exports, total Cuban exports and percentage US share of Cuban exports, Dudley Seers (ed.), *Cuba: The Economic and Social Revolution* (Chapel Hill: The University of North Carolina Press, 1964), p. 8.

7.  The Dance of the Millions refers to the boom period of 1919–20 when sugar prices, in the wake of the dislocation of the First World War went up to the record amount of 22.6 cents per pound. See Hugh Thomas, *Cuba, or the Pursuit of Freedom*, (London: Eyre and Spottiswoode, 1971), pp. 544–56.

8.  See Domínguez, 1978, p. 27.

9.  See Seers, 1964, p. 13. Much of this openness was due to the Reciprocal Trade Agreement with the US which opened the economy to US foodstuffs and manufactures, stifling the development of Cuban industry.

10. For real per capita income see Domínguez, 1978, p. 74; for unemployment, see Seers, 1964, p. 12.

11. See Domínguez, 1978, p. 75.

12. Ibid., 1978, p. 90.

13. Thomas, 1971, p. 616.

14. Ibid., p. 990. See also Theodore Draper, *Castroism: Theory and Practice* (New York, Washington, London: Praeger, 1965), pp. 31–2.

15. Szulc suggests that it was the failure of 9 April which starkly revealed to Castro the organisational weaknesses of 26 July and led him to the conclusion that he would have to forge close links with the communists, who retained the loyalty of a part of the working class. See Tad Szulc, *Fidel: A Critical Portrait* (New York: Avon, 1986), p. 343.

16. Domínguez, 1978, p. 436. In 1946, 83 per cent of all squatters in Cuba were located in Oriente. See ibid., p. 435.

17. See Thomas, 1971, p. 339.

18. For the perception of Machado as being benevolent to black Cubans, see Thomas, 1971, p. 683. For the similar perception of Batista see ibid., p. 122. When black volunteers were found among members of Fidel Castro's group after the failed Moncada attack, they were chastised by members of the army

for following the *blanco* Castro against Batista who was a *mestizo*, and therefore one of their own.

19. See Thomas, 1971, p. 423.
20. Ibid., p. 425.
21. Among the humiliating features for newly independent Cuba, the Platt Amendment prevented the Cuban government from accumulating debt without guarantees that the interest would be served from ordinary revenues, granted the US the right to buy or lease land for coaling or naval stations and most famously, granted the US the right to intervene in order to protect Cuban sovereignty and a government capable of protecting life, liberty and property. See Eric Wolf, *Peasant Wars of the Twentieth Century* (London: Faber and Faber, 1971), p. 255.
22. See Domínguez, 1978, p. 68.
23. Domínguez notes, for example, that between 1900 and 1932, except for some insignificant silver coinage in 1914 and 1920, neither the government nor any other institution under it such as a central bank, created money. There was no control over banks or their reserves and the exchange rate was out of the government's control because the US dollar could freely circulate in the country. See Domínguez, 1978, p. 33.
24. C. A. M. Hennessy, 'The Roots of Cuban Nationalism', in Robert F. Smith (ed.), *Background to Revolution: the Development of Modern Cuba*, pp. 19–29.
25. See Wolf, 1971, p. 261.
26. See Domínguez, 1978, p. 36 for a description of how the lottery as an institutionalised form of corruption worked.
27. See ibid., p. 40.
28. See Thomas, 1971, p. 587.
29. See ibid., p. 580.
30. Ibid., p. 587.
31. Ibid., p. 587. Domínguez illustrates in detail how Machado closed the door to this circulation of elites. Looking at the incidence of re-election to the House of Representatives for a second term, he notes that between 1910 and 1924, i.e. before Machado's presidency, the proportion of those re-elected remained stable, averaging 38 per cent. Machado's cooperative party system, however, led to a significant increase to an average of 53 per cent, 'a change that may have been seen by some politicians as further evidence that the incumbents had changed the rules of the political game in order to freeze others out of power indefinitely'. Domínguez, 1978, p. 42.
32. Thomas, 1971, p. 581.
33. See ibid., p. 586.
34. See ibid., pp. 589–9.
35. See Domínguez, 1978, pp. 113–115.
36. Ibid., p. 94.
37. Ibid., p. 126.
38. Thomas, 1971, p. 779.
39. See Wolf, 1971, p. 273. The best-known defence of independent intervention, although it is no longer popular, is to be found in Regis Debray's *Revolution in the Revolution: Armed Struggle and Political Struggle in Latin America* (New York: MR, 1967), in which he elevates the guerrilla *foco* as general strategy for successful revolution in Latin America.
40. Thomas, 1971, p. 594.

41. Domínguez, 1978, p. 116.
42. See Thomas, 1971, pp. 594–5.
43. See Sheldon B. Liss, *Roots of Revolution: Radical Thought in Cuba* (Lincoln and London: University of Nebraska Press, 1987), p. 8.
44. This essentially argues that Fidel Castro betrayed the true aims of the Cuban Revolution which were essentially to restore democracy. See, for example, Theodore Draper, *Castroism: Theory and Practice* (New York, Washington, London: Praeger, 1965).
45. See Draper, 1965, p. 37.
46. See ibid., 1965, p. 38.
47. See Thomas, 1971, pp. 272–3.
48. See Philip Bonsal, *Cuba, Castro and the United States* (University of Pittsburgh Press, 1971), pp. 151–3.
49. See Szulc, 1986, p. 89. Szulc is I think, right on the view that clear recognition for an alliance with the communists began after the failure of the 9 April 1958 general strike led by the urban arm of 26 July. He also is correct that actual cooperation began in the weeks after the taking of power in January 1959. But the long-distanced view of a Marxist perspective is hard to support in the light of the consistency of Castro's positions and its continuity with the past.
50. Domínguez, 1978, p. 147.
51. See C. Fred Judson's discussion on the Generation of the Centennial and other post-revolutionary Cuban myths in 'Continuity and Evolution of Revolutionary Symbolism in *Verde Olivo*', in S. Halebsky and J. Kirk (eds), *Cuba: Twenty Five Years of Revolution: 1959–1984*, (New York: Praeger, 1985), pp. 233–50.
52. See Sidney Mintz, 'Foreword' in Ramiro Guerra y Sánchez, *Sugar and Society in the Caribbean: An Economic History of Cuban Agriculture* (New Haven, London: Yale University Press, 1964), p. xxii.
53. See Liss, 1987, pp. 50–3.
54. See Thomas, 1971, p. 277.
55. See Nelson Valdéz, 'Ideological Roots of the Cuban Revolutionary Movement', in Susan Craig (ed.), *Contemporary Caribbean: A Sociological Reader* (Trinidad, 1982), pp. 211–42.
56. Thomas, 1971, p. 22; see also Szulc, 1986, p. 75.
57. See Szulc, 1986, p. 143.
58. In Columbia Castro was eyewitness to the *Bogotazo*, the spontaneous outburst of rage following the assassination of presidential candidate Jorge Gaitán. See Szulc, 1986, pp. 113–23, Carlos Franqui, *Diary of the Cuban Revolution* (New York: Viking, 1980), pp. 9–19.
59. See Szulc, 1986, p. 339.
60. See Antoni Kapcia, 'Marti, Marxism and Morality: The Evolution of an Ideology of Revolution', in Richard Gillespie (ed.), *Cuba After Thirty Years: Rectification and Revolution*, (London: Frank Cass, 1990), p. 166.
61. See Szulc, 1986, p. 21 for his sense of welfare.
62. Ibid., p. 29.
63. Thomas, 1971, p. 413.
64. See Jenny Pearce, *Under the Eagle: US Intervention in Central America and the Caribbean* (London: Latin American Bureau, 1981).
65. See Thomas, 1971, pp. 654–5.
66. See Richard M. Saunders, 'Military Force in the Foreign Policy of the Eisenhower Presidency', in *Political Science Quarterly*, Spring 1985, p. 99.

67. Thomas, 1971, p. 279.
68. See ibid., 1971, p. 486.
69. Nixon had concluded after speaking with Castro on his visit to the US in April 1959 that he was controlled by the communists. See Szulc, 1986, p. 537.
70. Bonsal, 1971, p. 24.
71. Domínguez notes a study which shows that catholicism – the major religion – was weaker in Cuba than in most of the other countries of Latin America, that only 17 per cent of all those with a religious affiliation attended church regularly. At the same time, alternative religions, in particular the Afro-Cuban *Santeria* was strong and not only among black Cubans.
72. See Thomas, 1971, p. 260.
73. Fidel Castro Ruz, Sierra Maestra, 1957, in Ernesto Guevara, *Reminiscences of the Cuban Revolutionary War*, Harmondsworth: Pelican, 1969), p. 212.
74. See James O'Connor, 'On Cuban Political Economy', *Political Science Quarterly*, Vol. 79, 1964, p. 241.
75. Szulc, 1986, p. 375.
76. Domínguez, 1978, p. 204.
77. Church influence deteriorated even more as the revolution became more radical. After the Bay of Pigs debacle in which some priests participated, many church officials were expelled and the Catholic University and some 300 private church schools closed. In recent years, however, a dialogue with the church has been initiated and relations, if not warm, are much improved. See John Kirk, 'From Counter Revolution to *modus vivendi:* The Church in Cuba, 1959–1984', in Halebsky and Kirk (eds), 1985, pp. 93–113.
78. See Domínguez, 1978, p. 137.
79. Saul Landau, 'Notes on the Cuban Revolution'. *The Socialist Register*, 1989, p. 295. See also Nan Elsasser and Nelson Valdez, 'Dancing With Fidel: Santeria Gods in Cuba', *Arete*, Vol. 1, no. 6, p. 32.
80. Max Azicri, *Cuba: Politics, Economics and Society* (London, New York: Frances Pinter, 1988), p. 235.
81. In 1957, the traditional parties formed a junta of National Liberation in Miami in an atempt to outflank the growing support for 26 July. In December, Castro vehemently denounced it, effectively destroying its credibility. See Thomas, *The Cuban Revolution*, pp. 186–7. For his conflict with the Civic Resistance, the urban arm of 26 July, see Szulc, p. 332 and for his effective neutralisation of effective opposition from the Revolutionary Student Directorate, see Szulc, p. 375.
82. See Szulc, 1986, p. 372.
83. For the 1962 crisis, see Thomas, 1971, p. 601; for the microfaction crisis, see K. S. Karol, *Guerrillas in Power: the Course of the Cuban Revolution*, (New York: Hill and Wang, 1970), pp. 468–9.
84. *Latin American Regional Reports, Caribbean Report*, 24 August 1989, p. 1.
85. See for a discussion, if not a conclusion on this incident, Alistair Hennessy, 'The Cuban Revolution: A Wider View', in Gillespie (ed.), 1990, p. 14.
86. See for a detailing of the US instigated assassination attempts and destablisation attempts, *US Senate. Select Committee on Intelligence Activities. Covert Action. Washington DC*, US Government Printing Office, 1976.
87. Domínguez, 1978, p. 148.
88. See ibid., p. 148.
89. See for a similar conclusion, Domínguez, *Order and Revolution,* p. 335 and Karol, *Guerrillas in Power*, pp. 531–3. Karol also argues that Fidel's in-

creasing loyalty to the Soviet Union's ideology and policies after 1968 reflected the fact that he was 'clearly defending a system of political power and economic priorities that contained automatic safeguards against the revival of heresies in Cuba', ibid., p. 529.

90.  See René Dumont, *Is Cuba Socialist?*, (London: Andre Deutsch, 1974), p. 102.
91.  Ibid., p. 90.
92.  Ibid., p. 108.
93.  Karol, 1970, p. 241.
94.  See, for example, Roberto González Echevarría, 'Criticism and Literature in Revolutionary Cuba', in Halebsky and Kirk, (eds) 1985, pp. 154–73.
95.  See John King, 'Cuban Cinema: A Reel Revolution?', in Gillespie (ed.), 1990, p. 141.
96.  Ibid., p. 146.
97.  See Jean Stubbs, *Cuba: The Test of Time* (London: Latin American Bureau, 1990), pp. 78–9.
98.  See Karol, 1970, p. 494.
99.  See Domínguez, 1978, p. 177.
100.  Ibid., pp. 274–5.
101.  Ibid., p. 275.
102.  For a description and balanced critique of the gradual process of institutionalisation and the first elections under *poder popular*, see Domínguez, 1978, pp. 191–259.
103.  Domínguez, 'Revolutionary Politics: The New Demand for Orderliness' in Jorge Domínguez (ed.), *Cuba: Internal and International Affairs* (Beverly Hills, London, New Delhi: Sage, 1982), p. 20.
104.  Domínguez, 1982, p. 64.
105.  See Ross Danielson, 'Medicine in the Community', Halebsky and Kirk (eds), 1985, pp. 45–61.
106.  Marvin Leiner, 'Cuba's Schools: 25 Years Later', in Halebsky and Kirk (eds), 1985, p. 33.
107.  Ibid., p. 36. Leiner also mentions some of the problems associated with the educational sector, some of which reflect the authoritarian features of the society. Most important is his criticism that principals of secondary schools are still selected according to their 'political history'. See p. 39.
108.  See Domínguez, *Order and Revolution*, pp. 224–7. See also, for a somewhat different view, Carlos Moore, *Castro, the Blacks and Africa* (Berkeley: University of California Press, 1988).
109.  Claes Brundenius, 'Cuba: Redistribution and Growth with Equity', in Halebsky and Kirk (eds), 1985, pp. 193–212.
110.  Ibid., p. 204.
111.  Ibid., p. 209.
112.  See Carmelo Mesa-Lago, 'The Economy: Caution, Frugality, and Resilient Ideology', in Domínguez, 1982, p. 153.
113.  See Carmelo Mesa-Lago, 'Cuba's Economic Counter-Reform (Rectificacion): Causes, Policies and Effects', in Gillespie (ed.), 1990, pp. 118–19. The aggregate indicator of growth used in Cuban statistics is the Global Social Product or GSP which excludes 'non-productive sectors' such as tourism and involves significant double counting because it does not use value added.
114.  See Mesa-Lago in Gillespie (ed.), 1990, p. 124.
115.  See Joel C. Edelstein, 'Economic Policy and Development Models', in Halebsky and Kirk (eds), 1985, pp. 177–211.

116.   Mesa-Lago, in Domínguez, 1982, p. 150.
117.   See *Latin American Regional Reports: Caribbean Report*, 11 May 1989, p. 1.
118.   See Jorge Domínguez, *To Make a World Safe for Revolution: Cuba's Foreign Policy*, (Cambridge, Mass., London: Harvard University Press, 1989), pp. 71–7 and Karol, 1970, pp. 505–33.
119.   Joseph Collins and Medea Benjamin, 'Cuba's Food Distribution Systems', in Halebsky and Kirk (eds), 1985, p. 75.
120.   See Mesa-Lago in Gillespie (ed.), 1990, pp. 98–134, and Jean Stubbs, 1989, pp. 47–67.
121.   See Mesa-Lago in Gillespie (ed.), 1990, pp. 125–6.
122.   See Domínguez, 1989, p. 231.
123.   *Latin American Regional Reports: Caribbean Report*, 25 August 1988, pp. 4–5.
124.   *Latin American Regional Reports: Caribbean Report*, 25 February 1988, pp. 4–5.
125.   Ibid.
126.   See Gillian Gunn, 'Will Castro Fall?', *Foreign Policy*, no. 79, Summer 1990, p. 133.
127.   *Latin American Regional Reports: Caribbean Report*, 1 March 1990, p. 4.
128.   See Domínguez, 1982, p. 43 for FMC and CDR figures. See Fidel Castro, *In Defense of Socialism: The Thirtieth Anniversary of the Cuban Revolution*, (New York, London, Sydney, Toronto: Pathfinder, 1989), p. 1, for Territorial Troop Militia figures.
129.   See Domínguez, 1989, p. 4.
130.   Ibid., p. 117.
131.   Ibid., pp. 173–5.
132.   Ibid., p. 236.
133.   *Latin American Regional Reports: Caribbean Report*, 7 December 1989.
134.   See Fidel Castro, 1989, p. 17; Stubbs, 1989, pp. 101–5.
135.   See Domínguez, 1989, p. 158.
136.   See Jorge Domínguez, 'The Cuban Armed Forces, the Party, and Society in Wartime and during Rectification, (1986–88)', in Gillespie (ed.), 1990, pp. 45–62.
137.   See Gillian Gunn, 'Will Castro Fall?', *Foreign Policy*, no. 79, Summer 1990, p. 135.
138.   See Gunn, 1990, p. 137.
139.   See ibid., pp. 141–2.
140.   See *Latin American Regional Reports: Caribbean Report*, 1 March, 1990. The US Coast Guard cutter had apparently stopped a Cuban freighter in the Gulf of Mexico, purportedly searching for drugs. The freighter refused to stop and was raked by gunfire. Later in Mexico, an authorised search by the Mexicans found it to be clean.
141.   Such a likelihood, despite the recent 25-year agreement and Gunn's prognosis should not be ruled out. In the face of a deteriorating Soviet economy, the demand to cut loose the Cuban burden is growing. In April 1990, for instance, the Soviet party daily *Pravda*, called for a 'radical overhaul' of Soviet assistance which was a constant drain. See *The Independent*, 10 April 1990.

| Chapter 3 | # Nicaragua: Failed revolution, or advance to empowerment? |
|---|---|

> The truth is that we always took the masses into account, but more in terms of their supporting the guerrillas, so that the guerrillas as such could defeat the National guard. This isn't what actually happened. What happened is that it was the guerrillas who provided support for the masses so that they could defeat the enemy by means of insurrection.
>
> Humberto Ortega

The Nicaraguan Revolution, two decades after Cuba, presents a dramatically different picture. Unlike the weeks and months after January 1959, there was no *paredón*, the widely-used term which indicated popular support for the execution of Batista's collaborators and henchmen. No 'red terror' succeeded the 'white terror' of the dictator Somoza's final years in power.

> The death penalty has been abolished. The 7,500 captured Somozist Guardsmen, including the worst torturers, have a right to a proper trial and risk a maximum sentence of thirty years imprisonment. The International Commission on Human Rights regularly visits the places of detention. The liberty and safety of citizens is guaranteed by law. . . . Every person in detention is presumed innocent until 'duly found guilty'. Nicaraguan citizens have the right 'freely to enter and leave the country'.[1]

Although there were different interpretations of its meaning, the ruling party, the Sandinista National Liberation Front (FSLN) accepted from the beginning the principle of plural elections. Further, two electoral exercises, both considered fair by international observers, have been held and, most critically, on the second occasion in February 1990, the incumbent revolutionary party was defeated at the polls and conceded the government to the opposition alliance.

Over the past decade, three widely different views have emerged on the significance of the Nicaraguan Revolution. A view on the right, captured effectively in the report of the 1984 'Kissinger' Commission on Central America,[2] argued that Nicaragua possessed a Cuban-style, Stalinist regime which ensured a monopoly of power by the Sandinistas. Faced with the reality of a 1984 electoral exercise judged reasonably fair by Latin American standards,[3] persons supporting this position either typically chose to ignore it, or questioned its legitimacy on the basis of the somewhat substantial fact that important opposition groups had boycotted the elections.[4] Such an argument, of course, was not possible in 1990 as the united opposition alliance both participated and won, but the hard right nonetheless maintains that victory was possible as a result of overcoming the resistance of a quasi-Stalinist regime in Managua. Thus, Penn Kemble, two days after the election, proposed in the *Wall Street Journal* that

> Ordinary Nicaraguans and the anti-communist Contras who were willing to take up arms to pressure the Sandinistas to hold elections deserve most of the credit for Sunday's latest triumph of democracy. But the Bush Administration acquitted itself well. Vigorous military action in Panama to restore a democratically elected President showed the Sandinistas that the US is not the paper tiger they had come to imagine.[5]

A second view, the dominant, almost paradigmatic view on the left, has argued, despite differing opinions and sometimes sharp polemics on the class character of the FSLN, that the revolution is an example of the 'transition to socialism'.[6] From such a position the recent electoral defeat of the FSLN vanguard might perhaps be interpreted as a blocked transition, emphasising the role of the United States in the defeat and the reassertion of its traditional regional hegemony.[7] A third perspective, which is still to some degree in the process of detaching itself from the 'transition to socialism' label,[8] argues, or more accurately, senses, that the Nicaraguan situation might well have thrown up something entirely novel.

Using a variant of such an approach, we can suggest that the outcome of the recent election needs to be reassessed. At one level, as a reassertion of US hegemonic power and will in the region, it is a defeat for the revolutionary party and for the notion of independence for small states. But if 'transition to socialism' is not what has been taking place in Nicaragua, then the democratic concession of power by the ruling vanguard may paradoxically present opportunities for furthering democracy, accountability and participation in a context which need not degenerate into liberalism nor fit the straitjacket of traditional social democracy. In other words, electoral defeat may have enhanced the potential for popular mobilisation, the escape from routine and bureaucracy, and may provide the opportunity for an advance toward negative capability. To arrive at this conclusion, however, we need to trace some of the important moments and features in the development of the Nicaraguan Revolution.

# The roots of revolution

Like the Cuban Revolution which preceded it, the origins of the Nicaraguan Revolution are to be found not primarily in economic causalities, but in a political crisis, resulting from blockages placed in the way of middle-class state-building elites. However, the peculiarities of the revolutionary situation meant that unlike Cuba, the forces 'down below' played a relatively autonomous role, which, together with the character of the leadership in the FSLN, a less entrenched available ideological context and an international conjuncture which excluded the likelihood of a single, overarching patron emerging, contributed to an outcome which, from the beginning had the potential to be less rigid and hierarchical than Cuba's.

## The historical context

Twentieth-century Nicaraguan politics cannot be understood, as Black suggests, without a grasp of the historical weakness of the Nicaraguan state. It was divided for most of the nineteenth century between warring fractions of Conservatives in Granada and Liberals in Leon, and little opportunity existed for the consolidation of an economic project or a unified political system. Instead

> The two cities developed independent power structures and economies, using their own separate ports for foreign trade. 'Both cities were like substitutes for a non-existent national state'.[9]

The actual fragility of the state was amply demonstrated in 1855 when the American adventurer and pro-slavery activist William Walker was able, at the invitation of the liberals, to enter and defeat the conservatives with only his 58-man 'American Phalanx of Immortals'. Walker soon turned against his liberal backers and installed himself as president, reintroducing slavery, seizing and then redistributing land to US citizens and declaring English the official language.[10] Walker, notably, was only defeated two years later by an alliance of local forces backed by the other Central American states and funded by the American railroad magnate Cornelius Vanderbilt, who had invested in the likely canal route across Nicaragua. This last factor is important because it points to the strategic significance of Nicaragua to the United States. Never seriously developed as a source of economic surplus in the way in which Cuba and the more classic 'banana republics' like Honduras had been, Nicaragua's prime importance was as a possible sight for an isthmian canal. With Atlantic access through the San Juan river and Lake Nicaragua, major construction would only have to take place on the thin strip of land dividing the lake from the Pacific Ocean, making it, for many, a far better prospect than the Panama route. Thus, while the plantation system spread through the Standard and United Fruit Companies in other Central American countries, the US sought to consolidate its rights of access to the future Nicaraguan canal. In 1850, the Clayton–Bulwer Treaty, over which the Nicaraguan government was never consulted, allowed for the United States and Britain to jointly control any future canal zone, and the Cass–Irisarri treaty of 1858 and the Dickinson–Ayon Treaty of 1867 extended US rights of free transit through the country.[11] It is not surprising then, that the first significant direct US intervention in Nicaragua in the twentieth century came in response to the first regime which seriously sought to address national economic development including taking steps to bring the future canal under the sovereign control of the Nicaraguan government.

The liberal leader José Santos Zelaya had come to power after a revolt in 1893 which ended some thirty years of conservative rule following the Walker debacle. The long period of relative peace and the fact that power had been in the hands of the more progressive wing of the conservatives, had allowed the development of coffee production for export and an accompanying coffee bourgeoisie. In turn, this new class, which felt itself stifled by the constraints of the conservative state, sought under Zelaya to modernise Nicaragua. Highly undemocratic, he nonetheless pushed ahead with infrastructural development in roads, railways, ports and communications to facilitate the growth of coffee exports. Zelaya's nationalism, however, ran afoul of the United States because it threatened that country's view of its hegemonic interests in the region. In March 1907, Zelaya's armies defeated the combined forces of El Salvador, Honduras and Nicaraguan exiles at the Battle of Namasigue, staking out his claim as an independent regional force to be reckoned with.[12] More importantly, after the US decided in 1903 to build the trans-oceanic canal in Panama, frustrating Nicaraguan expectations, he sought to negotiate loans with the British and offered the Germans and Japanese rights to build an alternative route through his country. This was considered by US Secretary of State Knox as an infringement of the Monroe Doctrine by entering into close relations with foreign powers and, in 1909, when conservatives rose up against Zelaya in the Caribbean port of Bluefields, they received the full backing of the US, leading predictably to his overthrow.

The end of Zelaya's 16-year tenure signalled the last attempt at a genuinely independent capitalist development, while the direct intervention of the US military helped to dictate the contours of Nicaraguan politics for the next 34 years, including the following features.

1) A highly dependent state, completely subordinate to the wishes of the hegemonic power. This is best illustrated in the Chamorro–Bryan Treaty of 1914 which gave the US exclusive rights in perpetuity to construct a canal on Nicaraguan territory, effectively eliminating competition with the Panama canal, rights to build a naval base in the Gulf of Fonseca and a 99-year lease on the Corn Islands off the Atlantic coast. In exchange the conservative government was given a paltry US$3 million which went immediately to pay outstanding loans to the US.[13] By 1916, following the earlier appointment of an American controller of customs and revenues, financial control of Nicaragua was in the hands of a triumvirate – the local Minister of Finance, and two North Americans, one of them a State Department appointee.[14]

2) The direct intervention of the propertied classes into the state, which forms a sharp contrast with the Cuban situation where intermediate interests defined the state, as their exclusive preserve and cooperated with the bourgeoisie on the basis of establishing a stable business climate.

3) Nonetheless, the relative weakness of the business and planter interests as a bloc, due to the perpetuation of the sharp liberal/conservative conflicts after Zelaya's era.

4) The opening at the top, as a result of these weaknesses for other, intermediate interests to seek a share in state power, but at the same time, the relative weakness of the middle as a consolidated class of state-builders, again, in contrast with the Cuban example.

5) In this context, therefore, intermediate interests could only seek state power in alliance with other forces. Both Anastasio Somoza and Augusto Sandino can be seen as fractions of a weak, but definite intermediate strata, the former seeking power through close alliance with the hegemonic power, the latter, in an accelerated process of development with the lower classes.

The 1920s were a period of crisis for US policy in Nicaragua. The presence of US Marines, introduced supposedly to maintain peace between the warring factions, had become increasingly ineffective. In 1912, liberal General Benjamin Zeledon had risen up against the US-backed conservative Diaz regime only to be defeated by an American force of close to 3000 Marines;[15] between 1913 and 1924 there were no less than ten revolts and the country remained under martial law for almost the entire time.[16] Faced with a costly, politically damaging and increasingly ineffective occupying force, the Americans chose to withdraw with least damage by putting in place a new electoral system and creating a National Guard as a supposedly neutral force. The winners of the 1925 US-supervised elections, however, were not the conservatives, but a weak alliance of liberals and dissident conservatives. As the coalition government foundered in October 1925, conservative General Emiliano Chamorro, who had been president from 1916 to 1920, returned to overthrow the regime and enraged Washington by trying to bring the emergent National Guard under his control. The withdrawal of American support led to the collapse of the Chamorro coup, but the American choice for a new President, the old standby of 1909 Adolfo Diaz, was completely unacceptable to the liberals, who revolted in 1926, setting up a constitutional government in the Atlantic port of Puerto Cabezas. On this occasion, the inevitable US military intervention was unable to defeat the liberal rebellion and instead US envoy Henry Stimson was forced to negotiate a treaty between the conservative President Diaz and the Liberal General Moncada, including an amnesty, the handover of arms to the Marines until the organisation of the National Guard and US-supervised elections the following year.[17] All the liberal generals, except one, were signatories to the peace treaty. Augusto Cesar Sandino, who had joined the rebellion in 1926, refused to sign until all American troops had withdrawn from the country, leading to a direct confrontation between his Army in Defence of the National Sovereignty of Nicaragua (ESDN) and US forces. Between 1927 and 1933, with distinct setbacks and lulls, the ESDN was able to wage an effective guerrilla campaign against the occupying forces which Black correctly identifies as a parallel with the later war in Vietnam. Thus, the US, with overwhelming superiority in manpower and arms, was never able to defeat Sandino's 'Crazy Little Army', based as it was on the popular support of the peasantry in the Segovias and the Rio Coco region;[18] a significant outpouring of international solidarity was generated for the ESDN and, on 1 January 1933, US troops were eventually forced to withdraw without winning a military victory.[19]

The amicable peace treaty signed between the undefeated Sandino and liberal President Sacasa could not hide the sharp contest which continued to exist in the country. Sandino had negotiated favourable terms, including the partial retention of arms by his forces and the ceding of the northeast third of the country to his former army to set up an agricultural cooperative. This independent position, however, was strongly opposed by the new head of the National Guard Anastasio Somoza. Backed by Washington and the previous president Moncada, Somoza's influence had blossomed because his fluency in English had led to him becoming an intermediary in discussions between the government and the Americans. As Sacasa's weak presidency floundered, Somoza increasingly became the power in Managua and in 1934 on his fourth visit to the capital to hold discussions with Sacasa, Sandino was assassinated by the National Guard, followed up the next day by the murder of 300 of his supporters at their base camp at Wiwili in the North.[20]

Sandino's assassination signalled the rise of the Somocista dynasty which would last, with cosmetic intervals, for the next 43 years, but we can suggest that he contributed at least two important features to the eventual revolution of 1979. Unlike Fidel Castro and the Cuban state-builders who derived their immediate experience from the conspiratorial efforts of Guiteras, ABC and others, the FSLN could turn to the Sandino experience, which had relied for its very existence on the popular support of the mine-workers and peasants of the north and east. And, while Sandino's thought was never the activating ideology of the Nicaraguan revolution in the way José Martí's was in Cuba, it is important to note that his eclectic ideological position went beyond the patriotism of Bolívar and the relatively reformist positions of Martí to address the social question. Thus, Hodges notes that

> Although Bolívar's patriotism was neither superficial nor shortsighted, it had its limitations. In its most profound sense, Sandino believed, a concern for the national honour includes the well being of each citizen. Patriotism would give all an equal stake in the nation. We have here the germs of his definition of patriotism in which the 'sacred' right of the weak includes individuals, not just sovereign peoples. Thus, as he became bolder, Sandino peeled off another layer of his patriotism to reveal its communist content.[21]

Thus, a quarter-century before the formation of the FSLN, Sandino had left a revolutionary legacy which in its practical and ideological reliance on popular support went significantly beyond the Cuban heritage. Before discussing that in detail, however, we need to look at the character of the Somoza regime and the nature of the eventual crisis which led to its destruction.

## Features of the Somocista state

The death of Sandino signalled the first stage in the rise of Anastasio Somoza (Tacho 1) to power. The methods which he used to move from the position of Jefe Director of the National Guard to President of Nicaragua, are a good indicator of those adopted throughout his term and also of his not-insignificant political skills. Black correctly suggests that

> The conventional image of a one-dimensional tyrant is as misleading a description of the founder of the dynasty as it was of his son. In fact, Somoza was a politician of great and cynical intelligence; . . .[22]

Initially supported by the US Ambassador Arthur Bliss Lane and former President Moncada of the Liberal Party, Somoza recognised that this was not enough to gain the presidency. He used his own fascist-oriented force, the *Camisas Azules*, armed by the National Guard, to terrorise the opposition and burn down one of its newspapers; when truck drivers went on strike and President Sacasa threatened to call out the Guard, Somoza promised demagogically to the strikers, that he would bring out the Guard to support them; the weak Sacasa was forced to resign in June, 1936 and the interim President – chosen by Somoza – put back elections six months in order to overcome a constitutional provision which prevented the head of the Guard becoming president before that time had expired; when the elections – closely supervised by the Guard – were held, Somoza romped home by 107 201 votes against 169 for his opponent Arguello.[23]

Two common myths seem to exist about the Somoza dictatorship. The first relates to its relationship to the United States and argues that Somoza was a puppet, at the bidding of the hegemonic power. Walter LaFeber, for example, posits that 'As every President after Hoover knew, (the) Somozas did as they were told'.[24] This is mistaken, as the real position seems to have been that Somoza so ingratiated himself with Washington in international relations as to carve out an autonomous sphere of operations for himself at home. This was most vividly demonstrated in his willingness to commit Nicaraguan troops to fight wars on behalf of the US. At the outbreak of the Second World War, he firmly declared his country's support for the Allied cause; a similar commitment was made in the Korean War, in which Nicaraguan troops saw active service, as they did in the American-led 1965 invasion of the Dominican Republic; further, Somoza was only too willing to allow the US to use Nicaraguan soil as a launching-pad for insurgencies against neighbouring countries, as was the case in both the CIA-backed overthrow of the Arbenz government in Guatemala in 1954 and the attempted invasion of Cuba at Playa Giron in 1961.[25] Shirley Christian seems to be closer to the mark when she suggests that 'Somoza . . . pioneered something that his sons would perfect: the manipulation of the US Government for the greater good of the Somozas'.[26]

But this autonomy did not mean that the regime could be described as a hermetic dictatorship along the lines, for example, of Trujillo in the Dominican Republic. Instead, Somoza allowed a definite, though limited circulation of elites, in which the parameters of power were clearly defined, with access above a certain level restricted to the ruling family and its closest associates, but with a definite space for other aspirants below that level. This approach did not emerge all at once. Middle-class intellectuals, the so-called 'Generation of 1944' broke with the Liberal Party in that year precisely because Somoza had decided to seek another term in office, indicating the extent to which upward aspirations would be restricted; in the same year, conservative demonstrations in Managua and Leon were violently put down by the National Guard; when Somoza again sought to run for President in 1947, even the US were willing to heed the complaints of the opposition and he was forced to seek a pliable substitute. Leonardo Arguello, his old opponent from the 1936 election, was chosen and duly elected, but proved too independent and within 25 days of taking up the reins of office, he had been deposed and Somoza was once again fully in charge.[27] Such a blockage at the top, roughly analogous with Batista's 1952 coup, might have been the prelude to a revolutionary crisis, but Somoza headed off such a possibility by partially opening up the state to his opponents in the Conservative Party, thus securing a limited circulation of elites and his family's rule for almost three decades.

In this sense, the conservative/liberal 'Pact of Two Generals' of 1950[28] cannot be underestimated. A new constitution was written: it gave formal guarantees of free competition and respect for private property; it provided the minority party with one-third of the seats in the Congress despite the actual electoral results; with the only legal parties being the liberals and the conservatives and with everyone understanding the meaning of majority and minority, it guaranteed the bourgeoisie a stable business climate and limited access to the state, once Somoza's dominance was accepted.

With this imperfect but relatively stable system of circulation at the top, Somoza was able to implement his peculiar brand of personalist dictatorship. With US support in the background, absolute control over his own party, the Nationalist Liberal Party (PLN) and a tame opposition, Somoza accumulated wealth through his personal army, the National Guard:

> Somoza . . . had converted the Guard into a personal instrument through an institutionalised blend of privilege, corruption and intimidation, and the growth of the Somoza state was determined by the consolidation of the Guard. By 1939 the model was complete, . . . An enormous quota of state power had been amassed by the Guard over the previous decade: first, military control of communications, then internal revenues and the railways, and later the postal service, immigration, the health service, liquor sales and prostitution, permits for all arms imports, including even industrial dynamite. Loyalty to Somoza was a prerequisite for the upper ranks, and any officer who became too popular, was transferred or dismissed before he could become a threat, . . .[29]

With the Guard safely under his control, Somoza was able to cultivate, for purposes of fulfilling the constitution and to satisfy US legislators and public opinion, a veneer of electoral popularity and legitimacy. Thus, it was obligatory for all government workers and employees in Somoza-owned businesses to be members of the ruling party, the PLN; there was no such thing as a secret ballot in elections; those who voted for Somoza or his stand-in were given a safe conduct card called *La Magnifica* on which their future employment and other benefits might depend.[30] With the powerful tools of the army, the party and the tacit approval of the opposition, Somoza used graft, favours and direct physical pressure to accumulate a massive fortune, estimates of which varied at the time of the Sandinista triumph of between US$500 and 900 million.[31]

> At the end of World War II, . . . Somoza . . . was already the largest cattle rancher and one of the largest coffee and sugar cane producers. After the war the family extended its activities first to mining concessions – in alliance with US firms – and beef exports, followed by cement, textiles, milk products, shipping and airlines, ports, tobacco, slaughter houses, fishing operations, securities, construction, finance, manufacturing industry and real estate speculation. By the middle of the 1970s, the Somoza family formed the third financial group in the country.[32]

One group of persons who, for social and historical reasons, felt themselves to be natural heirs to the state apparatus, seemed to have been excluded from this partial system of circulation, which worked for both Somoza and the traditional bourgeoisie in the Conservative Party. Thus, middle-class intellectuals, whom we can call potential state-builders, had split away, as mentioned, from the PLN to form the Independent Liberal Party (PLI) in 1944. One of their leaders, General Carlos Pasos, had even led an armed movement which had been easily defeated. Younger liberal rebels formed the Democratic Youth Front (FJD) as a more radical alternative to the PLI. In 1944, however, the middle-class alternative was too weak and too narrowly based. Thus, Bermann notes that PLI support was 'largely confined to intellectuals, professionals and artisans in the traditional liberal base of Leon'.[33] Working-class opposition, which might have developed on an independent foundation with the formation of the communist Nicaraguan Socialist Party (PSN) in 1944, was never realised. Somoza manoeuvred skilfully, first to recognise the PSN as a means of forestalling unity with the middle-class opposition groups and, later, when that opposition upsurge had been defeated, driving the PSN underground as an anti-communist measure.[34] In the absence of a powerful, Cuban-style middle-class resistance to the regime and with no significant allies from below, the frustrated and excluded middle-class intelligentsia resorted to ineffective armed movements and ultimately assassination as a means of asserting its place in the Nicaraguan sun.

On the evening of 21 September 1956, the young poet Rigoberto Lopez Perez, acting alone, shot Tacho Somoza while he was partying with friends at a club in Managua. It is of more than passing interest to note that 21 years later, in the main political platform of the FSLN before the seizure of power, that this action is seen as the beginning of the 'revolutionary ascent' which eventually led to victory.[35] This is not quite true. It did of course, identify the social stratum close to the top which felt itself most excluded from the fruits of office and which, with new economic and political developments, would lead the revolutionary struggle at a later period. However, in 1956, the assassination was far more an indication of the successful nature of Somoza's partial system of circulation and its imperviousness to more conventional forms of struggle. In another way, though, the FSLN position is also on target if it recognises that it is crisis up above, within the state *per se*, and between the state and excluded elites who see themselves as a part of the state, which is the primary generator of revolutionary crises. This, I suspect, however, was not the FSLN's interpretation.

## Middle-class elites and the route to victory

The fact that there was middle-class exclusion generated an exclusively middle-class rebellion. The FSLN was only the tenth in a series of movements with the aim of overthrowing the regime between 1958 and 1963; between 1958 and 1960, there were over sixty armed actions against the dictatorship.[36] Most commentators on Nicaragua, particularly those from the left, prefer to deny the obvious continuity of middle-class resistance to the regime which dates back to at least 1944 and instead, emphasise the ideological distinction of the FSLN because its leaders were Marxists. Thus, the FSLN themselves argue that the difference between their early movement and the other guerrilla groups is that they were the 'first armed organisation with a consistent ideological character and the proposal of a revolutionary programme for the construction of a socialist society'.[37] Weber proposes that because the FSLN had sought to organise and defend the working classes, it is a 'revolutionary organisation of the Nicaraguan Proletariat'.[38] The position adopted here is not that ideology was unimportant in the formation of the FSLN or in the outcome of the revolution, but that ideology does not transform the underlying reality that the FSLN leadership consisted of middle-class aspirant state-builders with organic links to the middle-class movements of the immediate past.

The founders of the FSLN, Carlos Fonseca, Tomas Borge and Silvio Mayorga, were all former university students who, alienated from Somoza, had joined the PSN as a vehicle for his overthrow. Frustrated with lack of militancy in the PSN's orthodox communist positions, and inspired by the example of the Cuban revolution, they formed the FSLN in 1962–63 as a Castroite guerrilla organisation to overthrow the dictatorship.[39] The first incursions into guerrilla warfare were a complete disaster. In 1963, the FSLN column of some 60 men was routed in the Coco River region due partly to its inexperience, but also to the fact that it had little contact with the local peasants who gave them no logistical support.[40] Learning from this experience, the party temporarily retreated from military activity and begun organising among students, workers and peasants and at the time of the second major military confrontation at Pancasan in 1967 there was far more peasant support in logistical and fighting positions. Nonetheless, when the confrontation with the Guard came, the poorly-armed and relatively iso-lated guerrilla column was badly mauled, losing 13 members, including Silvio Mayorga, one of its founders.[41] While there are definite disputes as to whether the FSLN in this early period followed a classic foco strategy or not,[42] it is fair to argue that in 1963 the FSLN was closer in strategy and tactics to the overtly middle-class, anti-Somocista movements which had preceded it and in 1967 this was less so, but it would be very premature to suggest that between the two dates they had somehow crossed a threshold and become proletarianised or peasantised. Two events in 1967, however, would hasten a revolutionary situation, but the far more important of them was completely outside the hands of the FSLN.

## From Luis to Tacho II

In February 1957, five months after his father's death, Luis Somoza, Tacho's elder son, was overwhelmingly elected as President of Nicaragua. While his inauguration confirmed the dynastic nature of *Somocismo*, it also signalled an interlude of political reform which is an important phase in the eventual revolution. Thus under Luis, many of those who had been jailed after his father's death were released. He relinquished control of the Guard, which was handed over to his younger brother, Anastasio Somoza Debayle, or Tachito, later to be called Tacho II. More significantly, he reintroduced a one-term provision in the constitution and at the end of his term, conceded office. The Guard, of course, remained in the hands of his brother and Schick, his successor, was a Somoza nominee from the family's Liberal Party, but the reforms had more than cosmetic value, because they geared expectations for even greater movement at the top. Other important devel-opments took place in this period. Through the forties and the first part of the fifties, cotton production had grown rapidly in response to postwar shortages in Europe and in the 1950s this contributed to the displacement of over 180 000 peasants from traditional small farming to agricultural labour and to urban unemployment.[43] In the 1960s, under the influence of the Alliance for Progress, the programme designed by President Kennedy to forestall potential Cuban revolutions, and the Central American Common Market, formed in 1960, significant new investments flowed into the coun-try and particularly into the capital, Managua. The average annual growth rate for Nicaragua in the 1960s was 7.2 per cent and from 1970 to 1978, 5.8 per cent – among the highest in the world for that period.[44] But the new industries, particularly in petrochemicals and foodstuffs, were capital-intensive and did little to solve growing unemployment in Nicaragua.[45] Naturally, the Somoza family and the best-placed elements of the bourgeoisie in both established parties benefited the most from the influx of capital. In the cotton-boom period, the big financial groupings BANIC and BANAMERICA were established and established their dominance in the financial sphere, but less appreciated as an important development in this period was the growth of the middle class to fill the new managerial and professional positions opened up in the industrial sector and in the state, awash as it was with Alliance funds. In 1963, only 1.4 per cent of the economically active population had been professionals, technicians, managers or administrators; by 1971 this had increased to 6.2 per cent.[46] While a rapidly transformed rural economic picture and growing urban unemployment in the sixties and seventies were important features in Nicaraguan politics, the most significant feature was this numerically small but dramatically increased middle, which was the natural social basis of the FSLN leaders and had been the stratum closest to the top which had been deprived of access to the state in the 1950 arrangements. Newly assertive at the National Autonomous University's campuses in Managua and Leon, they elected the pro-Sandinista Federation of Revolutionary Students (FER) to both student governments in 1969.[47] If, after the expectations created by Luis Somoza and Schick, the avenues to upward mobility and power were to be closed, then this newly-assertive middle could be expected to play a major role in any confrontation. If, further, the arrangements for limited circulation at the top were to be abrogated, then such an assertive middle could hope to gain important allies 'up above', creating fissures in the ruling bloc and precipitating a revolutionary situation. This is what happened in 1967 when Tachito Somoza, against the advice of his more realistic brother, sought to re-establish alongside the reality of Somocismo, the authority of a Somoza as head of state.

The decision by the Nationalist Liberal Party (PLN) to nominate the younger Somoza as its candidate for the 1967 presidential elections, not the 1972 earthquake, as is so often argued, was the critical moment in the generation of the revolutionary crisis. This political act, which cannot be reduced to economic causalities, undermined the written agreement between ruling elites on the sharing of power and the unwritten expectations of emergent elites of access to power. The manifestation of this incipient fissure at the top can be seen in the formation for the election campaign across traditional social and political lines of a National Opposition Union, including conservatives, independent liberals and the new Christian Democratic Party, with the conservative Fernando Aguero as Presidential nominee.[48] The new alliance was able to mobilise some 60 000 supporters to a rally in Managua on 22 January 1967, but when the crowd began to march on the Presidential Palace, the National Guard opened fire, killing some 40 marchers and wounding at least 100 more.[49] Somoza, of course, went on to win the elections, but the violence of January had two effects: firstly, it served to isolate the conservatives, whose tactics were impotent in the face of Somocista violence, and drove a wedge between them and other sections of the bourgeoisie both inside and out of the Conservative Party. This trend was consolidated in 1971, when, approaching the end of his term, Tachito, like his father in 1950, struck a deal with Aguero which would on this occasion, allow power-sharing right up to the executive level. A three-man junta was set up in May 1972, including Aguero as its conservative member, until a constituent Assembly could formulate the new constitution, but Somoza retained control of the National Guard. This time around, however, the 'pact' did not serve to heal, but rather exacerbated splits. Younger elements of the bourgeoisie began to group around Pedro Joaquin Chamorro, who later formed the Democratic Liberation Union (UDEL), and Aguero and his supporters who had compromised with the regime were derisively called *zancudo* (mosquito) conservatives.[50] It can, however, be suggested that Somoza had temporarily avoided crisis by retaining some alliance with the most influential and wealthiest sections of the bourgeoisie in the Conservative Party, but even this was eliminated after the 1972 earthquake.

## The 1972 earthquake: geological and political fissure

The December 1972 earthquake devastated Managua, causing upwards of 10 000 deaths, levelling the centre of the city and leaving more than 250 000 homeless.[51] At the same time, it destroyed the last remaining vestiges of alliance at the top and created a chasm in the ruling elites which is a typical prelude to a revolutionary crisis. Somoza saw it as an opportunity to make advances on both the political front, by reclaiming his position as leader of the country and, on the economic front, by making decisive incursions into spheres of the economy not yet under his control. Despite the continued existence of the triumvirate which had been established earlier in the year, Somoza again became *de facto* leader by taking up the position of President of the National Emergency Committee and changing his title from Jefe Director of the National Guard to Jefe Supremo of the Armed Forces.[52] Using his new position as head of the emergency committee, he was able to dispense the emergency funds (including $US78 million from USAID and $54 million from the Inter-American Development Bank (IDB)) effectively to corner the lucrative market for the reconstruction of the city for his own companies. The notion of *competencia disleal* (disloyal competition) became the common cry among elements of the bourgeoisie grouped around the Higher Council for Private Enterprise (COSEP) as Somoza used state power and privilege to buy damaged and destroyed plant and businesses at bargain-basement prices.[53] But the earthquake also, for the first time, created the basis for coalescent dissatisfaction below, particularly among the workers and unemployed of Managua. In typical fashion, Somoza had offered the Guard, in order to maintain their personal loyalty, a stake in the numerous possibilities for fraud and profit offered by the earthquake. Guard officers and men were involved in selling 'free' aid and supplies at exorbitant prices on the black market and exercised increasing brutality against the displaced persons.[54] It is not surprising in this context that a study done after the earthquake by mental health experts from Washington, DC, found a 'rise of aggressiveness, depression and sense of revolt among the people'.[55]

The 1972 earthquake and Somoza's incursions at the top, opened up a rift which had already been created by the method of his return to power in 1967. This crisis at the top, facilitated by a permissive world context in a situation similar to Cuba's in the 1950s, led to revolution, but the outcome was very different. Middle-class state-builders, struggling for power in a revolutionary situation, operated within a new ideological context and benefited from the conjunctural moment and matters of chance so as to emerge in power with a greater potential for democracy and flexibility. More importantly, the rolling and accumulating revolutionary crisis led to the appearance on the historical stage in a way completely different from Cuba, of the popular forces from below as actors with their own relative autonomy.

## The FSLN and the people

Two developments took place in the FSLN after the Pancasan disaster which allowed it to move from being, like other movements before, just another ineffectual dissatisfied group of middle-class elites to being the leading organised force in the 1979 revolution. The first of these emerged in 1973 with Ricardo Morales Aviles' assessment of the political situation in Nicaragua, *La Dominación imperialista en Nicaragua*, which argued that the 'structure of domination' in bourgeois society was threatened when the antagonisms between the ruling and opposition fractions of that class came to a head. It followed from this, as Hodges argues, that 'intrabourgeois antagonisms were more important than the struggle between the bourgeoisie and the popular forces in explaining the crisis of political hegemony'.[56] This position developed in opposition to another held by Jaime Wheelock which placed emphasis on the internal unity of the bourgeoisie and the proletariat and the need to engage in immediate struggle on a class basis.[57] That Morales Aviles' position eventually won out meant that the FSLN, which otherwise would have been isolated from the real forces which generated the revolutionary crisis, was instead able to exploit the intrabourgeois antagonisms on its route to state power.

The second development, the direct lesson of Pancasan and less directly of Che Guevara's death that same year in Bolivia, was the need to abandon the foco approach and develop popular support. The forging of links with the peasantry, the establishment of an underground network in the cities and the assiduous avoidance of armed actions between 1970 and 1974, allowed the FSLN to accumulate forces, train cadres and gain a minimum network of support at the same moment that the crisis up above was maturing.[58] This did not mean that the small, harried and still largely isolated party had somehow gained the confidence of the people, or more overtly, had become the vanguard of the people.[59] After Pancasan, the FSLN grew closer to the popular agenda, but it was their recognition of the crisis up above and the necessary tactics to exploit it which made them an effective revolutionary party. The unprecedented uprising from below served to dramatically modify the way the post-revolutionary society developed.

Early writers on the Nicaraguan Revolution, such as Weber(1981) and Black (1981) have argued, in an attempt to keep faith with Marxist theory, that the working class was the leading force in the process and/or that the FSLN was the organisation of the working class. Later, more reflective studies, particularly Vilas' well-documented *The Sandinista Revolution*, recognising the weaknesses of such an approach, have sought to redefine or clarify the notion of proletariat to fit the peculiar nature of the Nicaraguan upsurge.[60] What we should speak about in the Third World context, Vilas and others argue, is a new concept of the 'people' which is both a political and historical concept. While the people is a far more useful construct to explain the popular uprising, evident in even Vilas' approach, if not in the results of his study, is the notion of determined history, that somehow popular uprising and revolution leading to the transition to socialism are inevitable occurrences. Instead, we can suggest that a rolling series of events, each feeding on the other, none reducible to the economic, though generally tracing their roots to the crisis up above, dragged 'the people' on to the historical stage and transformed the nature of the revolution.

Among the most important points to note in this process is the fact that no profound economic crisis preceded the popular upsurge. The years preceding the revolution had been years of growth, albeit a decelerating one, and it was not until 1978, when the country was already gripped in a civil war, that negative growth was experienced.[61] It is true, as Vilas points out, that wage levels were low and that the movement away from the land and the tendency towards urbanisation had increased poverty, but this was not significantly different to the situation in the rest of (non-revolutionary) Latin America. If an economic crisis connected into the 'crisis of capitalism' cannot be identified as the motor force, then we have to begin examining non-economic factors, with significant ideological damage to an economically determined notion of the events.

Among the main factors which would have enhanced movement from below was the existence of a permissive world context. President Jimmy Carter had come to power in 1977 and his support for human rights not only undermined Somoza, as we shall examine in more detail later, but might well have provided an impetus for the popular movement by removing the likelihood of American intervention as a possible restraining factor. It is difficult to support this contention, except to advance it as one factor in an alternative approach. Far more significant was Somoza's actions against the people. After the December 1974 raid on the house of Somoza *confidante* Chema Castillo which led to, among other things a US$2 million ransom, and the release of political prisoners, Somoza imposed a 33-month state of siege. The brutality unleashed in this period, more than any other action, served to secure popular resentment against the regime. Napalm and defoliants were used to track down and eliminate the FSLN militants, peasant huts were burnt and an estimated 3000 people killed during the period of the state of siege.[62] While the January 1978 killing of Pedro Joaquin Chamorro is correctly seen as a critical catalyst in solidifying upper-class opposition to Somoza, less attention is placed on the effect it must have had on popular opinion. For, if Chamorro, the doyen of an old, conservative dynasty, could be killed with impunity by what at the time appeared to be the Guard, then no one was safe.[63] By the time full-scale war broke out in 1978, there was a further logic which pulled the people, particularly those in the ever-expanding war zones, increasingly into combat. Somozas' Guard, isolated from the people and directly responsible only to their leader,[64] did not hesitate, as more popularly-based armies might have done, to commit openly genocidal acts. Over 50 000 people died during the war, most of them killed when the FSLN withdrew from a position and the Guard attacked the remaining civilians for giving shelter or in indiscriminate bombing raids.[65] It was far better in this context to support the FSLN and fight, rather than cower at home and die, eliciting this reaction, typical of the period, from a mother in the town of Esteli:

> and I told my children that it would be best for them to go into the Frente (FSLN) because, if they didn't, the Guard would kill them anyway – just for being young, y'know.[66]

Eventually, the war itself began to have its economic impact. Faced with inevitable disruptions to the production of cotton and coffee, the two main export crops, the government had to apply for an International Monetary

Fund standby loan of some $66 million; in exchange, the preconditions included an immediate devaluation of the cordoba, which led to a 40 per cent increase in the price of basic foodstuffs – an obvious cause for acceleration in the midst of an already severe war.[67]

Other factors served to influence the pace and character of popular intervention in different ways. Prominent among these was the very weak-ness and small size of the FSLN itself. In 1977, Weber estimates that all three Sandinista tendencies numbered no more than 200 persons and there were no more than 500 when they entered Managua in July 1979.[68] Small size by itself is not an indication of support or influence, particularly when referring to a vanguard-type organisation, which the FSLN aspired to be; but other factors tend to support the proposition that the FSLN did not organise the people, but rather, the mobilised people gave their tactical support to the FSLN. The Christian *Communidades Ecclesiales de Base* (CEBs) or Base Communities, espousing liberation theology, had developed since 1965 with an ideological approach[69] and an organisational base which was supportive but independent of the FSLN. By 1979 there were more than 300 CEBs active throughout the country.[70] Marchetti's comments capture the close, yet ambiguous relationship between leader and presumably led in 1979:

> in Nicaragua, the Sandinistas did not have party structures to depend on. The alliance between the Christian churches and the revolution was really cemented during the insurrection against Somoza, because the Parish structure served as the organisa-tional base. . . . in a sense, the parish replaced Lenin's idea of a cell.[71]

Indeed, the most 'Sandinista' of organisations, the Sandinista Defence Committees (CDSs), which unlike the Cuban CDRs, were not set up by the revolutionary government after victory, but grew out of the revolutionary struggle,[72] reflected this autonomy from the vanguard. Far more self-help units than products of FSLN organisational strategy, this independence, as we shall discuss, would extend into the post-Somoza period. To conclude an appreciation of this overall picture of the autonomy of the 'people' from the vanguard, we need only look briefly at the course of the actual revolutionary civil war itself.

If we choose the FSLN's December 1974 raid on Castillo's house as the beginning of the final offensive and conclude that at this state the crisis above had already matured, then what we see emerging is a three-pronged struggle to gain recognition, prominence and ultimately dominance in the new, highly unstable situation. Two of these forces were reasonably well-organised and defined: the middle-class state-builders represented by the FSLN, who were nonetheless subject to peculiar forces which we shall discuss; and the traditional bourgeoisie, the liberal wing of which in COSEP, UDEL and other organisations, was seeking to place its own mark on the situation. The third, or popular force, which did not exist as a tight organisation, but neither as an inchoate mass also struggled to define an independent position.

In December 1974, the Sandinista action, which was sharply criticised by the Wheelock (proletarian) wing of the party, as adventurist, nonetheless did serve to identify the FSLN as a realistic and militant pole of opposition, particularly in a context where demonstrations and constitutional measures by the bourgeoisie had failed to have any impact on the regime.[73] Further, the state of siege led, as we have suggested, to growing popular dissatisfaction among the thousands whose families had been killed or experienced brutality at the hands of the regime, although the FSLN too, was to pay a heavy price as its leader Carlos Fonseca was killed in 1976. The October 1977 offensive, led by the Tercerista (Ortega) wing of the FSLN, had a similar propaganda impact. Although the fighters were poorly armed and the results were minimal, it kept the FSLN in the public eye in a developing revolutionary situation while the tactics of the other trends, the Prolonged Popular War (GPP) and Proletarian were still addressing an old situation where accumulation of forces was the priority.[74] The liberal bourgeoisie, for its part, struggled to find organisational form and tactics that would win over popular opinion and forestall popular action from below, but such an option increasingly did not appear to exist. After the murder of Chamorro in January 1978, the COSEP business grouping called for a 'civic stoppage' which was only partially successful because of the non-participation of big business and the inevitable need to reopen because of loss of earnings in other sectors.[75] With Chamorro's death and the fall in influence of his organisation UDEL, other groups such as Robelo's Nicaraguan Democratic Movement (MDN) and in July 1978 the Broad Opposition Front (FAO), sought to carve out a leadership role for the bourgeoisie. But while bourgeois influence remained relatively strong until January 1979,[76] its unwillingness to side with the popular wave, sharp divisions between those who had sided with Somoza and those who sought an alternative path and to a degree, continued reliance on external support to dictate national events, meant that from as early as Chamorro's death the writing, in retrospect, was already on the wall.

Not coincidentally, a month after the bourgeois-led shutdown, the residents of the largely Indian community of Monimbo rose up spontaneously against the regime. As a result of clashes with members of the National Guard over the previous days which had led to the death of a young boy, the residents of the highly homogenous and historical community laid down barricades on 25 February. After several days of minor skirmishes, Somoza decided to take over the *barrio* with force. Over 200 people were killed in an action in which the FSLN played no organisational role and in which its cadres for the most part did not participate.[77] This then, was how the insurrection developed. In the August 1978 Palace occupation, the FSLN led and in addition to winning important financial resources for the final offensive and freeing top leaders, reinforced the impression that it was the only organisation capable of resisting the Guard; the September uprising in Matagalpa was spontaneous as Monimbo had been earlier in the year; the 9 September Tercerista offensive in a number of cities, while it was led by the FSLN, involved spontaneous activity by the urban population which had been gaining in confidence and experience over the previous months.

By the time the three FSLN tendencies had united in January 1979, the bourgeoisie had been effectively isolated; thus in May, when the final offensive began, the FSLN was in the lead, but the people, with their own experience of spontaneous organisation and initiative, were playing an autonomous role, totally different from the picture of the Cuban revolution and recognised by the main military commander of the FSLN, Humberto Ortega, who noted in a candid interview less than six months after the victory that

> The truth is that we always took the masses into account, but more in terms of their supporting the guerrillas, so that the guerrillas as such could defeat the National Guard. This isn't what actually happened. What happened is that it was the guerrillas who provided support for the masses so that they could defeat the enemy by means of insurrection.[78]

As in Cuba, one other factor was critical for a successful revolution and that was a permissive world context.

## Permissive world context

In attempting to grasp the particular features of 'permissive world context' in the Nicaraguan case, we should recall that Nicaragua's value to the United States had, throughout the century, been primarily strategic in character.[79] Once a decision had been taken to build the canal at Panama, the alternative route through the San Juan river, and by extension, Nicaragua, became more important as the place where a competitive canal should *not* be built. Under Somoza, Nicaragua's value rested in its absolute fealty to the US, captured in the famous phrase attributed to Roosevelt that the elder Somoza was 'a son of a bitch . . . but he's our son of a bitch'.[80] Whether this was actually said may be contended, but the substance of US policy closely followed its line. In the highly unconstitutional arrest and dismissal of Arguello from office in 1947, for example, the US initially went along with other Latin American countries in not recognising Somoza's replacement. Completely in tune with the growing Cold War atmosphere in the US, Tacho quickly called a constituent assembly, got them to pass a new constitution with anti-communist clauses and rounded up many of his opponents on the basis of a 'communist conspiracy'. Within months, the US had restored formal relations, forgiving the crimes of the recent past and ignoring the wishes of the newly-emergent democratic regimes in Latin America.[81] Bermann correctly assesses the value of Somoza to the US when he notes that 'Tacho was better than a puppet. He did the right thing without prompting'.[82]

In the late 1970s, this attitude to Nicaragua and the Somoza dynasty changed qualitatively – if only, as events would prove, temporarily. Virtually all the literature on the revolution recognises that a shift of some sort took place in the period before 1979. Weber, for example, not immune to dominant Marxist thinking at the turn of the decade, argues that the events in Nicaragua indicated a shift in the regional balance of forces in favour of revolutionary movements. He places far less importance on the role and policies of the Carter administration with its human rights emphasis, which he dismisses as an '*ad hoc* ideology designed for US moral rearmament after the disaster of Indochina. . . .'[83] Jeanne Kirkpatrick on the other hand, proposes that it was Carter's policy which 'brought down the Somoza regime',[84] while other writers have argued that Carter's policy failed precisely because it did not try to bring down Somoza and replace him with a more liberal leader.[85]

All of these approaches sense the peculiar 'window of possibility' which opened up during the Carter Administration, but by focusing only on US policy or, conversely, on revolutionary movements, they fail to appreciate the outlines of an overall picture. Further, by focusing on the single case, instead of recognising that similar conjunctures have occurred in the past, they fail to recognise a *permissive world context*, which is a temporary, albeit recurring warp in the vigilance, unity of purpose and attention of the hegemonic power. This occurs in the context where regional and more distant neighbours are sufficiently strong and unified to provide logistical and diplomatic support and finally, where the revolutionary state-builders are sufficiently skilful to take maximum advantage of these contradictions while they last, for, as suggested, the warp is only temporary.

A first point to note is that the change in policy to Somoza, as Pastor argues, did not begin with the Carter period, but after Nixon's resignation following the Watergate debacle. The new Secretary of State for Inter-American Affairs, William Rogers, had taken up the job on the provision that the CIA would not act without his knowledge, as had been the case in the overthrow of the Allende government in Chile, and that he would be able to change several ambassadors. Turner Shelton in Nicaragua was soon replaced by James Theberge who immediately told Somoza that he would be watching how USAID funds were spent more closely and began a dialogue with the moderate opposition.[86] This sequence of events is important because it shifts the focus from the peculiarities of Carter and his policies to examine deeper bipartisan shifts which were taking place in response to both internal and external developments. Internally, the secrecy and paranoia of the Nixon administration, culminating in the secret bombing of Cambodia and the break-in to the Democratic Party offices in the Watergate Building, had created a groundswell of popular and legislative opinion against strong executive government. Externally, the failure of the Vietnam war effort with its significant human cost, had brought into question the previously acceptable notion of the US as the international policeman of the 'free world'. Both of these channels led to the same conclusion, at least from 1973, that the US should significantly moderate its policies and alter its approach to the kind of regimes considered acceptable to support. Carter, therefore, was the logical continuation and culmination of this position. At the head of the new agenda was a notion of human rights which contradicted the previously dominant view that dictatorships should be supported regardless, once they were opposed to communism, a position which struck at the heart of the relationship with the Somoza dynasty. Equally relevant was Carter's attitude to intervention, which opposed the US acting to destabilise regimes in the way Nixon had acted against Chile and instead called for multi-lateral diplomacy with the neighbouring Latin American countries. Thus, Pastor notes that

> Carter's preferred policies had two dimensions. First, the United States should encourage democracy and dialogue among competing groups within a country but should not mediate or arbitrate that dialogue. Decisions on the political future of Nicaragua should be made by Nicaraguans, not by the United States. . . . The goal was to seek more balanced relationships. The United States would state its concerns, for example, on human rights, but it would not determine who should govern.[87]

While it is evident that within this policy the Carter Administration struggled to get what it considered a moderate and acceptable, i.e. non-Sandinista leadership to head any post-Somoza government,[88] the measures taken, impelled as they were by a less aggressive national mood, served both to undermine Somoza and to encourage the popular upsurge. In June 1977, for example, the Administration, seeking to block further military aid to Somoza, was eventually able to reach a compromise with conservatives in Congress that it would not sign any new military aid agreement without an improvement in the human rights situation.[89] In response to this pressure, Somoza moved to lift the state of siege which had been in effect since the December 1974 FSLN raid, and changed his cabinet to make it more 'representative'. The FSLN, correctly reading the Somoza manoeuvre as a typical attempt to moderate in order to stay in power, but also, from the greater freedom which the new conditions allowed, launched their small but significant, September 1977 offensive.[90]

In the region, significant changes were taking place, reflected in the increasingly assertive policies of Venezuela under Carlos Andres Peréz and Mexico under José López Portillo. Both countries, awash in petrodollars, were seeking to establish themselves as sub-regional forces in their own right, while in Panama, the nationalist Torrijos government sought to establish a broader definition of its independence and, in Costa Rica, the Carazo Government retained the well-established tradition of caution towards its dictatorial neighbour to the north. This new conjuncture fitted, if somewhat awkwardly, with Carter's emphasis on multi-lateral diplomacy but, as events proved, when even Carter veered towards more traditional methods of solving the problem, the new regional alliance was willing to go beyond and resist Carter policy. Thus, when on 22 June 1979, on the verge of a Sandinista victory, Secretary of State Cyrus Vance proposed that a 'peace-keeping force' be sent to Nicaragua, with the exception of military-ruled Argentina, the Organisation of American States (OAS) Assembly over-whelmingly rejected the idea.[91] And, in addition to the critical supply of arms and safe areas in Costa Rica, without which it is questionable that victory would have been possible, the decision by the Andean pact on 16 June to recognise the Sandinistas as 'legitimate combatants', making them legally equivalent to Somoza, served significantly to undermine the US effort to marginalise and neutralise the left-wing movement.[92] Operating in this favourable window, the FSLN could have made the fatal error of emphasising its Marxist ideological credentials and longstanding links with Cuba and regional revolutionary movements. Instead, led by its Tercerista trend, it recognised the need to form alliances with the local bourgeoisie and used its closest allies in the Group of Twelve (Los Doce) as intermediaries in its discussions with regional leaders.[93] In the end, a combination of these factors (US reticence to intervene, differences between members of the administration on the correct policy to follow,[94] solid opposition to intervention and logistical support for the FSLN in Latin America), provided the opening for a Sandinista victory, forced home by what Pastor aptly describes as a 'sudden shift in the balance of military power'.[95] But this window was only temporarily open, as the very act of revolution itself contributed to a change in American foreign policy which began in Carter's final years and surpassed, in many respects, traditional Cold War positions under Ronald Reagan.

# The post-revolutionary landscape

Three forces competed for power in the revolutionary situation and all three emerged in the post-revolutionary landscape. The bourgeoisie, by definition, was divided. The pro-Somoza elements had lost and in the case of those closest to him, their property and land had been taken away and most were either in exile or, in the case of the Guard, in prison. The big bourgeoisie in BANIC and BANAMERICA, who had never been a part of the revolution, remained sullen but powerful in the national context. An intermediate bourgeoisie, represented by people like Alfonso Robelo and his Nicaraguan Democratic Movement (MDN), felt themselves and were to an extent, a part of the revolutionary movement. But Robelo, who sat initially on the governing Junta of National Reconstruction (JGRN), would resign within a year, as the revolution moved to the left. A third force, represented by the Group of Twelve of businessmen and professionals, were closer to the FSLN and many would remain so throughout the regime's stay in power.

At the other end of the spectrum was 'the people', a somewhat amorphous and open-ended concept of the majority of Nicaraguans, many of whom, particularly in the urban areas, had entered the revolutionary struggle independently. Into the post-revolutionary situation they brought their own rudimentary organisations and ideas which did not necessarily correspond, as we shall argue, with those of the vanguard. Finally, we can identify the FSLN and since they were the leading force, had sacrificed tremendously and were seen by tens of thousands of people as their own party, it is necessary to focus on some of the organisation's peculiarities to understand the outcome of the revolution.

# Peculiarities of the FSLN

If we begin with the notion that the FSLN was essentially an organisation representing middle-class state-builders, we nonetheless have to modify this to recognise that historical sequence, available ideological context and fortuitous circumstances all came together to produce a vanguard less wedded to routine and with a greater potential for flexibility than, for example, its immediate forebears in the Cuban Revolution. If one reads the 1977 'General Political and Military Platform of the FSLN', there is very little to suggest that the incorporation of Sandino's name into the Frente's title had in any way altered its essentially Marxist–Leninist framework. Thus, the platform speaks about the inevitable triumph of the 'cause of the proletariat' and socialism, identifies the present stage as one of a 'revolutionary-democratic process' and speaks of the proletariat as the 'fundamental and determinative class for bringing about profound revolutionary changes in the present capitalist system of exploitation and oppression'.[96] Most significantly, its vanguard policy, clearly outlined in the document, unambiguously identifies the organisation as Leninist:

> The Sandinista vanguard, in assuming its historical role, should correctly assign duties among the masses and intermediate or immediate peripheral sectors or those that have its trust. We are trying to create a mass struggle without enlarging the FSLN.[97]

If this is wedded to the 1969 *Historic Programme of the FSLN*, then a clear picture is seen of a typical Marxist–Leninist programme adopted to the realities of Third World underdevelopment along the lines of the Soviet 'socialist orientation' theses.[98] The programme called *inter alia* for participatory democracy, nationalisation of the commanding heights, state control over planning, an independent foreign policy, with the only albeit important novelty, that under agrarian reform no mention is made of state farms, but only the redistribution to poor peasants of capitalist and feudal estates.[99]

In the post-revolutionary situation, the very clear notion of the Leninist vanguard has been less emphasised (although never completely subordinated) and in its place has arisen the more confusing approach of a mixed economy, with pluralism but under revolutionary hegemony. The notion of revolutionary hegemony itself has caused tremendous theoretical problems, for as Vilas recognises, in the absence of a relatively large proletariat, a hegemonic project presumably led by that class, has, at best, questionable leadership.[100] In reality, the vanguard party becomes the protector of the revolutionary hegemony and the obvious question is, 'Who will guard the (van)guardians?' Even Corragio's recognition that in every society there are structural limits to pluralism and that pluralism is always defined within a hegemonic project,[101] throws light on the complexity of the problem, but fails to answer this question. Rather than assert the obvious, that despite Leninist preconceptions there has been a degree of pluralism in Sandinista policy from the very beginning, as Corragio does, the more relevant discussion should be directed to why the Sandinistas have not travelled the Fidelista route toward the concentration and monopolisation of power. A number of factors seem to be responsible.

The first, simply put, is that no Fidel emerged. Carlos Fonseca Amador, the leader of the movement from the early sixties, had died in combat in 1976 and it is possible that had he survived, he may have developed along the lines of Fidel. Nicaragua did, after all, have a tradition of *caudillismo* most evident in Somoza himself. This, however, is unlikely, as Fonseca never possessed nor indeed seemed to aspire to, the overarching power which is the hallmark of Fidel. Before he died, Fonseca was already a part of one tendency competing for influence among the cadres.[102] A supporter of the Prolonged Popular War (GPP) group along with Tomas Borge and Henry Ruiz, it is hard to imagine him establishing absolute authority in what looked like essentially a debate among equals. Death, imprisonment and dispersal seemed each in its own way also to have worked in favour of the decentralisation of power. By 1979, two of the three founders, Mayorga and Fonseca, had died; Borge, the other founder, had spent considerable time in prison as had Daniel Ortega; scattered in Cuba, Costa Rica and elsewhere, at one point in 1970–71, only one leader of the movement, Oscar Turcios, was operating freely in the country.[103]

More important was the split of the Frente into three trends after 1977. At a moment of revolutionary upsurge, this split, as Weber suggests, did not seriously weaken the movement, but led in a sense to a sort of division of labour:

> The Terceristas assumed responsibility for military initiatives and the policy of alliances, while the GPP and 'proletarian' tendencies conducted mass organisational work in the *barrios*, the university, the factory and the plantations.[104]

When the movement reunited early in 1979, the leaders of these three trends, who were equally represented on the new Directorate, could argue with some justification that they had all contributed to fostering the revolutionary situation and this must have immeasurably strengthened a spirit of collective leadership, tolerance and compromise, features in short supply in the Cuban revolution.

In addition, the FSLN benefited from a possible and cumulative ideological context which had learnt many lessons from previous errors. Ironically, it was the Cubans who gave the Sandinistas much advice on being cautious in the economy and not making too rapid an advance towards socialisation,[105] and as Daniel Ortega suggested, the Sandinistas had learnt their own lessons on the possible progressive role of the church from the experiences which had accumulated since the Cuban revolution.[106] As Serra suggests, the active participation of the church in the revolution and not international events such as Vatican II, forged an alliance between the FSLN and the progressive clergy,[107] a development which would have been highly unlikely twenty years earlier. Although, as the 1969 and 1977 programmes suggest, the FSLN tended to be very selective in the use of Sandino's heritage, they were nonetheless, through Sandino, heirs to an independent, non-statist brand of revolutionary thought and action. As we have shown, Sandino was not a Martí nor a Bolívar, but drew his inspiration more from the tradition of the Mexican anarchist Flores Magón.[108] This was later syncretised with the magnetic-spiritualist philosophy of the Spanish/ Argentine Victor Trincado and with theosophy into his own brand of spiritual communism.[109] Hodges effectively contends that these anarchospiritualist streams have re-emerged in the liberation church and, surviving alongside the FSLN's Marxism, act as a circumscribing force defining, unlike any force in Cuba or the Soviet Union, the limits of power of the 'new class'.[110]

Other ideological factors of the moment helped to define and moderate the FSLN's definition of the vanguard and hegemony. Thus Weber's contention that the FSLN learnt a great deal from the most immediate international experiences in communism, including the anti-bureaucratic uprisings in Poland and Hungary, the horrors of Cambodia and the experiences of post-revolutionary Vietnam is worth consideration.[111] By the early eighties, once in power, it must also have been very evident to them, unlike Cuba twenty years before, that state-centred socialism of the Soviet variety and indeed, the moribund features of the Cuban economy, could only be a model in terms of what to avoid on the road to national liberation.

Building on this point, one further factor with ideological overtones is worth consideration. From the beginning, the FSLN could not rely on a Soviet patron in the way the Cuban revolution relied for its survival on Soviet economic assistance and an unwritten security regime between the US and the Soviet Union.[112] This hard fact, together with the country's location on the continent, which required the utmost flexibility with neighbouring countries in both the accession to and retention of, revolutionary power, is important in understanding why FSLN ideological positions have never been able to harden into the far more orthodox assertions which exist in Cuba. Thus, unlike Cuba, Soviet economic assistance to Nicaragua between 1979 and 1987, fluctuated widely from year to year and socialist assistance for the whole period never amounted to more than 55 per cent of the total.[113] This lack of reliance on any single country has given the regime greater room to manoeuvre in international relations, reflected in a policy which is far more independent of Soviet concerns than was imaginable in Cuba for that period.[114] If however, the vanguard operated with an historical legacy which provided it with a greater opportunity for flexibility and innovation, it was nonetheless a vanguard party and we need to look at how it functioned in the new situation to lead to a result which was far different from that proposed in either the 1969 or 1977 documents.

## *From hegemony to popular pluralism*

As a result of the rapid military advances made in the closing weeks of the insurrection, the undoubted leadership role which they had played and the last-minute attempts to frustrate the transition to power by Somoza stand-in Francisco Urcuyo,[115] when the FSLN entered Managua on 19 July, although nominally a minority on the governing Junta,[116] they were far more powerful than was apparent. While Daniel Ortega was the only named FSLN member on the Junta, both Moises Hassan and Sergio Ramirez supported Frente positions, effectively making the two private-sector representatives, Violetta Chamorro and Alfonso Robelo, a permanent minority. At the same time, the absolute defeat of the Guard, which doubled as a police force, meant that in the pivotal military and security spheres, the insurgent FSLN forces wielded virtually absolute power.

In this framework, we can argue that immediately before the seizure of power, FSLN policy vacillated between its officially Leninist, commandist programme and other more disentrenched notions of popular participation and involvement, spurred on by the degree of popular insertion which had occurred in the revolutionary offensive. Thus, in the famous retreat from Managua to Masaya of 29 June, it was the semi-autonomous block committees of Masaya – the forerunners of the CDSs – which dug air-raid shelters, set up medical units and organised solidarity marches in support of the FSLN. However, while the 1977 programme had spoken about the *Frente* 'assigning' duties to the people, essentially a top-down relationship, a central function of the committees reflected an inversion of the relationship of the traditional vanguard to its mass base. Thus Black notes that

> One function of the committees in particular, marked the relationship between the people and the Frente: the committees were charged with identifying any abuse of power, any failure by a Sandinista to show respect for the civilian population.[117]

While flexibility existed from the very beginning, we nonetheless argue that the correlation of forces after the seizure of power enhanced the tendency towards commandism and monopoly, reflected in a narrow interpretation of the concept 'hegemony'. However, by 1984 this rendition of hegemony, purportedly directed against the bourgeoisie, had been severely undermined, not only by bourgeois resistance and external pressure, but significantly by popular resistance to commandism and centralised authority. After 1984, the revolutionary project, besieged as it was from external aggression, nevertheless proceeded on a less statist path with meaningful devolution of power from the centre.

Various random pieces of evidence support the view that the concept of a commandist vanguard still had significant influence in the Sandinista leadership after 19 July 1979.

(1) In an oft-quoted statement in *Barricada* of 24 August 1980, Humberto Ortega defended the traditional 'vanguardist' view that elections were not to be a channel for genuine rivalry for political power, but a means of choosing the best among the vanguard:

> (our elections) . . . are very different from those demanded by
> the oligarchs and traitors, the conservatives and liberals, the
> reactionaries and imperialists, that whole riff-raff, as Sandino
> used to call them. . . . Keep it firmly in mind that these elections
> are to consolidate revolutionary power, not to place it at stake.
> For power is in the hands of the people, through its vanguard,
> the FSLN.[118]

(2) When a group of former conservative youth chose to form a party called the Sandinista Social Democratic Party, claiming that Sandino's name was a national legacy, the FSLN argued that the legacy of *Sandinismo* belonged only to the FSLN and, through the Junta, passed a decree forbidding groups other than the FSLN and its affiliates to use the name.[119]

(3) In late 1979, the building workers' union the SCAAS, headed by Alejandro Solorzano, a leader of the communist PSN, sought to negotiate new wages for its members. Despite the fact that the PSN gave broad support to the revolution, the FSLN established a rival union which was promptly recognised by the Ministry of Labour as the only legitimate union representing building workers. It was only after massive demonstrations in January 1980 in favour of the SCAAS that the Sandinista union was pressured to give up its legal entitlement, opening the way for recognition of the popular choice.[120]

(4) Better known as an issue and central to the overall survival of the regime, were the initially heavy-handed policies towards the non-Hispanic residents of the Atlantic Coast. As Close points out, the Frente sought to impose its interpretation of the problems of the highly-underdeveloped Atlantic Coast as essentially class-based on a people who had traditional and deep-seated reservations towards the 'Spaniards' of the West Coast and who saw their problems in ethno-national dimensions.[121] Early errors included attempts to replace the existing organisation, The Alliance for Progress of Miskitos and Sumos (ALPROMISU), with Sandinista mass organisations. This was met with resistance and the FSLN backtracked and, together with leaders of the various ethnic groups, formed MISURUSATA (Miskitos, Sumos, Ramas and Sandinistas United) in November 1979. While at first this seems to have helped relations between the *costeños* and the revolutionary government, things soon deteriorated, with the Sandinistas accusing the increasingly nationalist demands of MISURUSATA as supporting counter-revolution, leading to greater hostility from the people on the coast to the FSLN. Eventually, in 1981, after a series of increasingly violent clashes, relations broke down completely, with MISURUSATA leaders joining the nascent Contra forces in Honduras and thousands of Miskitos fleeing, willingly or unwillingly, across the border with them.[122] While this is not an attempt to make a definitive judgement on the causes of the rapid deterio-

ration of relations in 1980 and 1981, many of which are obviously due to the activities of the growing US-backed counter-revolution, we can suggest from the evidence, that Sandinista vanguardism was at least partially responsible for these early mistakes, some of which, under the impact of popular resistance, would later be corrected.

(5) The final example of vanguardist policy surrounds the question of land reform. Faced with the need to maintain existing production levels and hold together the economic alliance with the bourgeoisie, early FSLN policy sought to discourage the spontaneous land-seizures which had occurred during and immediately after the insurrection. While it can be suggested that, unlike the monopolistic position taken towards the SCAAS and the insensitivity to the Atlantic Coast, there was a certain logic in the policy of restraining land takeovers we shall suggest that it was essentially a part of the early tendency to rely more on decree from above rather than demand from below. By February 1980, however, this had changed and, pressured by a massive demonstration by members of the Rural Workers Association (ATC), the government was forced to expropriate those estates which ATC members had already taken over although it made clear that no more land-takeovers would be tolerated.[123] More poignantly, the policy towards cooperatives, which initially favoured the more socialised form of production cooperatives, or CASs, over the credit and service (CCS) type, was forced, under the effects of the war and popular demand, to undergo significant moderation. In 1981, under pressure from the National Union of Farmers and Cattlemen (UNAG) the decision was taken to give peasants the right to choose the form of cooperative they wished to join, which by 1982 had led to the majority of cooperatives consisting of independent producers with only minimal credit and service arrangements.[124]

From the early stages, then, a pattern began to emerge. Vanguardist notions and entrenched ideological positions, when applied as policy, were confronted by popular resistance in ways completely alien to the experience of the Cuban revolution. In turn, Sandinista policy, particularly when that resistance came from below, proved itself to be not inflexible, but willing to seek a compromise even on matters which at first were stated as absolute principle. Under the impact of war, external blockade and economic disaster, this constant popular incursion into areas presumably reserved for the leadership has led to a significant devolution of power; this has combined with a strengthened political pluralism to largely negate initial concepts of the vanguard and of hegemony.

Four examples are sufficient to make the point. On the Atlantic Coast, despite the sanguinary war which had developed by 1982, the FSLN, as Close suggests, never labelled the Miskito people as a whole as counter-revolutionary, and offered an amnesty to all but the top command to return home in 1983,[125] leaving themselves the political space to negotiate. This policy of compromise bore fruit in December 1984 when in a remarkable *volte-face*, the newly-elected FSLN government recognised the *costeños'* claims to greater autonomy and set up a National Autonomy Commission to draft new constitutional proposals. In May 1987 the draft autonomy bill was passed by 1200 representatives of six ethnic groups in Puerto Cabezas. It created two elected governments, one in the North and one in the South, and gave them significant control over education, local economic efforts and some police functions. The central government retained control over large-scale development projects although the revenue from such efforts would be shared.[126] By 1985, land reform policies which had already been significantly amended by peasant demands were even further modified. The first five years of Sandinista policy had been oriented towards collective forms of ownership, but after 1985 individual ownership, without the requirement of being a member of a cooperative, was allowed.[127] The increasing demand for land was brought sharply home to the government when, in May 1985, 8000 peasants from Masaya demonstrated for land.[128] As a result of this, in January 1986, the Agrarian Reform Law was amended, liberalising the way in which idle land could be expropriated and allowing any landless *campesino*, whether a member of a cooperative or not, to be the beneficiary, once having guaranteed to work the land. With this, the FSLN hoped to shore up its support in both the war-zones and the areas of the country where land-hunger was greatest. As Close suggests, such a policy veers significantly away from the 'socialist' side of the agrarian reform balance, but when wedded to more profound changes in the political sphere, may mean that 'Nicaraguan agrarian reform may be striking off on a quite independent radical democratic path'.[129]

This confusion as to how precisely to define the revolution, evident in the early studies, but more prominent after 1985, is particularly pronounced in the body of literature on the left which has generally been supportive of the regime. While most early studies of this type sought to identify Nicaragua as an example of the transition to socialism, the most insightful recognised its peculiarities. Thus Vilas, who preferred to classify the process as one not in transition to socialism but in *transition to development*, would only tentatively suggest that a proletarian project was a possible long-term goal of the revolution.[130] Fagen, Deere and Corragio, in their more general work on the 'transition', which draws heavily on the Nicaraguan experience, asked rhetorically, 'where are the Models?'[131] and suggested that increasingly what was becoming apparent in studies of these processes was the need for 'increasing caution in claiming that answers are definitely known or pathways clear'.[132] Baumeister, who specialises in the agrarian reform and in keeping with this understandable lack of clarity in grasping the direction of the mid-eighties Sandinista project, found it 'hard to predict',[133] is still closest to an explanation. He suggests that what was happening was the '*kulakization*' of Nicaraguan agriculture, or the farmer road to capitalism:

> The presence of well-off peasants and medium-sized capitalist producers, the strengthening of the poor and the peasantry through cooperatives and the general support of agriculture through new investments make possible a broad-based, democratic and non-oligarchical capitalism.[134]

Whether this would go beyond capitalism to consolidate the Sandinista model of transition, he argued, would depend on the state's capacity to organise a vast cooperative movement, which is precisely not the path that the revolution took after 1985. What instead seems to separate the Nicaraguan process from a purely liberal, representative form of capitalism, is the unprecedented popular incursion into all aspects of the state's business, which lends support to Close's suggestion of a novel alternative, composed essentially of a market economy of cooperatives and variously sized producers alongside a radical and mobilisational plural democracy.

The most graphic illustrations of a possible alternative path are to be found in politics. The so-called mass organisations, which developed before and after the revolutionary insurrection, far from being the vertically directed and controlled organs of the Cuban revolution, have, as Ruchwarger suggests, carved out a significant area within which they possess relative autonomy in relation to the Sandinista leadership.[135] While there continued to be tension between the Frente and these organisations and the limited development of the productive forces hindered their effectiveness, independent activity, such as the aforementioned demonstration by the ATC in 1980, continued to be the norm, rather than the exception. At the same time, the CDSs, vilified by opponents of the revolution as totalitarian spy-mechanisms, had, as West argues, by virtue of their neighbourhood policing functions and critical independence from the FSLN leadership shifted the 'power locus' away from the state towards

> a new politics, a new form of state unrecognized (indeed suppressed) within more traditional Western capitalist liberal-democracies or Soviet state-capitalist one-party communism, which respectively maintain the public–private split with private dominance, or attempt to eliminate the private and civil liberties entirely.[136]

Without question, the 1984 elections represented a significant stage in a process of entrenching pluralism and decentralising power. While the US Department of State chose to emphasise the poignant fact that some of the most significant opposition parties had chosen not to run in the elections and that there had been some harassment of the opposition in the run-up,[137] their negation of the elections was more closely connected to their agenda of support for the armed Contra opposition. Far closer to the truth and the historical significance of the process, was the well-researched study by the American-based Latin American Studies Association, which found that

> Without question the November 4 election was the cleanest held in Nicaragua since 1928, when US marines were organizing and supervising the balloting. . . . As of the close of business on November 7, not a single formal complaint about voting or vote count irregularities had been presented at the Supreme Electoral Council by any party. Spokesmen for several of the contesting opposition parties contested the cleanness of the elections.[138]

If one is to approach this process of devolution as a dialectical one in which the gradual outlines of a new synthesis began to emerge, then the 1987 Constitution, discussed and approved in hundreds of public assemblies involving upwards of 100 000 persons,[139] was an even more important indication of change than the 1984 elections. While the new law contained the expected references to the mixed economy, political pluralism and non-alignment in international relations, it contained no reference to a vanguard and its only reference to the FSLN is that it was founded by Carlos Fonseca. While Title V, National Defence, entrenches the Sandinista Army (EPS) in the constitution and has been sharply contested as an example of the entrenching of the vanguard, Title 1, including the definition of political pluralism, confirmed what had already been put into practice in 1984, the right of all political parties which were not Somozist to exist and, by extension, to seek political office.[140]

## The 1990 elections

By the end of 1987, the Nicaraguan revolution was faced with a severe paradox. The last determined Contra offensive of October 1987 had ended in failure. The government, with its 62 000-man army, a militia force with over 100 000 persons, new Soviet weapons, good intelligence and recent experience of fighting a guerrilla war on the same territory, seemed more impregnable than ever.[141] The Esquipulas II[142] peace accords of August 1987, which, negotiated by the Central American countries among themselves, held out for the first time the possibilities of real peace, seemed to vindicate for the FSLN and many Nicaraguans the policy of resistance to the US which they had followed. This was confirmed with the temporary ceasefire signed in the village of Sapoa in March 1988 which ended the majority of fighting in the war with the Contras.[143]

While, on the one hand, peace seemed at hand and the FSLN seemed stronger than ever before, the reality was that the government presided over an economy that had been shattered by war,[144] low international prices for its staple products[145] and early redistributive policies which had enhanced the tendency toward inflation even before the war had begun.[146] Although very important advances were made in the first three years in health, education and social services,[147] and, spurred on by international assistance, the GDP grew at an average of 5 per cent per annum in this period, by 1983 when the Contra war[148] began in force, this picture was reversed. Inflation, the most dramatic indicator of the collapse of the Nicaraguan economy and which at 219 per cent, was ten times greater than anywhere else in Central America in 1985 had increased to 911.9 per cent in 1987 and then took on the hyperinflationary figure of 35 000 per cent in 1988.[149] Equally dismal were the other indicators that showed that gross domestic product had fallen in seven of the last eight years of FSLN government, reaching in 1989 levels unknown since 1960; urban wage levels were 10 per cent what they had been at the start of the revolution; international indebtedness had grown to seven times the level inherited by the Sandinista government; and all the laudable social programmes which had been instituted at the beginning of the revolution had gradually been eroded.[150] During 1988 and 1989, the government instituted drastic measures to reduce the size of the budget, mainly through reductions in the size of the armed forces and through a series of major devaluations which served to reduce inflation, which, beginning the year at 92 per cent, had fallen in the last quarter to an average of 20 per cent.[151] While, therefore, at the end of 1989 hyperinflation had receded and the worst symbols of the crisis – long queues and empty shelves – were not as visible, the reductions in the budget had meant that unemployment was on the increase and social services, which had already been seriously dented, were in an even more difficult state than before. In this sense, we can conclude that despite very limited success on the battlefield, the US-backed programme of limited war, embargo and propaganda barrage, had bled white the Nicaraguan economy and achieved an important measure of success. Also prominent on the government's mind in this period must also have been the changing international perspective. In the late eighties, Vilas, always a perceptive commentator and an accurate gauge of thinking at the leadership of the FSLN, wrote a useful article on the economy appropriately entitled, 'Troubles Everywhere . . . .'[152] In it, recognising the critical nature of the economy, he reasserted the 'socialist orientation' thesis that 'Assistance from the "advanced" revolutions is essential to guarantee the *initial viability* of social revolutions in less-developed and highly dependent economies'.[153] While Nicaragua, as we have suggested, never relied totally on the Soviet Union for assistance – indeed, in the first two years little if any help came from this direction[154] – this picture changed in 1984 and 1985. Faced with declining assistance from multilateral and Western sources, the latter actually falling below the $200 million mark for the first time since 1980 in 1984, socialist assistance, especially Soviet oil, increased dramatically to over $1 billion in 1985.[155] With this increased dependence and no alternatives, the June 1987 decision by the Soviets to cut Nicaragua's oil supplies by 40 per cent[156] – quite probably an early casualty of *perestroika* – must have been a final blow for the Sandinista's programmatic view of socialist transition. It must also have been a critical accelerator in the government's decision to negotiate peace, for if the oil supplies were cut, then the war could not be pursued. This was made even more explicit in a *Latin American Weekly Report* of August 1987, which suggested that the Mexicans (who, along with the Venezuelans, had stopped supplying Nicaragua with oil because they were owed too much)[157] would be willing to resume supplies if Nicaragua pursued peace negotiations.[158]

This was the background to the 1990 elections, which the FSLN lost to the *Union Nacional Opositoria* (UNO) led by Violetta Chamorro de Barrios, receiving 40.8 per cent of the popular votes and 39 seats to the UNO's 54.7 and 51 seats.[159] If the 1918 decision by Lenin and the Bolshevik Party to disperse the Constituent Assembly and rule on the basis of revolutionary power had been seen as the critical precedent on the attitude of revolutions to elections and the suffrage, then the 1990 Nicaraguan election has set a new precedent. An incumbent, if beleaguered revolutionary party has conceded defeat in a freely contested poll and in so doing has contributed to changing the horizons and possibilities envisioned within the notion of revolution. Such a precedent can obviously only be confirmed when the party loses and it does so at great risk, for there is no assurance that in six years' time it will be able to resume its chosen project. But in conceding defeat, it has enhanced its prestige and provided the space within which, perhaps, to win again and resume a less encumbered, ideologically entrenched project of democracy under more favourable circumstances.

One of the many noteworthy features of the elections was the large errors exhibited in the pre-election polls, many of which showed the FSLN and its Presidential candidate Daniel Ortega winning by a clear margin. Interestingly, while many of these polls were conducted by non-Latin American organisations, two regionally-based polls, discounted at the time, showed that Chamorro would be the winner. A Venezuelan-based poll gave Chamorro a 40 to 29 per cent lead while a Costa Rican poll gave her a 37 to 30 per cent lead,[160] leading one commentator to suggest that

> Pollsters were clearly deceived by voters, who, fearing reprisals, voiced support for Ortega when surveyed, but used the security of the ballot box to express their real desire for change.[161]

This comment may explain one reason for the loss of support, in that despite the devolution of power of the last five years, power in the state, particularly in the military, remains firmly in the hands of the FSLN and many people might still harbour deep suspicions that this power might once again be used to proceed on more centralist, statist directions. Such attitudes might explain the unwillingness to give honest opinions of voting intentions. A further possible reason for the defeat, connected to popular reservations about the statist intentions of the leadership, was volunteered by a Sandinista army officer, who said that

> All the top people got themselves a house, a car, shopping privileges in the dollar store and free electricity and water . . . the people knew that and resented it because they were suffering and have nothing.[162]

But while fear and resentment were probably factors in the defeat, we can suggest that by far the more significant factor was the wrecked economy, which, despite the rescue measures of 1989, had reached the stage where many people, certainly enough to swing the FSLN's support from 63 per cent to 41 per cent, were willing to try any alternative to one which had failed to bring prosperity, despite the promising start in 1979–81. Further, with the FSLN in power, there was no assurance that the Contra war which was temporarily on hold, but which had, up to 1987, led to more than 43 000 deaths and $3.6 billion in damage,[163] would not begin again with all the terrible implications for the soldiers and peasants of the border areas and, of course, the already shattered economy. In retrospect, what is more remarkable about the election is that the FSLN was able to retain the loyalty of more than 40 per cent of the people in the face of implacable US hostility and the collapse of the economy. This might be explained by suggesting that as the result of a dialectical process of unravelling sequences the Frente has moved from being a middle-class-led vanguard party which had the support of the people in 1979, towards a yet incomplete process of becoming a *tribune* for the people in 1990, with greatly decreased power in the centre and enhanced participation at the base.

If the post-election panorama is therefore to be viewed as simply another, albeit complex stage of the revolution and not the end of the revolutionary adventure, we can suggest the following as the existing correlation of forces. In charge of the government, but without absolute power in the state, is the UNO coalition, which, while dominated by the bourgeoisie, still possesses the internal weaknesses typical of coalitions. Thus, within weeks of the electoral exercise, Vice-President Virgilio Godoy was criticising Violetta Chamorro publicly for retaining Humberto Ortega as head of the Armed Forces at least until negotiations for the disarmament of the Contras had been completed,[164] while two members of the business organisation COSEP, turned down ministerial positions for the same reason. While, therefore, the FSLN consisted of a fairly solid block of 39 seats, the UNO was composed of a diverse group of 14 organisations ranging from the far right to the far left, its main unifying philosophy being to remove the incumbent government.[165] At the other end of the spectrum is the FSLN which, as a result of its strength in the armed forces, its influence over popular organisations and in particular among the young, remains a formidable force. There is, of course, some truth in the view that with the loss of control over the government and therefore of patronage, FSLN influence will fall,[166] but there is another imperative which may lead to the increase, and indeed deepening, of Sandinista prestige and this hinges, as is usually the case in Nicaragua, on the land question. As part of their election pledge, the UNO, treading lightly on sensitive ground, had offered to recognise land which had already been distributed to small farmers, but where government-expropriated land was still idle it would be returned, where possible, to the former owners.[167] This has elicited an immediate response from the thousands of small farmers who benefited from the land reform and who in the post-election scenario now look to the FSLN as a tribune and line of defence against the government.[168] There is also fear in Sandinista circles that, in the wake of a returning and demobilised Contra army, their supporters may become targets for recriminations in the near future; this led to the decision to distribute weapons freely in the weeks between the elections and the inauguration of the new government. According to Alexis Guido, a 16-year-old FSLN supporter in Matagalpa,

> The guns are to fight against the Contras if they attack, but if the UNO people come around making trouble, we will be ready for them.[169]

Such a policy may become counter-productive, backfiring against the FSLN and laying the basis for civil war or, more likely, common banditry. However, when viewed from the perspective of the historic devolution of power which has been taking place at least since 1984, it may strengthen the basis of a popular response to the bourgeois project of the UNO coalition.

In summary, the peculiar articulation of the social forces which emerged from the Nicaraguan revolution has contributed to a process of increased empowerment and the devolution of central authority in that country. Out of the electoral process, this trajectory might change and Nicaragua could resume its more traditional role of dependent capitalist appendage of the United States. The almost immediate lifting of the trade embargo against Managua, President Bush's call on Congress to give $300 million in new aid and the indication that the sugar quota would be restored for the 1990 crop,[170] are all early indicators of United States intentions to strengthen and consolidate a regime more acceptable to its interpretation of hegemony. The present picture, however, suggests a dynamic process in which no force is sufficiently powerful to dominate absolutely and in which, despite their wishes, the UNO government will have to entertain and come to terms with the organised and semi-autonomous popular power and the power of the partially disentrenched FSLN.

Two comments, both from leaders of the Frente Sandinista, are perhaps, most descriptive of the present juncture. Speaking immediately after the electoral defeat, Lenin Cerna, Director of the Interior Ministry's State Security Police said candidly, 'Here there is going to be a new government . . . but you can't change the regime'.[171] Shortly after this, Sandinista Commandante Carlos Nuñez noted that

> Those who at this time have a triumphalist position have not realised that the reconstruction of Nicaragua is possible only with the participation of all Nicaraguans.[172]

The first statement is true if it refers to the 'regime' not as the Sandinista government or even its continued influence in the army, but the regime of popular involvement which the people, acting autonomously from the FSLN, have imposed on Nicaragua. The second view can also be interpreted as insightful if it recognises that it is the spirit of compromise in a context of the tension of different forces which has allowed Nicaragua, despite economic disaster, to become the first revolutionary state to allow a peaceful electoral transition of power, which by itself has helped to redefine the meaning of revolution.

## Notes

1.  Henri Weber, *Nicaragua: The Sandinist Revolution*, (London: New Left Books, 1981) p. 108. Weber quotes from the *Statute of Rights and Safeguards* adopted by the Junta of National Reconstruction on 21 August 1979. It is useful to recall, in contrast to the early days of the Cuban Revolution, Commandante Tomas Borge's comments on the new government's attitude to murderers and torturers from the National Guard. His response was, 'Our vengeance towards our enemies will be the pardon, it is the best of all vengeance.' Tomas Borge, 'Our Vengeance Towards Our Enemies will be the Pardon', in Peter Rossett and John Vandermeer (eds), *The Nicaragua Reader* (New York: Grove, 1983).

2.  See 'The Kissinger Commission on Nicaragua' in Rossett and Vandermeer (eds) *Nicaragua: Unfinished Revolution: The New Nicaragua Reader* (New York: Grove, 1986, pp. 15–18. A similar perspective is also present in Shirley Christian, *Nicaragua: Revolution in the Family* (New York: Vintage, 1986) and Jeanne Kirkpatrick, 'A Paranoid Style of Politics' in Rossett and Vandermeer (eds), 1983 pp. 14–18.

3.  See The Latin American Studies Association, 'The Electoral Process in Nicaragua: Domestic and International Influences', in Rossett and Vandermeer, 1986, pp. 73–107.

4.  See US Department of State, 'Sandinista Elections in Nicaragua' in Rossett and Vandermeer (eds), 1986, pp. 62–73.

5. Penn Kemble, 'Say Goodnight Danny', *Wall Street Journal*, 27 Febuary 1990. The December 1989 US invasion of Panama was carried out purportedly to protect American lives, to install Guillermo Endara, who was considered to have won the May 1989 presidential elections, to capture strongman General Manuel Noriega and take him to the US to face drug-trafficking charges and to 'safeguard US responsibilities in defense of the Panama Canal'. See *Latin American Regional Reports: Mexico and Central America Report*,18 January1990.

6. See, for a left position, essentially critical of the insufficiently 'proletarian' character of the regime, James Petras, 'Nicaragua: The Transition to a New Society', *Latin American Perspectives* 29, Spring 1981, pp. 74–94. For an opposite perspective, arguing for its proletarian and democratic character, see Weber, 1981.

7. Such a position would be similar to that expressed by Joe Eldridge and Alex Wilde when they argue that the election was not a vote for the opposition alliance led by Violetta Chamorro but a vote 'for relief from Washington's unmitigated hostility'. *The New York Times*, 9 March 1990, 'Nicaragua Votes for end to Washington's Siege'.

8. See, in particular, David Close, *Nicaragua: Politics, Economics and Society* (London: Frances Pinter, 1988), which is perhaps the clearest expression of Nicaragua as a genuinely novel alternative, although much of the more recent literature which begins with a 'transition to socialism' approach sooner or later reaches a point where serious questions are asked as to whether Nicaragua can fit neatly into any Marxist or Leninist framework and whether the model therefore needs to be revised. See in particular, Eduardo Baumeister, 'The Structure of Nicaraguan Agriculture and the Sandinista Agrarian Reform', in Richard Harris and Carlos Vilas, *Nicaragua: A Revolution Under Siege* (London: Zed, 1986); Richard Fagen, Carmen Deere and Jose Luis Corraggion (eds), 'Introduction', *Transition and Development: Problems of Third World Socialism* (New York: MR, 1986) and Carlos Vilas, *The Sandinista Revolution: National Liberation and Social Transformation in Central America* (New York: MR, 1986).

9. George Black, *Triumph of the People: The Sandinista Revolution in Nicaragua*, 1981, p. 5. Black's quotation is from Sergio Ramirez, *El Pensamiento Vivo de Sandino*, Fifth edition (San Jose: EDUCA, 1980), p. vii.

10. See Black, 1981, p. 6 and Karl Bermann, *Under the Big Stick: Nicaragua and the United States Since 1848* (New York: South End Press, 1986), pp. 51–72.

11. See Black, 1981, p. 7.

12. See Bermann, 1986, p. 139.

13. See Black, 1981, p. 9 and Donald C. Hodges, *Intellectual Foundations of the Nicaraguan Revolution* (Austin: University of Texas Press, 1986), p. 123.

14. See Black, 1981, p. 9.

15. Ibid.

16. See Bermann, 1986, p. 126.

17. See Black, p. 13.

18. See Hodges' discussion of this (1986, p. 231) where he argues that Sandino was the father of the strategy of 'prolonged people's war' practised later in Asia and at certain stages by the FSLN itself, which, unlike the foco strategy, advocates greater emphasis on popular support and less on the small guerrilla group.

19. See Black, 1981, pp. 16–21 and Hodges, 1986, pp. 107–158.

20. See Black, 1981, p. 24.
21. Hodges, 1986, p. 77.
22. Black, 1981, p. 24.
23. Ibid., p. 29.
24. Walter LaFeber, Inevitable Revolutions:The United States in Central America (New York: Norton, 1984), p. 230.
25. See Christian, 1986, p. 28; LaFeber, 1984, p. 22, Bermann, 1986, pp. 230–1.
26. Christian, 1986, p. 28.
27. See Black, 1981, p. 29.
28. See Bermann, 1986, p. 239, Black, 1981, p. 32.
29. Black, 1981, p. 50.
30. See Bermann, 1986, p. 237.
31. See Black, 1981, pp. 34–6, 62–4.
32. Vilas, 1986, pp. 87–8.
33. Bermann, 1986, p. 238.
34. Ibid., p. 248.
35. 'General Political–Military Platform of the FSLN for the Triumph of the Popular Sandinista Revolution (May 1977)', in Jiri Valenta and Esperanza Duran (eds), *Conflict in Nicaragua: A Multi-Dimensional Perspective* (Boston and London: Allen & Unwin, 1987), p. 294.
36. Hodges, 1986, p. 219; Black, 1981, p. 76.
37. 'Unidad de Combate "Juan Jose Quesada"', Mensaje no. 2 al Pueblo de Nicaragua, communique, 27 December 1974, in Black, 1981, p. 78.
38. Weber,1981, p. 19.
39. Black, 1981, pp. 76–7.
40. See Hodges, 1986, p. 220.
41. See Black, 1981, p. 81.
42. Hodges (1986, p. 223) argues that if the Debrayist as opposed to the Guevarist interpretation of the foco is used, i.e., one relying less on popular support, then the FSLN did not follow a foco strategy. This, however, is inaccurate if we look at the different levels of attention given to popular support in 1963 and 1967.
43. See Black, p. 37. Between 1950 and 1971, the population of Managua quadrupled, from 110 000 inhabitants to almost 400 000. See Vilas, 1986, p. 101.
44. See Robert Pastor, *Condemned to Repetition: The United States and Nicaragua* (Princeton: Princeton University Press, 1987), p. 43.
45. See Black,1981, p. 40
46. Vilas, 1984, p. 67.
47. Hodges, 1986, p. 229.
48. Bermann, 1986, p. 252.
49. Bermann, 1986, p. 252. The rally was considered the largest ever held in Nicaragua.
50. Ibid., p. 253.
51. Widely varying accounts exist on the actual extent of deaths and displacement. Thus, Bermann (p. 253) suggests 20 000 dead and 400 000 displaced. Vilas' figure of 250 000 displaced seems more realistic in that the larger figure would have included virtually the whole population of Managua in 1972. See Christian, 1986, p. 35, for deaths and Vilas, 1986, p. 101, for displacement.
52. Black, 1981, p. 61.

53. Ibid., pp. 60–4.
54. Ibid., p. 59.
55. Bermann, 1986, p. 255.
56. Hodges, 1986, p. 206.
57. Ibid., p. 209.
58. Ibid., pp. 226–9.
59. Various permutations of this vanguardist position appear throughout the literature. See especially Black, pp. 75–119, Roger Burbach and Orlando Nunez, *Fire in the Americas: Forging a Revolutionary Agenda* (London: Verso, 1987), p. 65 where they argue, trying to subordinate the peculiar role of the middle, for a 'Third Force', including the middle class and intellectuals as the leading force in Latin American Revolutions, or Vilas, p. 122, where he posits that the FSLN was the articulation of the masses into a revolutionary political organisation.
60. See Vilas, 1986, p. 21.
61. Ibid., Table 3.1, p. 92.
62. See Black, 1981, p. 89.
63. One of the ironies of the revolution is that most evidence indicates that Somoza was not behind this particular atrocity, although it played such an important role in the accumulation of forces. See Christian, 1986, pp. 54–5.
64. See Vilas, 1986, p. 112.
65. See Weber, 1981, p. 52, and *Report on the Human Rights Situation in Nicaragua*, InterAmerican Commission on Human Rights, General Secretary, OAS,Washington, DC, 1978.
66. Testimony of a mother of Esteli, in Vilas, 1986, p. 122.
67. See Black, p. 148.
68. Weber, 1981, p. 55.
69. See Hodges, 1986, p. 295–7.
70. See Luis Serra, 'Ideology, Religion and the Class Struggle in the Nicaraguan Revolution', in Harris and Vilas, 1985, p. 152.
71. 'Church and Revolution in Nicaragua: An Interview with Peter Marchetti', *Monthly Review*, July/August 1982, Vol. 34 no. 3, p. 45.
72. See Weber, 1981, p. 77.
73. See, for example, Black's discussion of the negative impact of the failed 1967 march on the Presidential Palace and the ineffectiveness of the Chamorro-led attempt to declare Somoza's 1974 election illegal through the courts. Black, 1981, p. 61.
74. See Black, pp. 60–1.
75. See Weber, p. 41.
76. Ibid., p. 41.
77. See Black, pp. 113–15.
78. 'Nicaragua – The Strategy of Victory: Interview by Marta Harnecker with Humberto Ortega', in *Sandinistas Speak* (London: Zed, 1981), p. 58.
79. See Weber, 1981, p. 34.
80. Bermann, 1986, p. 228. The actual article in which Somoza was reputed to have said this, appeared in *Time* in November 1948, nearly four years after Roosevelt had died. There is some question therefore as to whether these words were actually used, although in substance, they reflected US policy. See Pastor, 1987, p. 3.
81. See Bermann, 1986, pp. 236–7.
82. Bermann, 1986, p. 239.
83. Weber, 1981, p. 138.

84. Jeanne Kirkpatrick, 'US Security and Latin America', *Commentary*, January 1981, p. 36, in Pastor,1987, p. 5.
85. See, for example, William LeoGrande, 'The Revolution in Nicaragua: Another Cuba?' in *Foreign Affairs*, Fall 1979, p. 28, where he says that Carter 'laboured mightily . . . to prevent the accession of a Sandinista Government in Nicaragua'. In Pastor, 1987, p. 5.
86. Pastor, 1987, p. 39.
87. Ibid., pp. 77–8.
88. See, for the best 'inside' view of the twists and turns in US diplomatic policy to ensure a favourable revolutionary outcome, Pastor, 1987, especially pp. 76–166.
89. Ibid., p. 54.
90. See 'Interview with Humberto Ortega', 1981, p. 60.
91. Weber, 1981, p. 52.
92. See Pastor, 1987, p. 138.
93. See Christian, 1986, p. 43, Pastor, 1987, p. 138.
94. In June 1979, on the eve of the revolutionary victory, influential foreign relations adviser Brzezinski had argued for intervention as a counter to the Soviet invasion of Afghanistan. Faced, however, with the OAS rejection of a multilateral peacekeeping force and the Andean pact's decision to 'recognise' the FSLN, a position supporting no unilateral intervention, held by Secretary of State Vance, prevailed. See Pastor, 1987, p. 148.
95. Pastor, 1987, p. 169.
96. 'General Political–Military Platform', in Valenta and Duran, p. 306.
97. Ibid., p. 309.
98. See for example, Rotislav Ulyanovsky, *Socialism and the Newly Independent Nations* (Moscow: Progress, 1974) and K. N. Brutents, *National Liberation Revolutions Today* (Moscow: Progress, 1977).
99. See 'The Historic Programme of the FSLN' in *Sandinistas Speak* (London: Zed, 1981), pp. 13–22.
100. See Vilas, 1986, p. 42.
101. See Jose Luis Corraggio, *Nicaragua: Revolution and Democracy* (London: Allen and Unwin, 1986), p. 28.
102. See Hodges, 1986, p. 245.
103. See Hodges, 1986, p. 245.
104. Weber, 1981, p. 57.
105. See Weber, 1981, p. 91. Also Black, 1981, p. 196 where Castro on his visit to Nicaragua urged the FSLN leadership to 'avoid the early mistakes we made in Cuba, the political rejection by the West, premature frontal attacks on the bourgeoisie, economic isolation'.
106. See for a discussion of the differences in approach to religion in the Cuban and Nicaraguan revolutions, John M. Kirk, 'From Counterrevolution to Modus Vivendi: The Church in Cuba: 1959–1984', in Sandor Halebsky and John M. Kirk (eds) *Cuba: Twenty Five Years of Revolution: 1959–1984* (New York: Praeger, 1985).
107. Luis Serra, in Harris and Vilas, 1985, pp. 154–5.
108. See Hodges, 1986, p. 14.
109. Hodges, 1986, p. 14.
110. See Hodges, 1986, pp. 297–8.
111. See Weber, 1981, p. 134.
112. See Jorge Dominguez, *To Make a World Safe for Revolution* (Harvard: Harvard University Press, 1989), pp. 34–60.

113.  See Michael Conroy, *The Political Economy of the 1990 Nicaraguan Elections* (draft), Texas, 1990, p. 10.
114.  Two well-known examples of this independence include the decision to retain diplomatic relations with South Korea (see Close,1988, p. 164) and the Abstention on the UN vote condemning the Soviet invasion of Afghanistan. Both Cuba and Grenada, the latter experiencing revolution in the same year as Nicaragua, voted with the USSR against the measure. See Pastor, 1987, p. 201.
115.  See Black, 1981, p. 179.
116.  The five-person Junta includes Violetta Barrios de Chamorro, widow of the murdered editor of *La Prensa,* Joaquin Chamorro, Alfonso Robelo of the Nicaraguan Democratic Movement (MDN), Moises Hassan of the leadership of the United People's Movement and the National Patriotic Front–FSLN front organisations created in the last months of the war, Sergio Ramirez of the 'Group of Twelve', with the only acknowledged FSLN member being Daniel Ortega of the former Tercerista tendency. Although the FSLN appeared to be outnumbered by 'moderates', Ramirez was in fact a member of the Frente and Hassan – on the left – supported their positions. See Black, 1981, p. 171.
117.  Ibid., p. 168.
118.  Weber, 1981, p. 118.
119.  See Christian, 1986, pp. 154–5.
120.  See Weber, 1981, pp. 122–3.
121.  See Close, 1988, p. 53.
122.  Ibid., p. 55.
123.  See Diana Deere, 'Agrarian Reform, Peasant and Rural Production, and the Organisation of Production in the Transition to Socialism', in Fagen, Deere and Corraggio,1985, p. 126.
124.  See Deere, 1985, pp. 128–9. In 1982, independent producers organised in credit and service cooperatives made up 63 per cent of the total membership of co-ops and, by July 1984, of 1 million hectares or 20 per cent of the total cultivable land which had been distributed, 42 per cent had gone to production cooperatives while 54 per cent had gone to individual producers.
125.  See Close, 1988, p. 56.
126.  *Latin American Weekly Report,* 14 May 1987.
127.  See Close, 1988, pp. 93–9.
128.  Ibid., p. 96.
129.  Ibid., p. 98.
130.  See Vilas, 1986, p. 268.
131.  Fagen, Deere, Corraggio (eds), 1986, p. 16.
132.  Ibid., p. 17.
133.  See Baumeister in Harris and Vilas, 1986, p. 24.
134.  Ibid.
135.  See Gary Ruchwarger, 'Sandinista Mass Organizations and the Revolutionary Process', in Harris and Vilas, 1986, p. 114.
136.  W. Gordon West, *Vigilancia Revolucionaria: A Nicaraguan Policing Resolution to the Contradiction Between Public and Private,* mimeo, 1986, p. 27.
137.  See US Department of State, 'Sandinista Elections in Nicaragua', in Rossett and Vandermeer, 1986, pp. 61–73.

138. See the Latin American Studies Association, 'The Electoral Process in Nicaragua: Domestic and International Influences' in Rossett and Vandermeer, 1986, p. 84.
139. Close, 1988, p. 140.
140. See ibid., pp. 140–3.
141. See *Latin American Weekly Report,* 20 October 1987.
142. See Elia Kuant and Trish O'Kane, 'Nicaragua: Political Parties and Elections 1990', *Working Paper,* CRIES, Managua, 1990.
143. See Michael Conroy, *The Political Economy of the 1990 Nicaraguan Elections,* draft, 1990, p. 1.
144. Fitzgerald suggests that by 1985 the Contra war had led to 13 443 deaths with an aggregate loss in foreign exchange earnings of $1.23 billion. See E. V. K. Fitzgerald, 'An Evaluation of the Economic Costs to Nicaragua of US Aggression: 1980–1984', in Rose Spalding (ed.), *The Political Economy of Revolutionary Nicaragua* (Boston, Mass., London: Allen & Unwin, 1987), pp. 195–213.
145. Between 1980 and 1987, Nicaragua experienced a decline in the prices of its traditional exports of 7 per cent, which, when combined with an 18 per cent decline in goods produced and exported, led to a 40 per cent decline in earnings. See Conroy, 1990, p. 8.
146. See for a discussion of the weaknesses of redistributive policies and policies of accentuated class struggle in the context of new revolutions, Forrest Colburn, *Post-Revolutionary Nicaragua: State, Class and the Dilemmas of Agrarian Policy* (University of California, 1986), pp. 8–19 and for the particular problems associated with Nicaragua, pp. 121–31.
147. See, for example, Rossett and Vandermeer, 1983, pp. 322–56, which takes a good global look at the main changes in these areas.
148. See for an assessment of US policy to Nicaragua and the Contras, Holly Sklar, *Washington's War on Nicaragua* (New York: South End, 1988).
149. See IDB statistics in *Latin American Regional Reports: Mexico and Central America Report*, 18 January 1990.
150. See Conroy, 1990, p. 2.
151. Ibid., p. 23.
152. Carlos Vilas, 'Troubles Everywhere: An Economic Perspective on the Sandinista Revolution', in Spalding (ed.) pp. 233–46.
153. Vilas in ibid., p. 246.
154. See Conroy, 1990, p. 9.
155. See Conroy, 1990, p. 10.
156. See *Latin American Weekly Report,* 11 June, 1987.
157. The US had, according to *Latin American Weekly Report*, told the Mexicans that if they resumed selling oil to Nicaragua it would have been considered a hostile act. See *Latin American Weekly Report,* 11 June 1987.
158. See *Latin American Weekly Report,* 13 August 1987.
159. *Latin American Regional Reports: Mexico and Central American Report,* 29 March 1990.
160. *Latin American Regional Reports, Mexico and Central American Report,* 29 March 1990.
161. *Latin American Regional Reports, Mexico and Central American Report,* 29 March 1990.
162. Larry Rohter, *The New York Times,* 1 March 1990.

163.  See *Latin American Weekly Report,* 23 July, 1987.
164.  See *Latin American Regional Reports, Mexico and Central American Report,* 10 May 1990.
165.  See Kuant and O'Kane, 1990, p. 11.
166.  See Larry Rohter, *The New York Times,* 1 March 1990.
167.  See *The New York Times,* 14 March 1990.
168.  *The Los Angeles Times,* 6 March 1990, quotes Daniel Nunez, leader of a Sandinista Farmer Union, as saying that 'a rancher who went to inspect lands in Matagalpa province last week was chased away by farmers shooting into the air. . . . Farmers who voted for the Sandinista Front said that they trust the party leadership will continue to defend them from the opposition, which will soon be the government.'
169.  Richard Bourdeaux, *The Los Angeles Times,* 8 March 1990.
170.  See *The Miami Herald,* 14 March 1990.
171.  Julia Preston, William Branigin, *The Washington Post,* 1 March 1990.
172.  See *The New York Times,* 19 March 1990.

# CHAPTER 4

# Grenada: the pitfalls of 'popular' revolution from above

So what we did we did in their interest, even though they did not necessarily understand why we were doing what we were doing.

Maurice Bishop

If, of the two examples discussed so far, the Nicaraguan Revolution is at one pole of popular involvement and the Cuban at another of popular subordination, then the Grenadian Revolution extends beyond the Cuban pole, redefining the meaning of revolution from above and starkly illustrating the pitfalls of a path where middle-class state-builders, acting autonomously, attempt to impose a revolutionary project in a paternalist manner. At first glance it is difficult to understand why so much attention has been placed on a tiny, obscure island in the southern-most part of the Antillean chain with a population of less than one hundred thousand persons. Yet, a growth industry has developed around Grenada, with new books appearing at short intervals highlighting in some cases novel aspects of the revolution, in others, simply regurgitating or distorting material which has already been rehashed. The significance of Grenada for English-speaking West Indians is fairly obvious. As Gordon Lewis has pointed out in one of the most important of the recent studies,[1] Grenada was chosen to be the first English-speaking Caribbean country to experience a successful *Golpe*, the first whose Prime Minister was assassinated and the first to have experienced invasion from the United States. While this might be significant from the perspective of Kingston or Port of Spain, it is understandable if the casual observer in Caracas, Barranquilla or Managua might not laugh knowingly and argue that the islands had simply lost their virginity and entered the mainstream of Latin American history for the first time. Yet the significance of the rise and fall of the revolution goes beyond this. Flawed as it was, the Grenadian revolution, as Maurice Bishop's successful 1983 trip to the US showed, was becoming a dangerous model of an alternative approach to development and, more, of successful resistance to US hegemony in what is usually considered in Washington a US lake. It should also be remembered that from the perspective of the early 1980s, the success or failure of Grenada lay to a degree at the cutting-edge of the struggle against communism. For the US Departments of State and Defense, the vast documentation left by the New Jewel Movement (NJM) and People's Revolutionary Government (PRG) and carted away after the invasion, illustrated how Leninist regimes worked, their weaknesses and how to combat them. As then Assistant Under-Secretary of Defense for Policy and Resources Dov Zakheim summarised it:

> Grenada was not only a boon to the ideologues; it was also important to those who practised realpolitik because of its geo-strategic dimensions. Grenada was one of the factors in what Brezhnev constantly referred to as the 'correlation of forces' in the world – that great balance sheet that assesses the relative standing of the two superpowers. More importantly Grenada represented another successful effort to find holes in the Monroe Doctrine. . . . In addition, Grenada was of potential military utility to the Soviet Union. . . . It mattered little whether the airport at Point Salines would be used primarily as a tourist facility, as the NJM claimed. It was the potential that the airport offered to the Soviets that worried American analysts.[2]

Early writing after the 1983 invasion took two forms. On the right, there was an overtly anti-communist perspective which saw the need to destroy the revolution at the level of ideas in much the same way as it had been shattered in October 1983 at the physical and political levels. Reich and Smith, for example, commenting on the economic performance of the PRG, which the World Bank itself had from time to time considered favourable, left no room open for a balanced assessment in their conclusions that

> Grenada kept two sets of books – a technique taught by the Cubans – and the World Bank and IMF were simply the victims of a hoax. The economy was actually a disaster from start to finish. All major productive sectors continually declined.[3]

As a vehicle for convincing public opinion, this approach suffered from a serious weakness. By denigrating and casting aspersions on the entire revolutionary process, such an outlook did not recognise that, in the Caribbean at least, Maurice Bishop, the murdered leader of the process, was considered by many a martyr, and among wide cross-sections of people – certainly in Grenada itself – the revolution was seen in a positive light. This was evident in the poll carried out by Emmanuel *et al.* in the wake of the events of 1983, which found that despite the trauma of the moment, 86.2 per cent of the people were favourable to Bishop's leadership and 77.2 per cent concluded that the PRG had always been popular.[4] Partly as a result of a desire to hold the centre, which, while favourable to the invasion, was at worst, ambiguous on the question of Bishop and the revolution, and out of a closer reading of the appropriated Grenada documents, a new, dominant view emerged which distinguished Bishop the 'moderate' from Coard the 'radical' or 'Leninist', with the former seeking *rapprochement* with the United States and the latter leaning towards the Soviet Union.[5]

As the debate evolved in the weeks and months after October 1983, it became clear that this view was not restricted to those who supported the invasion, but, in a modified form was also dominant in the centre and on the left of the international political spectrum. Thus, O'Shaughnessy found that the Soviet Union's unwillingness to criticise the Coard group was an indicator of its support for him and possible complicity in the events; Don Rojas, Maurice Bishop's last press secretary and as such, an influential spokesman, asserted that Coard had manoeuvred his supporters – members of the Organisation for Revolutionary Education and Liberation (OREL) – on to the Central Committee. Fidel Castro – close personal friend of Maurice Bishop and with his tremendous prestige as a revolutionary, seemed to seal the debate on the causes of the crisis and fall of the revolution when he concluded that it was as a result of the ambitions and criminal manoeuvres of the Coard clique:

> Coard worked with great subtlety. He did not work openly. He started placing cadre – that is, people from the group that had joined Bishop's party. He did not dissolve that group, he kept it as a faction. Very quietly and gradually, he placed his sworn followers in key positions in the Army, as political instructors, in the Ministry of Security and in some positions in the Party.[6]

Explicit in this interpretation of the *dénouement*, was the view that things had been going reasonably, or very well for the revolution and were it not for the personal and harmful intervention of ultra-leftists, Grenada would have marched on, albeit in the face of adversity, to achieve even more social and economic victories. George Louison, who was a leading member of the Party and the PRG, supported this view in 1984:

> I disputed that there was any crisis. Far from the people losing confidence in the revolution, they were beginning to settle down with the revolution and see it as a way of life. Even people who had reservations about the revolution in the early period were beginning to settle down with it. They saw that there were plans to deal with all the key problems in the society.[7]

Beyond this narrow, personalist *explicandum*, very few serious attempts emerged to examine the balance sheet of the revolution, the real problems which it faced in politics and economics and whether the conspiratorial thesis conformed with reality and, if it did, whether it was a sufficient explanation for the tragic ending of the process. Among the more important of these, Gordon Lewis[8] introduced the important point that the way power was seized – by a tiny group of insurgents – was critical in understanding the character of the process and, by implication, its ultimate failure. Lewis also severely criticised Leninism as an ideological and strategic guide for revolutionaries and argued that it invariably led movements which followed its principles into ideological dead-ends, a point further elaborated with great effect by Charles Mills.[9] Both Lewis and Manning Marable,[10] the former with a sensitivity derived from his long watch of Caribbean affairs from Puerto Rico, are sensitive to the intercession of social and historical factors in the making of the revolution and its final collapse, but in the end both come down on the side of the now familiar conclusion that personality and conspiracy were the decisive factors, stemming from the irreducible conclusion that 'Coard at bottom was Leninist, Bishop at bottom, populist'.[11]

Only Mandle, in his short work, Thorndike and Meeks,[12] go decisively beyond this position to place a more important role on the social formation within which the personalities operated and to raise serious questions on the nature and content of the personality and ideological clashes as they did occur. The failure of most of the studies to explore the relationship between actors and structures is a fatal error. The suggestion advanced here is that Grenadian society and its product, the Grenadian Revolution, operated within a deeply-entrenched social structure in which (a) a vast social, educational and linguistic gap existed between those at the top and those below; (b) this was mirrored in the continuation of paternalistic attitudes which emerged out of the nature of the Grenadian plantation system, was reinforced under altered conditions by the Eric Gairy regime and subsequently not shattered, but strengthened, by the revolution; (c) The nature of Grenada's external relations, its British history, island status, small size and marginality in hemispheric affairs, all contributed to enhancing this relative autonomy which leaders from Gairy to the PRG and Maurice Bishop felt they possessed; (d) the head of the not-so *ancien régime*, Eric Gairy, had shattered any notion of alliance at the top and had gone a significant way to monopolising power in the state, so when the PRG took power, they were already the inheritors of a monopoly, which, enhanced by the way power was taken, set them on a path of authoritarianism; (e) while accepting the general and fairly obvious conclusion that the revolution imploded from within, albeit under extreme pressure from without, the conspiracy notion is simplistic, can be strongly questioned on the basis of the existing evidence and when advanced as the sole cause of the crisis obscures the fundamental point, that there were serious flaws in the overall strategy of the revolution which transcended personality differences, which stemmed in part from ideological and strategic choices, but was also impelled by the structure of Grenadian society and the 'gridlock of events'; (f) finally, while Leninism deserves much of the criticism which Lewis and Mills place at its door, what was operative in Grenada was a cumulative and available ideological context which was partly Leninist, partly generated from national and international experience and partly derived from a certain West Indian intellectual culture of the 1970s, which exerted a far more powerful and determinate impact on the choices of the leaders and path of the revolution than did the narrower veneer of purely Leninist ideological precepts. Within this, however, there were moments at which important decisions might have been taken to embark on a less entrenched, hierarchical path of development. In 1979 after the revolutionary seizure, with the massive cross-class support; in 1981 after the suppression of the last of the violent counter-revolutionary activities and in the early stages of the 1983 crisis, opportunities existed to embark on different paths which might, perhaps, have led to different outcomes. To arrive at this conclusion, however, we need to retrace the historical path to the period in 1951, called 'sky red' by the Grenadian peasantry, when plantation workers and peasants made the sky glow red as they burnt estates in revolt against the old plantation order and placed their hopes in Eric Gairy, the hero of the moment.

## The 1951 Gairy-led uprising

In February 1951 Grenada experienced an island-wide uprising of agricultural labourers which included the burning of estate property, looting and physical attacks against individuals associated with the ruling order. Colonial Office sources estimated the damage at £195 000 incurred from fire, lost cocoa and nutmeg harvests and lost wages – a huge amount by the standards of the tiny island.[13] Marable is correct when he identifies the decline of Crown Colony government and the socioeconomic inequality of the Black majority as factors contributing to the 1951 crisis and ultimately the 1979 revolution, but this is only a partial explanation. To focus more carefully on the causes of 1951, the question which needs to be asked is, Why did Grenada escape the widespread social revolts which had taken place in other West Indian islands in the 1930s?[14] The answers to this question might be found in (a) the solidary structure of Grenadian society which contributed to quietude and inhibited the development of revolt from below; and (b) the weakness of the Grenadian middle classes, both in terms of size and ideological development, which prevented the early development of a state-building leadership which might have precipitated crisis up above.

As Marshall suggests, the Windward Islands of St Vincent, Dominica, St

Lucia and Grenada, because of their mountainous topography and relatively late incorporation into the sugar plantation economy, remained always somewhat marginal sugar producers. After slavery, when sugar became even less profitable, many estates foreclosed, providing the opportunity for land acquisition and leading to the expansion of the peasantry in these territories well into the twentieth century.[15] Peasant expansion, however, was not accompanied by growing peasant independence, far less political assertion in these territories. Instead, via an intricate system of semi-capitalist *metayage* type relationships, the peasantry was reconnected to the remaining estates, where they laboured for their white or fair-skinned landlords in exchange for patrimonial favours, effectively described by M. G. Smith:

> In return for planting and tending the young cocoa, worker tenants had rights to all bluggoes (bananas) on their plot; to cultivate ground provisions therein; to live on the estate rent free; to occupy all gardens near their homes; to rent the plots further afield at nominal rates; to tether stock in the estate; . . . He was also expected to provide them with credit when needed, to settle their internal disputes, to stand as godfather (*compère*) for their children and generally to support and assist them.[16]

Such a tightly-bound and prescribed relationship, magnified by the small size of the island, did not encourage the growth of an autonomous peasantry, but rather a submissive, subordinate rural folk with an outlook based on respect and duty. For the good planter, that is, the individual who fulfilled his obligations, the attitude of the spiritualist Norman Paul, in praise of the owner of the property he grew up on, was undoubtedly more the rule than the exception:

> Hampstead is over a hundred acres, over a hundred fifty labourers he had, men and women, all living on the estate – houses scattered all over the estate. They were free to hold their gardens and houses and everything on the estate. Well, he was one of the best gentlemen in this parish. I would not say in the parish, but in Grenada there wasn't another like him.[17]

While there was respect from below, there was, in the highest echelons of the society, a patronising detachment typical of those who genuinely believe in their superiority:

> Like their parents before them they are customarily educated abroad and have at best, a limited understanding of the local patois spoken by the folk. . . . In place of identification with the society in which they hold the highest status, they see themselves as white settlers in an essentially foreign and unpredict-

able country, whose people differ from them in race, language, culture, ideas and other ways.[18]

At the level of the state, this economic and social paternalism was duplicated in the politics of Crown Colony government, which, under the pre-Second World War ideology of 'trusteeship' sought to benevolently govern both the planters and the peasants from above. This rarely worked, and the Governor, as Lewis suggests, invariably came down on the side of the planters who regarded him as 'their most prominent social exhibit'.[19] Despite concessions made to the 'pure' Crown Colony system in 1914 and 1924, which allowed a small number of elected persons based on a restricted franchise to enter the legislature, it is fair to conclude as Munroe does, that 'the modifications were made in the nature of concessions to oligarchy, rather than, more simplistically, milestones on the return journey to democracy'.[20]

Solidity above, in this British/planter duopoly, was further assured by the weakness in the Grenadian case of a state-building middle. In the 1946 population census, less than 800 persons could have been classified as being middle-class, and, more pointedly, in that year there were only 13 physicians and 14 lawyers in the professional upper stratum from whence nationalist leaders were usually recruited.[21] Such a weak middle was able to produce the occasional quixotic spokesman, among them, T. A. Marryshow, who remains one of the outstanding advocates of West Indian regionalism but, without the support of a consistent social bloc, his nationalist position was at best inconsistent, or as described by Lewis, 'royalist–loyalist'.[22] There was therefore no middle to intercede either as peacemakers or on their own platform as Munroe described the organised Jamaican middle classes on the eve of the 1938 upheaval:

> Relatively self-conscious of themselves as a class with distinct interests, aware of relevant experience in other societies, possessed of their own leadership and organisational linkages, they were ideally placed to speak in 'responsible' terms to the colonial power on behalf of the articulate classes'.[23]

The Grenadian middle classes might have wished to fulfil this role, but were unable to do so. When crisis overtook this tightly-knit society in 1951, the revolting peasants did not therefore seek out Marryshow, but a man of their own colour and background. But their chosen leader, Eric Gairy, had independent interests which did not fit into the conceptions of his followers, of the planter class nor those of the British colonial power.

The causes of the revolt can be traced to the undermining of the solidary arrangements of the plantation society coupled to an economic contraction which generated dissatisfaction from below. Together with a change in the consensus and solidity of the ruling bloc, this allowed some limited movement in the state. A number of interlinked factors, some tracing their roots to the economy and others independent of it, worked together to generate revolt from below. During the Second World War, Grenada had prospered as a result of high prices fetched for cocoa, one of the two main exports, and living conditions were further improved for the majority as a result of the emigration of thousands of Grenadians to work on the oil-refineries of neighbouring Trinidad and Aruba and to build the American military base at Chaguaramas in Trinidad. But after the war, Trinidad severely restricted the inflow of migrants and with decreased opportunities, Grenadian workers began returning home. In 1945, for the first time in five years, the population actually began to increase again.[24] Returning workers affected the society in different ways. Whereas previously they had provided remittances for their families, they now formed a growing pool of disgruntled unemployed persons. More importantly, they had broken with the paternalism of the estates and had been party to the birth of modern trade-union relations in the Trinidad oilfields, indeed, one of their countrymen, Tubal Uriah 'Buzz' Butler, had been the leader of the Trinidad oil-workers in their 1937 revolt.[25]

Eric Gairy, the son of a plantation overseer in rural St Andrews, had developed his skills as a shop steward in Aruba and had returned to Grenada in 1949. With his literacy, knowledge of industrial bargaining and experience in the 'wider world', he was well-placed to play a role in the troubles that were to come. In early 1950, an incident occurred between the new British owner of an estate in the east of the island who did not understand the paternalistic relationship which the previous owners adhered to and the estate workers. When the workers had demanded their traditional rights, the owner proceeded to evict them from the estate. The local people called on Gairy to intervene and he carried the owner to court, winning some $3000 compensation for the tenants under the Tenants Compensation Ordinance.[26] With his growing fame and popularity, he founded the Grenada Manual and Mental Workers Union (GMMWU) in July of that year, fortunately, as it would turn out, for in December a major crisis occurred with the existing trade union. In 1950, the Grenada Trades Union Council (GTUC) had signed an ill-fated agreement linking the statutory agricultural wage to the price of cocoa. When the price of cocoa went up, so did the average wage, but the inverse also applied. In November of 1950 the price of cocoa fell and in the face of a rising cost of living, workers were supposed to accept a decrease in their take-home pay. This development destroyed the credibility of the GTUC at the same time as Gairy's union was calling for a 46.5 per cent increase in wages. Naturally, the employers refused to recognise the GMMWU which was operating outside the notions of duty and respect embodied in the GTUC positions, but the increasingly incensed workers were adamant. In February 1951, Gairy called the first island-wide strike in

Grenada's history, receiving the support of the vast majority of estate workers, who had rallied to his cause.

The 1951 upsurge is remarkable for the level of tenacity shown by the strikers. Throughout the last two weeks in February, the strike gained momentum, with increasing disruption to the economy and resistance to authority, despite the declaration of a state of emergency, the detention of Gairy and his deputy Blaize and the arrival of HMS *Devonshire*, whose sailors had been deployed in the capital, St Georges.[27] With a solid ruling bloc as had existed before 1945, even such an active upsurge could have been easily suppressed, given the overwhelming might of the British Navy and tiny size of the island. But in 1951, this was not the case. Whereas the doctrine of 'trusteeship' had envisioned a long-term relationship with the colonial power, after the war and under pressure from the United States and growing anti-colonial movements, the British had adopted the policy of 'partnership', implying incremental constitutional changes leading to an early independence.[28] These new positions were evident in the different attitudes taken to the increasingly militant strikers. The Governor, on advice from Whitehall, brought Gairy back from the sister island of Carriacou and sought to negotiate with him to appease his supporters. Such a position was anathema to the planters and businessmen, who considered this a dereliction of duty on the part of the British. At a meeting with their representatives, the Governor reported with more than a little concern that

> feelings ran extremely high and several of those present appeared on the verge of hysteria boasting, incidentally, that they went about armed and were in fact, armed at meeting with me. Their main contention was that the strike is nothing short of a communistic plot designed to overthrow society and that to treat directly with Gairy would mean the end of industrial and social peace in Grenada. They said government had 'abdicated' and they were prepared, if necessary, to take the power into their own hands.[29]

In the end, the Governor's position prevailed. Gairy, the only person who could convince the strikers to go back to work, spoke with them on 15 March. Two days earlier, the planters had agreed to recognise the GMMWU and both groups had expressed their willingness to sit on a wage-fixing council. In October 1951, Gairy's union, later to become the Grenada United Labour Party (GULP) swept to victory in the first elections under universal adult suffrage, taking seven out of eight seats and 71 per cent of the eligible vote.[30]

The 1951 upsurge set the stage for the 1979 revolution in the following ways: first, it established that there were sharp divisions between a deeply conservative and traditional planter class which saw no reason why things should not continue in the old way and the dominant British colonial

segment of the ruling bloc which, responding to a new international conjuncture, was hoping to extricate itself from its position in the state on the
most favourable terms. In order to do this, the British would have preferred
a more 'responsible' type of leadership of the Rhodes Scholar, Oxbridge-
educated type, as Grantley Adams in Barbados and Norman Manley in
Jamaica undoubtedly were. But after the 1951 events, there was not, nor
could there have been, an organised middle-class force able to command
significant popular support in Grenada. Ever pragmatic, the British were
willing to do business with Gairy, who they sensed, in the absence of any
clear ideology, would not present a threat on the crucial international front.
For the planter classes, this was heresy. Gairy was black, rural and poor and
should therefore know his place in the society. He had no right jostling with
them for power. For his part, Gairy knew these attitudes well and continued
to resist the hostility of those who considered themselves his betters. However, bound by the horizons of a limited education and a colonial consciousness, where even in the early sixties 67.4 per cent of the people polled
supported colonialism,[31] his primary objective was not to transform, but to
secure a place for himself and his closest supporters at the top. This
contradiction between a hostile traditional ruling oligarchy and an insurgent
and popular faction, caught up as it was in the racial and social tensions of
the society and in the context of a retreating colonial power, was the
definitive feature of the Grenadian state for the next thirty years. It meant in
effect, a prolonged and attenuated crisis up above, albeit one in which
power gradually moved away from the planters and consolidated in Gairy's
hands.

## *From popular revolt to people's revolution: the Gairy years*

In trying to interpret the evolution of the relationship between Gairy and the
Grenadian upper classes, Gordon Lewis asserts that if the latter had accepted the popular hero in the way similar strata in Jamaica and Barbados
had accepted their populist leaders, then they would have saved themselves
a lot of trouble.[32] This is to underestimate the gap which separated the
somewhat more modern, market-oriented societies of the larger territories
and the deeply paternalist traditions of Grenada. Also, in the Jamaican
context, neither Manley nor even Bustamante with their brown-skinned
and/or intellectual credentials were considered revolutionaries. Gairy,
however, was black and poor and though he was not a Marxist, spoke in his
own blend of 'God, Marx and the British Empire'[33] and could not therefore
be accommodated.

It can be argued that Gairy simultaneously represented three interests. At
the height of his powers in 1951, he represented all black Grenadians, who

for the most part found themselves at the bottom of the society and who gained vicarious pleasure as well as material benefits from his trade union and political fight. At the same time, he also represented a thin stratum of black businessmen who gradually came into their own as Gairyism strengthened its hold on the state and economy. Thirdly and critically, he represented himself: a poor black boy who had made it and now expected to have all the material things he had been denied as well as the respect which was granted to someone at the top of the social hierarchy. Singham captured this in his reporting of Gairy's attitude to corruption charges levelled against him in 1961:

> He said it was 'all right' with 'that crowd' for colonial governors to have their parties, but when Uncle (Gairy) had a few drinks with his friends they labelled it Squandermania.[34]

Himself conditioned by the structures of a paternal society, Gairy in turn, adopted the trappings of the patron. Singham's description of his role as leader of the GULP, captures accurately this elevation and autonomy of action which it gave:

> Gairy's political organisation has remained personal even during campaign periods, and he has always commanded more support than the candidates he nominated. There is no functioning central organisation. Gairy instead maintains personal links with all the constituencies, but necessarily through the local candidate. A Party supporter knows that if he wants action or decision he must see Gairy personally.[35]

Any attempt to understand his rise to power would be incomplete without a recognition of these features. If however, the broad representation had been the dominant aspect in the beginning, in the end, the personalist features had come to dominate if not monopolise, the Gairyite project.

Between 1951 and 1974, with notable setbacks, Gairy made slow and then more rapid advances against positions held by the oligarchy in the state and in the economy. Although he won both the 1951 and 1954 elections, the limited provisions for executive power in the evolving constitution allowed little independent room for Gairy to carry forward his scheme. It was not until 1960 when Grenada was given a new, 'advanced' constitution[36] in anticipation of West Indian Federation that the first serious attempts were made to consolidate his position. With greater room to spend funds and with significant control over appointments, Gairy's first task was to eliminate those persons in the civil service who stood in his way. In a memorable battle with the Financial Secretary, who initially hid documents from him, Gairy effectively made him redundant by re-routing his work through a newly appointed Principal Secretary.[37] With a similar tactic in the strategically important Public Works Department, he diminished the powers of its

Director while effectively making the Chairman of the Tenders Board – an appointee who reported directly to Gairy – the person responsible for the granting of all awards.

With greater control in the state, he moved rapidly to give deals and grant contracts to his closest cronies, drawn in large measure from the small black business class. Gairy decreed, for example, that all cement should be purchased from B. N. Davis and Company at inflated prices, while all government cars were to be insured by a previously unrecognised insurance company owned by black businessman Cecil Maitland.[38] All this had taken place within four months of winning the 1961 elections, but Gairy had overestimated his strength and gone too far. In January 1962 a Commission of Inquiry was established to examine charges of corruption in the government. It ruled in July that the Minister of Finance had 'contravened laws governing expenditure' and had 'deliberately destroyed the morale of the civil service'.[39] The constitution was suspended for three months and when new elections were called, Gairy's GULP lost, winning only four seats and 46 per cent of the votes to the Grenada National Party (GNP), a middle-class ensemble with close links to the oligarchy, which won six seats and 53.7 per cent of the votes.[40]

It was not until 1967 that the political climate favoured further advances. Under the provisions for Associated Statehood, the government became fully responsible for its internal affairs with Britain retaining control over only defence and foreign affairs.[41] Reversing the results of the 1962 election, Gairy rapidly moved to consolidate his limited advances of five years previously. In his demagogic 'Land for the Landless' programme, facilitated by the growing economic weakness of the planter class,[42] he was able to move effectively against his oldest opponents and by the mid-1970s, the state had managed to acquire more than 40 per cent of all estates in the country over 40 acres in size.[43] But this had been done, ironically, without a significant redistribution of land to the 'landless' and with an accompanying decline in the overall area of land under production. In 1961, 71 per cent of the cultivable land was under cultivation, but by 1975 this had fallen to 54.8 per cent.[44] By the late 1960s, then, Gairy who had started out as the junior and somewhat unwelcome partner in the ruling bloc, had wrested a position of dominance from the traditional oligarchy and, in the context of a receding colonial power, was virtually, though not completely in charge of the state.

From this plateau of success, however, grave weaknesses were already evident in his project. Moving from his success in the Land for the Landless programme, he strove to eliminate one of the few remaining power bases of the 'upper brackets' in the agricultural producer associations. Both the powerful cocoa and nutmeg associations grouped together farmers of all sizes in order to control the export of the commodities, but were weighted in their provisions in favour of the big planter. The system of proxy-voting in the Cocoa Association, for example, allowed one person, usually an influential big planter, to vote on behalf of a number of usually smaller growers.[45] Stating demagogically that he was acting in the interests of the small cultivators, Gairy moved instead to consolidate governmental control first over the cocoa, and later the nutmeg growers' associations. The latter attempt, however, was met with resistance as the big planters, fearing further loss of influence and strength, and the small growers, fearing government monopoly and abuse, formed an unprecedented united front to resist his efforts. Despite his passage of the Nutmeg Board (Dissolution) Act in 1975, placing the Board firmly in the government's hands, the growers fought back and, guided by their lawyer, Maurice Bishop, introduced a motion to declare the act *ultra vires*. At the time of the 1979 revolution, the unresolved issue was before the Privy Council.[46] More significantly, as it became evident to a new generation of Grenadian poor that Gairyism held little benefit in it for them, dissatisfaction began to grow in the lower classes, his traditional bedrock of support.

While the period between 1969 and 1974 cannot be characterised as one of economic crisis, with Gross Domestic Product growing between 1970 and 1973 by 9.6 per cent,[47] it was certainly one in which the conditions of the majority were aggravated. Unemployment in Grenada had actually decreased between 1960 and 1970,[48] but under the disorganising impact of Land for the Landless, a deteriorating balance of trade and increasing net immigration, unemployment by 1973 was definitely on the increase.[49] Accompanying this was a serious rise in the cost of living. The index of retail prices, which stood at 130.7 in 1969, had risen to 189.5 in 1973 and 269.4 in 1975.[50] This economic aggravation dovetailed with the growing wariness with governmental intervention and found a vehicle for its expression in the black power movement.

West Indian black power traces its immediate roots to Jamaica in 1968, when Walter Rodney, a Guyanese academic at the University of the West Indies and supporter of black power, was declared *persona non grata* by the Jamaican government for what was seen as his threatening posture against the *status quo*. The subsequent demonstrations by students against Rodney's exclusion from the island led to spontaneous riots which were quickly quelled, but it signalled a new militant mood at the grassroots level which found its echoes in the student population. It was in Trinidad and Tobago though, that black power reached its high point between February and April 1970. Initially sparked off as a student demonstration in solidarity with West Indian students detained in Montreal, Canada, it soon escalated into open rebellion against the Eric Williams regime, with a section of the army eventually attempting to carry through a military coup.[51] With its proximity and close demographic and economic links, Trinidadian black power ideas soon filtered over to Grenada to influence the increasingly dissatisfied young and unemployed population, especially around St Georges. The critical factor, as Meeks argues, was that

> Black power represented a potential force autonomous of Gairy's power and patronage precisely because it effectively utilised the symbols which he had monopolised for twenty years.[52]

For Gairy to retain his vital cornerstone and *raison d'être* as defender of black people, he would have to move to eliminate black power as an alternative ideological and organisational reference point, particularly in the context of the Jamaican and Trinidadian experiences, where the movement had forged cross-class alliances between the young intelligentsia and the urban poor. This he began to do in the weeks after the Trinidad revolt, stating in an infamous broadcast that black power could do tremendous harm, that when your neighbour's house is on fire, 'keep on wetting your house', and, ominously, that he had recruited the 'toughest and roughest roughnecks', regardless of their criminal record, to defend law and order in the country.[53] Two weeks later, the State of Emergency Act was declared, giving the government extensive powers for arrest, detention, search and seizure of property during emergencies.[54] The November 1970 nurses' demonstration was the first substantial manifestation of the nascent black power alliance, as it was the first indication of Gairy's determination to destroy it. Returning young middle-class professionals, nurses and unemployed youth participated in the enthusiastic demonstration,[55] which was ruthlessly broken up by Gairy's informal and illegal thugs in the 'Mongoose Gang'. The nurses' demonstration served as a catalyst for a deeper and wider resistance to the regime, arising out of the sense of outrage felt at the way a peaceful demonstration had been handled. Increasingly after 1970, in a manner similar to the last years of the Somoza dynasty, state-administered brutality, initiated by the Mongoose Gang and the uniformed police, became an independent factor of far more significance than the state of the economy, in generating revolt from below and consolidating dissatisfaction above. Eventually, in 1974, this development, acting on an already aggravated and attenuated crisis up above, would lead to a revolutionary situation of the classic kind which, however, was not carried through to completion.

## Middle-class state-builders

To appreciate the course and outcome of the 1974 revolutionary upsurge, it is useful to digress on the notion of middle-class state-builders and to examine how this stratum had evolved. The early structural and political weaknesses have been mooted as important features which provided space up above and allowed for Gairy's rise to power. By the late sixties, important changes were evident. Between 1960 and 1970, the number of Grenadians trained at university-level – admittedly still very small – had increased from 193 to 352,[56] forging a greater sense of community and consistency among an educated bloc. Inevitably, this growing sense of self-awareness, most evident in those newly-returning, was further forged in the resistance to the Gairy regime, which had been engaged in a long-term battle with the St Georges cadre of civil servants, professionals, merchants and teachers. And equally, Gairy perceived these young professionals as simply a new contingent of 'that crowd' against whom he had battled relentlessly and had almost defeated. At one level, then, this was a continuation of the 1951 struggle of fair-skinned against black, of urban St Georges against rural St Andrews, of English speakers against English creole speakers, of the decent, 'intelligent' Grenadians against the rural country bumpkins whom they and their Trinidadian middle-class counterparts ridiculed for their pronunciation of 'ship' instead of 'sheep', and 'bax' instead of 'box'. When these young professionals, like Maurice Bishop, Bernard Coard and Kendrick Radix, returned from the United States and Britain, they came with new ideas influenced by a cumulative and available ideological context of the late sixties, but they also entered a world with a dense structure of potentially constraining relationships. Their language, background, local education at the Grenada Boys Secondary School (GBSS) or Presentation College, and colour in some cases, identified them as occupants of high positions in the society, enhanced significantly by their travel and study abroad. For their part, they understandably inherited their parents' distaste for Gairy, because he had methodically fought against them, but also because he was a pretender to the throne. In the closely-knit world of the Eastern Caribbean middle class, the Grenadian contingent was deeply embarrassed by the fact that it was deprived of its 'rightful' share of power and at the same time, had to live under someone whom they considered a black buffoon. Ironically, Gairy's defeat of the planter class, by removing that pole of contention, may have strengthened the aspirations of the middle at the same time as new contingents provided fresh impetus for contestation of a 'place in the sun', and aggravated crisis up above.

## *The taking of power: 1974–79*

The 1974 revolutionary upsurge and independence lock-down was as much the rehearsal for the 1979 revolution as in a different time, place and scale, 1905 had been the rehearsal for October 1917. 1974 was a popular, broad-based, mass-driven upsurge, in which none of the insurgent forces was strong enough to dominate, nor was the incipient vanguard – the NJM –

strong enough to take power. 1979 on the contrary, took the form of a party-led, pre-emptive strike, in which the popular forces were at first passive and later entered the fray enthusiastically, but as followers. Had it been possible for power to be taken in 1974, then a different, perhaps Nicaraguan-type outcome, might conceivably have emerged. This was not the case and 1979 reinforced an inherited configuration of deeply-entrenched hierarchy and paternalism which was the Achilles' heel of the revolution and the underlying condition of its ultimate collapse.

Two developments accelerated the alignment of anti-Gairy forces which eventually led to the 1974 crisis. In the 1972 general elections, many young persons supported the GNP – the urban middle-class party of their parents, on the assumption that despite the increasing arbitrariness of the regime, the GULP could be defeated at the polls. Both Unison Whiteman and Selwyn Strachan, who would later become top leaders of the NJM and PRG, were actually candidates for the GNP, the latter running against Gairy himself. Both were decisively defeated, as was the party, with the GULP romping home with 58.8 per cent of the votes and 13 of 15 seats.[57] The general perception was that there had been massive vote-rigging,[58] cementing the view that Gairy could not be moved by constitutional means and opening the door for revolutionary perspectives. More significant as a precipitant, was the newly-elected government's decision to use the election as a mandate to carry the island into independence – an issue which had never been raised during the campaign. As Meeks suggests, this was the final nail in the coffin:

> Apart from the reservations concerning Grenada's viability as a state, for the GNP and the oligarchy independence meant the removal of the final constraint which would give Gairy a free hand to continue and consolidate his incursions against them. For the growing mass movement, it meant unfettered 'mongoose' power, further victimization and dictatorship. Neither those 'above' nor those 'below' were willing to allow Gairy to proceed unhindered into this new situation.[59]

When, in the following weeks, the British indicated that they would not interfere in the timing of Grenada's independence,[60] effectively removing themselves from the equation, the correlation for revolt had been established. Crisis up above, an absolute and irreconcilable rift between Gairy and the other, albeit subordinate elements in the ruling bloc, now enhanced by the final withdrawal of the British, was being accompanied by crisis down below – an active and increasingly mobilised cross-section of youth, workers and students, unwilling to put up with Gairyite arbitrariness and brutality and to proceed into independence under his monopoly rule.

Specific events and developments dictated the pace and potential of the 1974 revolution of which the most significant was the formation of the NJM. The New Jewel Movement was formed in March 1973 out of the amalgam of the Joint Endeavour for Welfare, Education and Liberation (JEWEL) and the Movement for Assemblies of the People or MAP. The new organisation was led by the middle who had studied overseas. Of the twelve members of the leading organ or Bureau in 1974, five had been to university, all outside the West Indies and three of these were lawyers. While it is true to say that persons who could be considered as workers, peasants or urban poor held positions in the Bureau, the most important posts were held by the educated elite.

Maurice Bishop, who studied as a lawyer in Britain, and Unison Whiteman, who gained his MA in economics at Howard, shared the leadership as Joint Coordinating Secretaries. Lloyd Noel, another lawyer, held the obvious position of legal defence, while the third lawyer, Kendrick Radix, was in charge of fund-raising and finances. Bernard Coard, whose MA in economics was from Sussex, and who would play a pivotal role in later events, was a member of the Bureau without portfolio, due no doubt to the fact that he lived out of the country, first in Trinidad and then in Jamaica until 1976.[61] While it has been suggested that the structure of Grenadian society weighed heavily on them, they for the most part, had returned from study overseas with a prevalent outlook which was, on balance, anti-hierarchical, de-emphasised the role of the single leader, and placed great stress on mass action and decentralised organisation. This 'outlook of 1974' had a perspective of an anti-bureaucratic, disentrenched, post-revolutionary state, but it possessed on overarching weakness, in that it had little concrete appreciation of the tactics appropriate for the taking of power.

## *Cumulative and available ideological context: the early phase*

Of the two trends which came together to form the NJM, Jewel, based in St Davids and led by Teddy Victor and Unison Whiteman, was closer to the rural pulse and possessed a far more black-power, self-reliant tradition, drawing freely on the evangelical, almost mystical view of black liberation which was an important trend in the Trinidad black power movement.[62] As late as July 1974, when most of the movement was headed in a different ideological direction, Teddy Victor still described the struggle in idealist, almost metaphysical terms:

> Right is right. No force can defeat right in the end . . . However,
> to lead, we must have self confidence. Most important is what

we see ahead; if we see gloom we'll get gloom. If we see bright days, we'll get bright days.[63]

Jewel, which gave its name to its already popular paper, brought in the first mass support, but the driving force in the alliance was undoubtedly MAP with its well-connected and economically independent core of lawyers and its more developed ideological platform. It was MAP's positions, based on an interpretation of C. L. R. James's concept of Marxism, which became the early platform of the party. Among its main features were:

(i)   a distaste for the single leader arising, in part at least, from the experience under monopolistic Gairyism and reflected in the joint leadership of Bishop from MAP and Whiteman from Jewel;

(ii)  a hostility to traditional elections, fostered again, from the Grenadian experience, but also informed by African socialist notions of the single party as a unifying national force, and the Marxian/Rousseauist view that deeper, participatory forms of democracy were superior;

(iii) an emphasis on decentralised state structures, evident in the central MAP thesis that the state should be reconstructed from the base up, through a system of village assemblies and also in the early NJM party structure, which gave greater powers to the monthly meeting of a coordinating council of delegates than to the weekly bureau meetings;

(iv)  a deep hostility to the official, international communist movement, reflecting in this the views of C. L. R. James in his long struggle with Stalinism in the Trotskyite and neo-Trotskyite left;

(v)   a disdain for conspiratorial forms of struggle, exhibited in the support for spontaneity and in the chosen tactic of the mass uprising for the seizure of power from Gairy.[64]

The chosen ideological perspective of 1974 was related, of course, to the specific experience of individuals, but a cumulative and available ideological context can be identified, with its boundaries delineated by black nationalism, an 'indigenous' orientation, and most notably by the absence of Leninism. Norman Girvan, a Jamaican academic, but whose experience as a student in London under C. L. R. James's influence paralleled that of Bishop and others, illuminates some of the events which helped to constitute this outlook:

the World itself was in the grip of powerful political currents. Kwame Nkrumah had broken the back of British imperialism in Africa. Earlier, Nasser had nationalized the Suez canal. Nehru and Tito had already rejected the cold war definition of the world which Truman and Stalin, and afterwards, Eisenhower and Kruschev had sought to impose. They declared neutralism as the guiding principles of their foreign policy. . . . In place of the struggle between 'freedom' and 'communism' or 'capitalism' and 'socialism', the fundamental contradiction in the world was recast as one between former colonisers and formerly colonised, rich and poor, imperialism and national liberation. The idea of the Third World was in the making. These developments were followed with tremendous interest in the Caribbean.[65]

As a dominant view among radical intellectuals in Grenada and many other parts of the Caribbean, this outlook had peaked by 1974. The failure of the earlier black power movement in Trinidad; the rapid accumulation of new world events and the failure of the 1974 upsurge itself, was transforming the agenda of available ideas and placing Leninist notions at the forefront.

The NJM's role in the 1974 events needs to be seen from the perspective that the party was less of a vanguard, leading and directing the people's struggle, than a tribune, providing a channel for discussion, mobilisation and action. This was evident even before the formal unification of the two trends, when in January 1973, Jewel and MAP jointly staged their 'People's Trial' at La Sagesse Estate. The owner, the Englishman Lord Brownlow, almost duplicating the events of 1951, had denied local residents their traditional rights of access to the only beach in the area. Jewel and MAP were able to mobilise some 800 persons to declare Brownlow *persona non grata* and break down the estate-gates leading to the beach.[66] On 20 April, just one month after its formal launching, NJM mobilised 5000 persons in St Andrews parish and blocked the runway of the airport at Pearls, protesting the shooting of Jeremiah Richardson, a local youth, by one of Gairy's secret police.[67] On 6 May, NJM held its People's Convention on Independence at Seamoon with a reported attendance of 15 000 in a total adult population of less than 50 000 persons, calling for meaningful independence under a system of people's assemblies and on people to return to their villages and prepare for the taking of power.[68] As Gairy's formal and informal police reacted with increasing brutality to the growing NJM constituency, beating and shooting suspected supporters of the movement,[69] mobilisation through the summer of 1973 was largely directed against police brutality, with the resultant growth in sympathy and support for the young party. The consolidating mass support and increasingly revolutionary drift of the movement could be seen in the 4 November People's Congress, where an estimated 10 000 persons supported a list of 27 crimes by the Gairy regime, called on the government to resign by 18 November and for a general strike beginning on 19 November if he refused to resign.[70] But despite the growing sympathy for the NJM, the party had little strength in the trade union movement nor in the business community and, in the weeks after the Congress, sought to forge links with these sectors through a series of meetings. Ironically, it was Gairy who did more than anyone else to build an alliance and also intensify the upsurge, when on 18 November, thereafter called 'Bloody Sunday', his secret police attacked and badly beat leading members of the NJM. Maurice Bishop, Unison Whiteman, Selwyn Strachan, Kendrick Radix and Hudson Austin were travelling to Grenville on the east coast to discuss tactics for the general strike with a group of local businessmen when they were set upon by some 80 secret policemen led by an inspector of police, badly beaten, detained and denied legal or medical attention overnight.[71] The following day the atmosphere had changed. Spontaneous lock-downs were taking place in St Georges and other parts of the island and there was general outrage directed at Gairy. But the NJM was unable, despite appeals to the people, to lead an organisational lock-down. A 'Committee of 22' trade union, business and middle-class organisations was instead set up to intercede in negotiations with the government and in effect, to steal the thunder from the more radical 'Jewel boys'. Whereas the NJM had called for Gairy's immediate resignation, the committee called instead for a commission of inquiry and the disbanding of the 'police aids'. Gairy outmanoeuvred the committee, first by agreeing to its demands if industrial normality was ensured and then, once this had occurred, refusing to implement the demands.[72] By 27 December, the die had been cast. Popular outrage was even more firmly directed against the regime, but at the same time, the moderate trend had been undermined by the failure of its tactic and Gairy's uncompromising stance, leaving it no option but to implement the NJM demand of immediate lock-down. From the beginning of the new year until late January, the popular tide flowed in favour of the NJM. Increasingly larger groups demonstrated on a daily basis, peaking with an estimated crowd of some 20 000 persons[73] – one-fifth of the entire population – on 21 January. But at its high point, the movement also exposed its critical weaknesses. The night before this demonstration, Gairy had gathered 500 members of the Mongoose Gang together and that morning, as the rally ended on the St Georges Carenage, they descended on the crowd with weapons. In the ensuing battle, a policeman shot Maurice Bishop's father Rupert to death as he attempted to protect some women and children in a building near the waterfront.[74]

With a martyr to its cause and an even greater level of revulsion directed against the regime, the likelihood of an early collapse seemed more imminent after the elder Bishop's death, but this was not the case. The NJM had tied itself into a single tactic for the removal of Gairy – the spontaneous mass uprising – and this had taken place, yet Gairy seemed as strong as ever. This was compounded by the fact that the party was one-year-old and naturally had limited organisational experience. It also had very few international contacts, a factor also directly related to its youthfulness, but also a product of its ideological outlook, which limited its contacts to a narrow band of black power and Pan Africanist organisations in and outside the region. So, when Bishop and Whiteman travelled around the Caribbean to solicit support for sanctions against Gairy, they were coolly received or ignored by the neighbouring governments.[75] Most critically, despite the NJM's dominance with students and the young unemployed on the streets, the actual lock-down still remained in the hands of the more conservative trade unions and the business sector. In the weeks to come these were the telling factors. Although the treasury was running low, Gairy declared independence on 7 February; by 20 February, electricity workers were back on the job; and on 29 March, when the dockers, who had held out to the end, finally caved in following their leadership's decision to resume work, the upsurge had been defeated.

## *From defeat to victory*

In 1975, Bernard Coard, writing under the pseudonym Chris Holness in *Socialism!*, the Theoretical Organ of the Jamaican Marxist group the Workers Liberation League,[76] strongly argued in Leninist terminology that the reason for the failure of the 1974 Revolution was the NJM's lack of a working-class orientation:

> This failure to organise the working class as an independent force with its own tactics and acting on its own behalf, was to lead at a most critical period in the revolutionary struggle, to NJM finding itself *objectively tailing*, the bourgeoisie. NJM's helplessness in the face of the bourgeois ordered end to the electricity and telephone workers' strike and, most critically, the dockers' strike, was the most telling proof of this fact.[77]

The conclusion from this was that working-class support and Leninist party structures would solve these weaknesses and ensure victory the second time around. By late 1974, the party had already started to reorganise itself along vanguardist lines, a task which was largely completed at the time of the seizure of power in 1979. While it is true to say that Coard was the critical person to introduce Leninist perspectives into the party, it is simplistic to conclude, as Lewis does, that he was somehow the genuine product, while Bishop remained a populist, or as Marable suggests, a 'marxist humanist'.[78] Instead it is suggested that Leninism, as understood and interpreted by the NJM leadership, won out decisively as an approach between 1974 and 1976 and this can only be understood in the context of the shifting equation of a cumulative and available ideological context. If Girvan's interpretation of nationalism and neutralism as the dominant ideas among young Caribbean intellectuals in the sixties is correct, then by 1970 this was changing. By then, all world events seemed to point to the efficacy of Leninist-inspired policies to ensure genuine independence and presumably beyond that, economic development.

In Vietnam in 1968, it was a Leninist organisation which, at tremendous cost, had inflicted a severe blow to the prestige of the US military; the Portuguese African struggles led by Cabral, Neto and Mondlane were inspired by Marxism–Leninism and not by the African socialism of a previous generation of leaders; after the weak economic showing in the sixties, the Cuban economy, boosted by high sugar prices, seemed at last to be fulfilling its socialist ideals, with social programmes unrivalled in the Caribbean; even failures and problematic experiences seemed to support the superiority of Leninist tactics. Thus, the conventional wisdom in young intellectual circles was that Allende had been defeated in Chile in 1973 because the Unidad Popular had been insufficiently firm, resolute and Leninist; by the late seventies, when the Manley regime came under tremendous pressure reminiscent of the Chilean experience, the same conclusions were drawn, that Manley needed to impose another dose of 'heavy manners', as he had done in 1976, in order to retain power; throughout the region at the micro-level, other events were happening to support this conjuncture. In Jamaica, the tiny WLL, which generally supported Cuban and Soviet positions, competed in the mid-seventies on an equal footing with the Maoist Youth Forces for National Liberation (YFNL) and the Trotskyite Revolutionary Marxist Collective, but by 1976, both of these organisations had become moribund and the WLL, while still small, had come virtually to monopolise the young radical intellectual constituency. Similar developments took place in St Vincent with the formation and growth of Yulimo, with the development of the Workers Revolutionary Movement in St Lucia and with the Dominica Liberation Movement. In Guyana, the parliamentary Marxist opposition, the People's Progressive Party (PPP) rededicated itself to a transformation into a Leninist organisation, while the Working People's Alliance – closer to the intellectual roots of the other organisations – struggled to define an independent Marxist position. Only in Trinidad, where Maoist tendencies had taken root in the progressive trade union movement and in Antigua, where Tim Hector's small Jamesist – oriented Antigua Caribbean Liberation Movement (ACLM) continued to dominate the left, can it be said that the trend towards Leninism was relatively weak. Further, the few actual revolutionary experiences in the Caribbean seemed to support the superiority and inevitability of Leninist tactics; from this perspective, the National Joint Action Committee (NJAC) was defeated in Trinidad and Tobago because it had no roots in the working class, no central organised core of cadres and no experience with insurrection.

Finally, the 1974 upsurge was seen to have failed for the same reasons and because there was no Leninist party to become the general staff of the working class and provide it with resolute, 'hard', revolutionary leadership. Bernard Coard may have been the person who first raised these theses as practical matters inside the NJM and he undoubtedly met with resistance from stalwarts like Victor, Lloyd Noel and Kendrick Radix, who regarded Marx as just one philosopher among many with no special importance of his own,[79] but it was met with sympathy by the majority, including Maurice Bishop, who were searching for a way around the impasse of defeat. More so, the confluence of ideas and events had made Leninism not so much a choice but an irresistible current for bright, thinking persons.

None of the leaders had deep theoretical roots in Marxism. Coard had only begun to read Marx seriously while in Trinidad in 1973 under the influence of Winston Suite and the small United Revolutionary Organisation. From 1974 to 1975 in Jamaica at the University of the West Indies, he read more extensively and was influenced by the emerging Leninist praxis of the WLL. Bishop had been influenced by the spirit, if not the letter of Jamesian thought while in Britain, but by the mid-seventies he seems to have been equally committed as anyone else in the leadership to the new path. In 1978 at a Bureau meeting, for example, he openly attacked those who were still in favour of the spontaneous, 'big bang' approach to struggle, without reference

> to patient, consistent organisational work and the need to consciously promote class struggle and build class consciousness.[80]

But the rapid shift to Leninism meant also a wholesale rejection of the previously dominant Jamesian model. Whereas that approach had failed essentially in its lack of tactics for the insurrectionary phase, its anti-hierarchical organisational structure, inclusion of a wide cross-section of people and agitational form of tribunals and conventions, had served the early party well. These were also thrown out in favour of a conspiratorial and hierarchical command structure with restricted membership and a hidden ideology.

Lewis has suggested that a spontaneous uprising along Luxemburgist lines could not have succeeded in Grenada.[81] The failure of the 1974 upsurge, which to some extent approximated this approach, supports this argument, as does Grenada's small size, which obviously militated against a long 'positional' struggle, without the necessary element of surprise. It therefore can be argued that in the specific context of Grenada, the only possibility for successful seizure of power would have to be the method of clandestine preparation and then surprise attack. If this was an inevitability, it brought great dangers with it from the point of view of democracy and accountability. This was the central tension on the final lap to insurrection.

Each Leninist measure which made the party more capable of taking power, also increased its tendency toward hierarchical decision-making and enhanced the autonomy of the leadership both from ordinary party members and the people.

In 1975, the creation of a Military Committee, with Teddy Victor and Hudson Austin as leaders, improved the party's preparedness for military struggle, but of necessity, increased the tendency towards secrecy.[82] From mid-1974, Coard had proposed a scheme of 'fighting membership'[83] of trained cadres for the party, but it was not until 1978 that a vanguardist system of selectivity was fully implemented, ending the old method of membership based on 'willingness to support'.[84] While a party composed only of trained and trustworthy comrades was a *sine qua non* for secrecy and successful insurrection in small, open Grenada, it also meant that hundreds of persons who considered themselves 'Jewel' and had been active workers in 1974, were now outsiders looking in, awaiting the instructions of the vanguard. The strict requirements of work, study and dues also weighed heavily against the poor, marginal and less literate, shifting the focus of membership more towards students and the middle. Chester Humphrey, an early member of the Bureau who had left for the United States in 1974 and only returned after the revolutionary victory, remarked at the time on the absence of many old fighters in the reconstructed party.[85] Baby Neckles, a St Georges working woman who had been a member of the early Bureau, for example, could not hold a place in the new structure and eventually left for the United States. In March 1979, there were no more than 50 full members in the entire party.[86]

The introduction of the Organising Committee (OC) in 1978 had a similar effect. Whereas in 1973 the OC was just one of a number of equal committees, it now became, under Bernard Coard's leadership, the heart and soul of the party, coordinating the growth of women's, youth and worker's committees and monitoring the vanguardist conversion. This undoubtedly increased the party's efficiency, both for insurrectionary purposes and to play a leading role in a new state, but it also shifted the centre of gravity of internal decision-making. In 1974, the monthly Coordinating Council meetings with village-level membership, monitored the Bureau's work and made it accountable to the popular base, while the regular congresses and conventions further ensured an ongoing renewal of the organic connection between party and people. No similar link existed after 1978, with decision-making conveyed from the Bureau or OC to the members beneath them and then to the people.

Equally damaging in the transition, was the NJM's adoption of a 'dual personality'. In 1974, the programme, structure, leadership and ideology of the party were all known to the people and published regularly in the party paper *The New Jewel*. With the conversion to Leninism, only the party member knew for sure that this had taken place. For the man in the street, Jewel was still the popular tribunal of 1974, but in reality, all the members and what they did were no longer known, the party structure was hidden and the true belief of its members under 'deep cover'. This both eroded the popular connection and increased the sense of sectarianism in those few privileged to possess the knowledge or 'science'. It also had the potential to generate distrust and betrayal, depending on the manner in which this divergence was revealed as, it is suggested, was the case at the time of the 1983 crisis and fall of the revolution.

In 1978, however, there was a strong argument in its favour. If Leninism was the necessary ingredient for victory, then it had to be implemented. If making it public, however, would stir up anti-communist sentiment in the population and attract the baleful attention of the United States, then the logical answer was to keep its implementation secret. Leninism prepared the party for insurrection, but at the same time it made it more hierarchical. The populist elements in the Jamesian approach had been thrown out with its tactical weaknesses. The NJM was preparing to take power but with an orientation which fit closely with the deeper, patriarchal structures and rhythms of Grenadian society, in which its top leaders saw themselves as state-builders and were regarded by the people as persons of high standing.

Two additional factors improved the chances for success. With the approach of the 1976 elections the NJM was faced with the decision as to whether to form an anti-Gairy alliance with the GNP and the newly-formed moderate United People's Party (UPP). Initial views weighed against forming an alliance with parties which were considered ideologically incompatible, but Bernard Coard's return to the island helped to change this view. Influenced by the WLL's decision to give 'critical support' to the People's National Party (PNP) in the 1976 Jamaican elections, and by the regional Marxist position supporting 'united fronts against imperialism', Coard was able to swing the NJM in favour of an alliance. In the election, despite overt rigging by Gairy, the People's Alliance was able to win 6 of 15 seats and 48.2 per cent of the vote to 9 and 51.8 per cent for the GULP. The NJM, the dominant party in the alliance, emerged with three seats to the GNP's two and the UPP's one. Maurice Bishop became the leader of the Opposition, with Bernard Coard and Unison Whiteman the other parliamentarians.[87]

This boosted the legitimacy of the NJM as it further corroded Gairy's claim to legitimacy. Bishop, as Opposition leader, now held a constitutional position and could credibly argue that had the elections been fair, he would have been the Prime Minister. On his travels out of Grenada in the following months, the reception given to his critique of the regime would be totally different to that of 1974, when he was regarded simply as the leader of a black power faction. A subtle difference of great importance for later events should also be noted. Whereas in 1974 Bishop and Whiteman had been joint leaders and whereas after 1976 Coard had become the moving force in deciding the organisational direction and tactical positions of the party, Bishop had now emerged as the international representative of the NJM and its genuinely popular leader. Two poles of authority were emerging. One centred around the party with Coard at its head and the other, with Bishop as its leader, on the question of national leadership. In 1976, this was embryonic, but in retrospect it is difficult to deny that there was the potential for further tension in this divergence of command. Gairy, for his part, was even further isolated, in that the NJM had managed, if only temporarily, to draw the political representatives of the alienated forces up above into an alliance under its leadership – quite the opposite of the situation which had held during the lock-down and street actions of 1974.

## Permissive world context

It is not coincidental that successful revolutions took place in Nicaragua and Grenada in the same year and this can best be understood from the perspective of a permissive world context. Many of its features, in particular the changing policy horizons of the Carter Presidency, have already been sketched in relation to Nicaragua and need not be repeated. Yet, there are special features of the permissive world context peculiar to the Anglophone Caribbean and Grenada which should be stressed. Among the prominent features is the fact that the English-speaking islands of the Eastern Caribbean were still extricating themselves from British colonialism and had therefore not been fully incorporated into the American geopolitical picture. US warships had steamed towards Trinidad at the height of the 1970 black power uprising but did not intervene. In Central America, Haiti and the Hispanic islands, there had been direct intervention but this did not take place in the anglophone territories.[88] While, after 1976, increasing attention was given to the leftward-moving Manley government in Jamaica,[89] much less attention was paid to the strategically minor Windward and Leeward islands. This is clearly evident in the surprise with which the revolutionary overthrow was met in Washington and, five years later, the equal surprise elicited by State Department officials when they reviewed the seriousness of purpose of the revolution evident in the captured Grenada documents.[90]

Grenada was a minor and obscure island in a hemisphere in which there were other pressing and immediate concerns, not the least of which was the gathering insurrection in Nicaragua. With this veil of obscurity and enhanced by the party's clandestine planning and rapid seizure of power, the revolution was able to 'sneak in' and present an international *fait accompli* before the US could concentrate its formidable diplomatic and military powers in that direction. With this, the character of permissive world context as a temporary warp needs to be emphasised. If the Grenada action had taken place after the Sandinista victory in June and not while the US was still deeply embroiled in averting such a victory; if, other things being equal, it had occurred two years later when the regionally influential Manley government was out of power and unable, therefore, to support a call for regional recognition, there might well have been a strike against Gairy, but its chances of success would have been minimal. A permissive world context did not exist at the time of the 1974 upsurge and indeed, did not fully emerge until Carter's election in 1977.

For Grenada, the possibility of utilising the opening was at its peak in the months before the June 1979 Sandinista victory. The actual decision to move may owe a great deal to Gairy's dictatorial whims and to chance, but in retrospect, it was taken at the best possible time. The 13 March Revolution itself and the subsequent overthrow of Somoza, then played independent and pivotal roles in bringing Carter's foreign policy into question[91] and in returning the US to a more traditional hegemonic policy. But the revolution had by then been made, and had gained critical regional recognition.

## *The taking of power*

On 10 March 1979, while gathered at a Bureau meeting, NJM leaders had picked up disturbing signs that Gairy was planning a major action against them. Their homes had been searched simultaneously and one Bureau member who had not been at the meeting – Vince Noel – had been arrested. On Monday 12 March, Noel was told by sympathetic police officers that if he wanted to save his life, he should escape from detention by nightfall. At 1.00 p.m. that day, Gairy left the island for New York, distancing himself from the events and further supporting the fear that something was about to happen.[92] Acting on this information, the Security and Defence Committee, consisting of Coard, Bishop, Whiteman and Austin, met and put into place its military plans which had been in the process of preparation for the past four years and decided in favour of a preemptive strike against the regime.

At first it was a split vote, with Coard and Austin in favour and Bishop and Whiteman hesitant to move; with this, another Bureau member, George Louison, was invited to break the tie and he voted in favour of action. All members then moved to activate the clandestine National Liberation Army, as the small group of 46 men in the military arm was called. There were only 16 rifles, two shotguns and a few pistols, with the remaining members armed with Molotov cocktails.[93] At 4.00 a.m. on 13 March the force, led by Hudson Austin, had captured the small and only army barracks at True

Blue. By 5.00 a.m. the radio station at Morne Rouge had been taken and by 6.15 Austin had announced the overthrow of the Gairy dictatorship. Later in the day, announcements on the air called on the police stations to surrender and encouraged people to assist in their capture and to volunteer to help the revolution at the newly-named Radio Free Grenada. By midday, some 3000 persons were directly assisting the insurgents and with only two casualties, the Gairy regime which had been in effective control for 12 years and in contention for 28, was overthrown.

In the specific situation of tiny Grenada, there is, as we have suggested, a strong basis to support Lewis's view that a prolonged, 'spontaneous', uprising along Nicaraguan lines was impossible. This is a moot question, but the reality was that the nature of the seizure of power, a rapid strike, carried out by a small group of secretly trained and armed men, belonging to a single party (albeit the leading party in the legal Opposition alliance), enhanced all the hierarchical features which were latent in the Grenadian matrix. Among them, it (a) elevated the position and autonomy of those leaders of the party, the keepers of the 'science', who in making the right, scientific, decisions, had proved to the ordinary members the infallibility of the doctrine and of themselves; (b) had thus legitimised Leninism where other theologies (Jamesism, black power) had failed; and (c) called on the people to support the revolution, but by the very juxtaposition of events, linked to the hierarchy of Grenadian society, brought them in as followers, not equals.

This structure of the revolution is captured in two quotes. The first, made by Maurice Bishop, indicates the extent to which the leadership – no doubt honest and well-intentioned – nevertheless saw themselves as both patriarchal and benevolent. Reflecting on the role of the party on 13 March to a private party meeting in 1982, he said:

> So what we did we did in their interest, even though they did not necessarily understand why we were doing what we were doing.[94]

The other quote is from Philbert Thomas, then a 61- year-old public works road-cleaner, whose sentiments on the overthrow reflected both the antagonism to the Gairy regime, and the messianic, almost genuflectory, respect given to those who had 'delivered' the Grenadian people. Commenting on the news of the overthrow, he said,

> Then, when March 13th came, it was a new day for all Grenadians, a new day! I jumped up and raised my hands to God, for we had been oppressed for 28 years.[95]

The Grenada revolution was a revolution from above, marginally distinguishable from a *coup d'état* by its execution by armed irregulars and by the willingness of the leadership to mobilise popular support, though firmly under its command. In the Cuban Revolution, middle-class elites had played a dominant role, but there were still popular checks placed on them by their initial dependence on the Oriente peasantry and the semi-autonomous character of the urban insurrection. In Nicaragua, middle-class elites, seeking to travel on a Cuban path, were instead confronted by an unprecedented popular upsurge which severely undermined their ability to rule from above. In Grenada, the NJM gave the revolution to the people who 'did not necessarily understand why we were doing what we were doing'. Faced with a patriarchal and hierarchical social and political structure, this rule from above, unless it was converted into a more organic and democratic movement of the people, possessed the same inherent fragility as the Gairyite state, derived from a shattered alliance at the top, with a similar potential for crisis when placed under pressure.

## *Jewel in power: a brief perspective*

Jay Mandle has described the political model which was adopted in revolutionary Grenada as one of 'paternalistic socialism':

> In this model . . . the leading party claims to embody within itself the interests and aspirations of the masses of the population. It therefore is to be relied upon to work hard and conscientiously to advance the people's interests. This is especially the case with regards to providing basic needs such as food, medicine and education. According to the theory, it is in the pursuit of these goals that the party will mobilise the people on the community level, both in order to facilitate the accomplishing of specific goals and in order to heighten consciousness. In this model then, there is no positive function to be filled by placing the party's leadership of society at risk through national elections. Such elections are seen to be divisive in any case, and if an opposition party were to be victorious, its success would only set back the process of revolutionary advance.[96]

This is an accurate description of the overall political stance of the NJM and the PRG, but it fails to capture an important dimension of the process. The very act of rupture with the old state and the hope for a better world which this stirred in ordinary people, together with the massive mobilisation of tens of thousands, even if under party hegemony, created a tension between the model and a competing, popular democratic impulse. In the end, this tension was resolved in favour of entrenched paternalism and authoritarianism, but it would be abstract and colourless, a conclusion as

Lewis suggests, from someone who had never seen the revolution at work,[97] to ignore the other aspect. There was an almost tangible revolutionary spirit, which tapped under-utilised energy, inspired the beginnings of a cultural revolution and raised the self-esteem of ordinary Grenadians at home and abroad.[98] This rekindled sense of self and of possibility, sorely absent in the old Grenada with its deep colonial and paternal traditions, is best exemplified in a calypso sung at the 1981 Carnival by Lord Melody, one of the older, traditional crooners:

> Since after the revolution
> We have a change in every direction,
> Look around us and you will see
> The rise in our economy,
> it's a miracle, some people does say,
> Believe it or not we are on our way.

> **Chorus:**   Grenada is moving fast
> We reaching somewhere at last
> Our motto we must remember
> 'Forward ever and backward never!'[99]

Community mobilisation and self-help projects were not inventions of the PRG, but had roots in the traditional rural culture, nevertheless under the revolution they were given new meaning as people increasingly saw themselves as part of a progressive, national community. It is fair to conclude that willingness to sacrifice for the nation grew during the revolution. Morrissey's mid-1980 study of schoolchildren in seven Commonwealth Caribbean countries found that 45 per cent of Grenadians listed Grenada as their favourite of forty countries, exceeded only by Belizeans, while only 14 per cent of Jamaicans put their island first. When further questioned, 13.3 per cent of the Grenadian youth said they had a desire to build their country, compared to only 1.7 per cent of the Barbadians and 0.7 per cent of the Trinidadians giving a similar response.[100]

With this important *caveat*, it is useful to identify three periods in the process. In the first, 1979–80, the PRG showed remarkable flexibility in tactics at the same time as there was justifiable cause for provisional forms of rule to maintain revolutionary power. In the second period, 1980–82, the unwillingness to move beyond authoritarian forms of control and Leninist organisational methods, led to a rapid deterioration in popular commitment and in the physical ability of the vanguard to keep on ruling in the 'old way'. In the third period, beginning with Bernard Coard's resignation from the Political Bureau (PB) and Central Committee(CC) in October 1982 and the collapse of the revolution a year later, the party, having sown the wind of a commandist and dogmatic policy, began, in the face of immense external pressure, to reap the whirlwind of institutional collapse. In the face of crisis, gravely damaging decisions were taken which, however, were not alien to the previous operational methods of the party, aggravating crisis and leading to tragedy.

The first weeks after the taking of power were accompanied by a degree of flexibility and innovation which augured well for the survival of the new government. Most strikingly, the Governor General was retained as head of state, maintaining the traditional link with Great Britain and the Commonwealth; a policy of non-victimisation was practised in the civil service and in the lower ranks of the police force, immediately neutralising or winning over Gairy supporters who had braced for a massive purge; and it was announced by Maurice Bishop, the new Prime Minister, that early elections would be held[101] – a statement which generated support in the neighbouring Westminster-oriented islands, but which would become a serious debit as the years passed with no indication of the promised ballot. There was, however, significant justification for the postponement of elections in the first year. If, as Bishop reiterated, and tens of thousands agreed with him at meetings around the island, the revolution was against Gairyism, then it had a right to protect itself. Gairy himself, despite his frantic attempts to rally support in the US, was not the only immediate fear of the PRG. The *Washington Post* in July had reported that the US government had considered slapping a naval quarantine around the island in the days after 13 March,[102] and suspicious incidents in the following months fuelled rumours that the CIA had started a destabilisation campaign. In May, there were simultaneous fires at travel agencies in the capital and in the Grand Anse tourist belt; in September and October the weekly *Torchlight* newspaper launched a sustained campaign against the People's Revolutionary Army (PRA), claiming that it had been harassing members of the Rastafarian sect; in November 1979, a police corporal was found with weapons and plans to attack targets in St Georges; then, in February 1980, a group of former PRA soldiers took over an estate in rural St Andrews and called for the people to rise up against the PRG.[103] Then, on 19 June 1980, when thousands had gathered to celebrate Heroes Day, a bomb, intended for the government, exploded under the Queen's Park grandstand, killing three young women and injuring 31 others.[104] In such a climate, where tasks of survival and consolidation had necessarily to be pre-eminent, it is difficult to condemn the PRG's tactics of arrest against the counter-revolutionaries and decisive action against what appeared to be a Trojan horse of destabilisation, in the closure of the *Torchlight*. As a temporary tactic, it is difficult to see how else the PRG, in an extremely tenuous and insecure position, should have responded, outside the framework of what it called 'heavy manners'. By the end of 1980, however, these had been crushed or dissipated and a new situation had emerged.

In late 1980 Ronald Reagan was elected to the US Presidency on an international platform directly geared at turning back the revolutionary movements which had made advances during the Carter years. Reagan and the New Right trends in the Republican Party blamed Carter for 'losing' Nicaragua and Grenada to the Soviet Union and called for the removal of the Soviet presence in the western hemisphere.[105] In the Caribbean itself, the new decade heralded a further strategic shift against the revolution as Michael Manley's regime was defeated at elections by the right-wing, pro-American Seaga government, and further elections in the neighbouring Windward islands strengthened the right and, by definition, an anti-PRG consensus.

With a demoralised counter-revolution and a gathering external alliance against Grenada, the PRG, from a purely tactical perspective, should have held elections in late 1981, allowing all, but perhaps the most violent counter-revolutionary elements, to participate. While, as the experience of Nicaragua in 1985 suggests, this would not have ended US-sponsored opposition to the PRG, it would have disarmed the ideological cutting-edge of the regional opposition and given the government some breathing space to address pressing economic difficulties and discuss deeper forms of democratic involvement.

There were other compelling reasons to hold elections. The government had predicated its economic model on the notion of a mixed economy,[106] with active participation by local and foreign capital. But despite the presence of a number of prominent business people in the government and the inclusion of the private sector in the frequent debates on the economy, private sector performance remained poor throughout the revolution.[107] Its laggardly performance might have been overlooked while lavish aid funds were flowing in for the airport and other projects, but beyond this temporary boost, the role of local business would have to play a far more central role. The suggestion here is that business went on a 'go-slow' because it was excluded from political power, which was monopolised in practice by the leaders of the party and government and that the only way to stimulate local investment would have been to give the 'national bourgeoisie' a fair chance to run its candidates in a national election contested by many parties.

The same perspective applies to other strata of the population. By 1981, the PRG, with its nationalist focus and success in channelling overseas funding into employment-generating and social welfare programmes, undoubtedly had the support of the majority. No polls were carried out during the revolution and attendance at public rallies, relatively massive as it was, is a highly subjective measure of real support. But if we begin with the (rigged) 1976 elections in which the Alliance had received close to 50 per cent of the vote, recognise that by 1979 the GNP was largely moribund and that by 1981 many Gairy supporters had defected as a result of social and economic gains, then a significant PRG support base, perhaps in the region of 55 to 60 per cent of the population, is a credible conclusion.

However, there remained a significant minority who were not Jewel supporters and who found no genuine representation in a system dominated by a single party. Many older people remained loyal to Gairy for his pioneering trade union work in the fifties. In the post-invasion elections which took place in a climate which was both anti-communist and heavily weighted against Gairy, the GULP polled 36.1 per cent of the popular vote,[108] a remarkable figure in the circumstances. Surely, a government confident in its economic platform, which had shown its ability over the previous two years to actually govern and which obviously had large, enthusiastic support among broad sections of the people, could have afforded to entertain opposition from parties, from which in the final analysis it had little to fear. The only suggested answer as to why this was not done is to be found in Mandle's notion of paternalistic socialism, woven into a cumulative and available ideological context which, in the path of Chile and Jamaica, placed dogmatic emphasis on the need to be hard and decisive, together with the elevation of the leadership above the society, which endowed them with a sense of 'correctness' and infallibility. This blind and resolute adherence to a policy of 'heavy manners' long after it was required, served to alienate many people. If action against the *Torchlight* might initially have been justified on the grounds of a national security threat, the refusal to reopen it after 1981 and the September 1981 arrest of 26 businessmen and prominent citizens for the publication of the *Grenadian Voice* on the grounds that it was CIA-supported,[109] can only be attributed to paranoia and rampant authoritarianism.

The PRG's response to this, of course, was that it was engaged in building an alternative democracy in which the divisions and schisms of the Westminster system would be transcended by a unified nation, actively involved in decision-making through participatory structures. At best, this approach, embodied in the parish and zonal councils, and most highly developed in the annual budget debates, was seriously flawed. Searle's and Hodges' ringing tribute to the new democracy in Grenada[110] begins by arguing that it had nothing to do with structures imposed from above, and then continues to present a diagram of the new system with the Political Bureau at the centre, followed by the party, the party-controlled Parish Coordinating Bodies and with community groups only given a position on the periphery of the model. Claremont Kirton, who was central to the organisation of the annual budget discussions, perhaps the most laudable exercise in the whole process, could nonetheless conclude that it was too 'top-down' in orientation and did not fully involve the people at the input level.[111] And Bernard Bourne, who was then a leading member of the party, supported this with a comment made in 1984:

> It was the party members themselves who organised these zonal
> councils which were to be organs of popular power for the
> people. But during the entire revolution never at one time did
> we show the people that we had confidence in them to do these
> things for themselves.[112]

At best, the model of participatory democracy was, in the Cuban tradition, a conveyor belt for letting the leadership know what the problems were
at the base, from which in their wisdom, they would then seek appropriate
solutions. As a means of allowing the people to decide policy, to provide
real opposition along lines advocated by Rosa Luxemburg,[113] or more substantially to change leadership, the structures were useless, nor were they
intended to do these things. This inability to seriously incorporate the
population into the process of decision-making was a two-edged sword. It
secured the monopoly of power in the hands of the ruling party, but it also
removed the people collectively from any sense of national responsibility.
If the PRG did its job of decision-making well and this was seen in social
and economic benefits, it would receive popular support. If, however, the
requisite benefits decreased, then government, which was solely responsible, would receive the popular opprobrium. Such events are commonplace
in multi-party democracies and the result is usually an electoral defeat for
the ruling party. But in Grenada there were no multi-party elections nor any
plans to hold them.[114]

These dogmatic and commandist positions, however, were even more
manifest within the party itself. When, on the day of revolutionary victory
in 1979, the members of the small party met at the radio station to assess the
way forward, they re-dedicated themselves to the religion of Leninism
which had brought them victory.[115] In 1982, when Bernard Coard's resignation from the Central Committee presented the leadership with its biggest
crisis, a similar decision was taken, that the route forward could not be a
petty-bourgeois one, but to place the party on 'a firm leninist footing'.[116]
Whereas Leninism, or rather, clandestinity, organisation and discipline, had
contributed immeasurably to the 1979 victory, it had little to recommend
itself as a method of organisation for the state after 13 March. If at the time
of the victory there had been only 50 members of the party, in July 1983 on
the verge of the collapse, there were still less than 100 full members and
some 300 candidates and applicants.[117] A paternalist approach to running
the state and rebuilding the economy, required a substantial cadre of trained
and dedicated party members to fill bureaucratic positions both in the party
and in the state. Not only did Grenada not have such a pool of skilled
persons, but the restricted party-entry requirements excluded many who
would otherwise have been able to make contributions, even within the
limits set by the leadership. In the lower echelons, a similar paradox was

evident. More people were needed in responsible positions on the farms, on the construction sites and in the army, but many supporters of the revolution were excluded from positions of responsibility because they were not considered ready for party membership. The simple result of this was all too obvious by 1982. Under the immeasurable strain of party work, study, voluntary work on weekends, innumerable rallies, not excluding the members' substantial jobs in the state or private sectors, party cadres began to collapse and persons close to the party refused to join the organisation for fear of themselves collapsing.[118] As early as May 1982, for example, women party members, faced with the additional burden of child-rearing, reported that the 'masses' were criticising them for neglecting their children, and appealed for clemency in the face of committee chairmen who criticised them for being undisciplined and 'petty bourgeois' for asking to spend more time at home.[119] In a model in which power came from the top and was concentrated in a few hands, this factor of physical collapse was a major one in the final demise of the revolution. It certainly was central, although not singularly responsible for Bernard Coard's resignation in 1982 which set off a chain of events ending in Maurice Bishop's murder a year later.

By 1982 serious political problems were surfacing, which traced their origins to the overly centralist approach to party organisation and the paternalist model adopted, but somewhat independently, the economy was also entering a period of increasing uncertainty. Most commentaries on the economy have either given it a positive gloss[120] or have resorted to blanket condemnation.[121] On balance, the economy was a success, but not in the way that the PRG had hoped. The initial perspectives of 1973 had envisaged an economic model based on agricultural diversification, import substitution, 'new tourism' and cooperatives,[122] largely paralleling the nationalist political positions of black power. By 1979 this had been abandoned for a traditional tourism-led model, uncomfortably wedded to a programme of 'socialist orientation'.[123] While the adoption of tourism as the leading sector was a realistic decision, given the limited options, and not a betrayal of the previous programme as Maingot suggests,[124] it nevertheless had serious weaknesses. Mandle effectively highlights the paradox in which a left-wing government had adopted a model of development which had been roundly condemned by the Caribbean left for its potential for reinforcing racial stereotypes and the questionable contribution which tourism could make to the economy with its limited multiplier effect.[125] A further dilemma was raised by Clive Thomas who suggested that a small state engaged in an anti-imperialist project could not seriously hope to consistently attract tourists from Western hard currency areas in the face of adverse and damaging propaganda.[126] This was supported by the steady decline of stop-over tourists between 1979, when 32.3 thousand arrived, and 1982 when only 22.7 thousand came.[127] At any rate, the real performance of the tourism sector would have depended on the completion of the new international airport at Point Salines, which with massive Cuban assistance, was still at least six months from completion in September 1983.

The economy grew by some 8 per cent during the revolution and unemployment fell from in excess of 30 per cent to somewhere in the region of 15 to 20 per cent.[128] While this is somewhat less extravagant than the PRG's estimate of a more than 35 per cent fall in unemployment and over 14 per cent cumulative growth, it is still impressive, especially in light of the severe international recession of the early eighties. This growth, however, was largely based on two factors: the notable ability of the government to attract loans from a wide variety of sources, and its success, in the absence of any serious corruption, in channelling these loans into productive and beneficial programmes. Other aspects of the economy were far less successful. Agriculture remained a shambles. The attempt to diversify crop production had made only marginal gains, while the cooperative movement was an outright failure.[129] In the end, Grenadian agriculture was still tied to nutmeg, bananas and cocoa, dependent on Britain and the European market and subject to drastic price fluctuations.[130] It was the massive infusion of over $168 million from sources as diverse as Cuba and the Soviet Union, Libya, Canada and the United Kingdom,[131] which allowed the PRG to carry out far-reaching social programmes in health, child care, education and housing. In the last full year of Gairy's government, he had spent EC$16.1 million on health, education and housing; in 1983, the PRG's projected figure for health and education alone was EC$29.7 million.[132] But as the airport approached completion, the amount of loans, many of which were directly tied to airport construction, would naturally begin to diminish.

Short of a massive spurt in tourist arrivals immediately after the completion of the airport, which Grenada's limited hotel capacity was unable in any case to absorb, there was bound to be a downturn in the economy as loan sources dried up. Equally, if other expected loans were not forthcoming, a similar contraction could be expected. This is exactly what happened in late 1982. With the non-appearance of important loans from the OPEC countries,[133] significant belt-tightening had to be introduced; for the first time unions began to report significant lay-offs.[134] In July 1982, the Central Committee, assessing the developing situation, noted the serious cash-flow problem resulting from the difficulties in mobilising external finance and that the increasing lay-offs had 'shaken the confidence of broad sections of the masses'.[135] By late 1982, then, two features of a crisis up above had emerged. The tiny vanguard, burdened by a constricting Leninist ideology, was beginning to collapse from overwork, and the economy, upon which rested the credibility of the paternalist leadership, was for the first time facing a severe bottleneck, with a reversal in the trend towards decreasing unemployment. Both of these tendencies were compounded and intensified, when Bernard Coard, reacting to the pressures of office, but also responding to a deeper divergence of directions within the party, resigned from the Political Bureau and Central Committee, setting the stage for the fall of the revolution a year later.

## The fall

In October 1983, less than three weeks after leaving Grenada, I stood speechless on the Mona campus of the University of the West Indies, as reports came in that Maurice Bishop, the leader of the revolution, a friend, and someone with whom I had met less than two months earlier, was under house arrest. The last time I had seen Maurice was in August at a convivial meeting with Bernard Coard and other senior party members to discuss the planning of a political education programme for workers throughout the country. As the news became more urgent in the following days, I often thought of that last meeting, the laughter, the animation, and what appeared to be a genuine shared sense of honesty and concern with building the revolution, along what was thought to be the best possible lines. I have never been able to reconcile the two events: the fraternity of the first and the absolute antagonism of the last days, and still often refer back to those recollections to help reconstruct the traumatic events which were to follow. On 19 October, when news on Grenada had already taken over the Jamaican airwaves, the most tragic announcement was made, that Maurice Bishop, Jacqueline Creft, Vince Noel, Unison Whiteman and others, had been killed on Fort Rupert in St Georges by soldiers of the PRA.

For me and the small group of Grenadians at the University who knew personally those who died and probably knew the soldiers who had killed them as well, the sense of loss was palpable. We waited numbly in a vacuum over the next few days, switching on and off the radio, knowing that the inevitable *coup de main* would come, but hoping against hope that it would be avoided. On 25 October, the US-led invasion, an event only possible because of the self-annihilation of the revolution, did come, and after four days of resistance, which the Americans in retrospect found surprising, but we who knew the revolution did not, the small PRA garrison surrendered and the revolutionary chapter had ended.

Ever since the house arrest of Maurice Bishop on 13 October, a 'conventional wisdom' has developed on the reasons for the collapse of the revolution, which, simple to comprehend as it is, and widespread as belief in it may be, is essentially flawed. Its main elements include all, or some of the following assertions:

(i) Bernard Coard retained a Leninist cell inside the NJM, composed of members of the early Marxist study group the Organisation for

Revolutionary Education and Liberation (OREL), which worked under his leadership and bided its time until power could be seized.[136]

(ii) There was no crisis in 1983. Those problems which did exist were blown out of proportion by the OREL trend to justify moving against Bishop, through the strategy of 'joint leadership' which would elevate Coard to equal status in the party and therefore effectively demote the former.[137]

(iii) The motive for the Coard/OREL manoeuvre lay in one, or a combination of the following: (a) Bishop was seen by them as too moderate, or moderating his position, bringing him into conflict with their ultra-leftist 'Leninist' perspective. This, then, was essentially a conflict between 'Marxist humanism' and Leninism.[138] (b) Bishop was pro-Cuban while Coard was pro-Moscow, and the crisis was essentially over different interpretations of strategy as defined by these two poles.[139] (c) Coard and Bishop had deep personality differences. Coard was ambitious but unpopular and was essentially using the party and the revolution to advance his own desire for power; Bishop was popular, but was too reliant on his popularity and naive as to Coard's intentions and manoeuvres.[140]

While there are obviously elements of truth and important insights in many of these positions, the conventional wisdom is on balance wrong, but rather than begin by countering each element separately, we can suggest the main outlines of an alternative explanation.

In a context of tremendous pressure from without and strait-jacketed by dogmatic decisions on state and party policy, by 1983 there was a genuine crisis within the revolution. Faced with the sternest test to its survival since 13 March, the entire party leadership, accustomed to ruling from above, sought to resolve the crisis *from above*, by tinkering with the structure and form of leadership. But such an approach failed to recognise that two diverging 'logics' had been at work, at least since the 1976 elections, but certainly since 13 March 1979. These were: the logic of the supreme leader and the logic of the vanguard party. Both logics operated within the parameters of 'rule from above', and as the differences intensified in September, both trends at first sought to keep them within the leadership and resolve them in a manner in harmony with hierarchy and bureaucracy. In the end, it was only the logic of the leader which could and did, appeal to the people, but it did so without rupturing the structures and norms of the deeply-entrenched paternalist relationship. It is my belief that there was no established conspiracy, there were no substantial ideological or tactical differences and, although personality differences did, of necessity, intercede, the overarching issue was the growing disconnection of the leadership *tout court* from the people, which, coupled with the depth of the crisis and the physical strain of paternalist rule, drove them to take irretrievable decisions. Once these were taken, the 'gridlock of events' followed its own logic, in which pride, misunderstanding, innuendo, external intervention and further rash action, each served to stoke the fire, leading like a Greek tragedy to the eventual *dénouement*. If this approach is not simple, for me it is the only satisfying one, able to explain that rapid transition from fraternity to antagonism which I noted in 1983, and have not forgotten.

## The existence of crisis

Three factors underline the contention that there was a severe crisis in 1983. Firstly, as suggested, the economy was facing a serious downturn for the first time since 1979, due to the non-appearance of expected loans and grants. These had been at the cornerstone of its success and with a model predicated on the paternal rulers giving quickly tangible benefits to those below, this development was immediately damaging to morale. Abundant evidence supports this position. The 'top secret' National Security Report to the PB of 18 March 1983 commented that there had been a 'dramatic collapse'[141] in the militia over the past eight to ten months; Fitzroy Bain, a CC member who died on the fort alongside Bishop, and who obviously had no interest in falsifying matters, reported in April that militia mobilisation in his parish of St Davids was 'weak' and that 'the people at present are very confused and uncertain about militia matters';[142] the August report of the party members in the Technical and Allied Workers Union (TAWU) which assessed the political 'balance of forces' in some TAWU plants, found alarmingly, that of 276 workers in the sample, only 44 at that time could be considered 'firm supporters' of the revolution;[143] Layne suggests that demoralisation and poor pay had reached its apex in the PRA, where in 1983 desertions, because of low pay and bad working conditions, had become widespread, many soldiers whose contracts had expired refused to sign up for another term and thus the very existence of the permanent units was in question.[144]

Secondly, this 'dramatic collapse' in morale and support was happening at a time when the tiny party itself, under the weight of overwhelming statal duties and constricting Leninist structures, was at the point of collapse. At the leadership level this was most evident:

> George Louison estimated that some 5 to 6 members of the CC had virtually lived in hospital over the previous year. John 'Chalkie' Ventour had spent almost a year in hospital for hepatitis; Ian St Bernard had spent 5 months in the Soviet Union trying to correct blindness in one eye; Dave 'Tan' Bartholomew

had spent 4 months there for a similar problem and a knee injury; Kamau McBarnette had been on 6 weeks sick leave in Cuba and then spent 3 further months in hospital in Grenada and Phyllis Coard had been in hospital for a gallstone operation which incapacitated her for 6 weeks.[145]

In a model predicated on rule from above, a collapsed party would certainly mean the collapse of the model and perhaps the entire revolution, particularly when the third factor is taken into consideration; for, at its weakest moment internally, the revolution was facing its sternest external test, as the generally hostile Reagan administration stepped up its bellicose statements and actions. In March 1983, in time for the fourth anniversary of the revolution, Reagan in a statement widely interpreted as the prelude to some form of action, accused Grenada of building, with Cuban help, a military airstrip at Point Salines and concluded by saying: 'It is not nutmeg that is at stake in the Caribbean and Central America, it is the United States' national security'.[146] This, of course, was only the most ominous in a series of hostile actions and statements which had occurred since his 1981 inauguration. In that year, the 'Amber and the Amberdines' military exercise, a thin code name for Grenada and the Grenadines, had sought to free hostages on Amber island and establish a government 'favourable to the way of life we espouse'[147] and, even as the fourth anniversary celebrations were under way in St Georges, reports had come in that the US' and its allies were holding manoeuvres in the surrounding waters, using Barbados as a staging area.

With a crippled party, unable effectively to mobilise the people in the face of a looming military confrontation, a demoralised population, increasingly resistant to mobilisation, and a credible military threat to its very existence, it is difficult to support the view that there was no crisis in 1983. The cutting-edge of the crisis was manifest in the physical collapse of the party, but the incipient crisis, the one which could not yet be seen from the outside, was nonetheless evident in the low mood of the people, which needs to be gauged against the credibility and scope of the threat which faced the process. A crisis situation required crisis measures, but before examining the measures taken, we need to scrutinise the notion of conspiracy.

## The absence of conspiracy

OREL was formed by high-school students in 1974, who had fought alongside the NJM in the anti-Gairy struggle, but were moving away from black power to Marxist–Leninist positions. Although formed independently of

Bernard Coard, when he returned in 1976, there was a natural affinity between his position and OREL's and close relations developed with its main leaders, including Liam 'Owusu' James, John 'Chalkie' Ventour and Ewart 'Headache' Layne. After some four years of more or less independent existence, however, OREL decided to merge with the NJM in 1978, on the basis that there was no need for two organisations with similar policies and that unification would strengthen the anti-Gairy movement.[148] Mention of OREL as an organisation then virtually disappears from the record until after the 1983 crisis, when many commentators, Castro most notably, argued that the group was never dissolved and functioned as a cell led by Coard, preparing to take over the party at the opportune moment. It is almost impossible to prove decisively that OREL ceased functioning, as there is no evidence to support the assertion that it continued, but a number of observations support the former contention.

The first, as suggested, is the absence of any discussion of OREL in the private party documents or in the national media after 1978. It seems almost impossible to imagine that nothing is said about this fact anywhere in the five years from 1978 to 1983. The second stems from this, and relates to the peculiarity of the tiny, micro-state of Grenada. The island's total population is in the region of 100 000 persons; some 10 000 to 20 000 live in and around the capital, St Georges; the party itself never had more than 100 full members, among whom were included people like Kendrick Radix, who had other more personal reasons not to like Coard. I contend that it would have been impossible to keep a secret cell functioning within the party and in Grenada, which is defined by the fact that even amorous liaisons can never remain secret for very long. It is particularly disingenuous for Castro to speak in one breath about this longstanding conspiracy and in the next say, 'The truth is we didn't know about the process that was evolving'.[149] From late 1979 until the end, Cubans were involved in virtually all areas of Grenadian society, including construction, health, the military, finance and agriculture and all Ministers, including the Prime Minister, had an open-door policy to the Cuban Ambassador, Julian Rizo. I contend that if a parallel, subversive organisation existed, it would have been impossible for the Cubans *not* to know. The need to maintain a separate trend, with its requirements of meetings, minutes, strategy and tactics, would seem also quite impossible given the already massive workload of the leadership.[150] Further, why the need for a separate cell, when any cursory examination of its available documents would show that the NJM in its structure, ideology and style, from at least 1977, was irrevocably, dogmatically Leninist? Obviously, if the party had remained torn between Jamesist and Leninist factions, such an explanation could be advanced. But this was not the case. OREL ceased to exist after 1978 and was resurrected after the demise because it provided a useful and simple explanation for what was in fact, a far more complex phenomenon, or alternatively, to find a visible and admittedly, credible scapegoat to obscure the deeper fact that the entire project of the revolution was seriously flawed.

The manoeuvring of people on to the CC was a subset of the conspiracy position and the argument used to support it is the fact that there was a general attrition of older longstanding NJM comrades and the promotion of younger ones, closely associated with OREL. James, Layne and Ventour all found places on the Political Bureau after 1982, while stalwarts like Radix and Vince Noel were demoted. The first point is that these were decisions of the entire CC, of which Bishop was the Chairman and were based on their own Leninist-derived criteria that leaders should be hard workers and leading members of mass organisations. Louison, interestingly, who generally supports conspiracy, in a candid interview in 1984, denied the notion that people were manoeuvred on to the CC of which he was a member:

> I think that over the years there were certain people who earned their position on the CC and there were certain people who could not function or pull their weight in the last days.[151]

With the load of work which the chosen model placed on the leadership, there seemed to be a natural attrition of those who had been in the party longest and were usually older, and a younger set, who had arrived at a slightly later date and were less jaded. The conspiratorial pattern of manoeuvred promotion is not evident. George Louison, who had risen fastest and after Coard's resignation had replaced him as the CC's study-group leader, was definitively not from OREL; in October 1982, following Coard's resignation, Radix was expelled for lack of work, but this was done under the leadership of his close personal friend Maurice Bishop; among the people who had been severely reprimanded by Coard at an earlier date for having militaristic tendencies[152] was Layne, an ex-OREL member; and in the final Central Committee which opposed Bishop on a number of measures were people like Selwyn Strachan and Hudson Austin who had been with Bishop and the NJM from the very start. On close consideration of the facts, the outline of a conspiratorial model as sketched by Castro, Rojas and others, becomes increasingly indistinct.

## *No sharp ideological differences*

Coard had introduced Leninism, but there is nothing to suggest that Bishop was a closet 'Marxist-humanist'. On the decision to attack in 1979, it is true that Bishop had wavered, but this says little about his ideological inclinations and more on his tactical position as to whether the moment was right. In many subsequent speeches, including the seminal 'Line of March' statement of 1982, he removed any doubts, if they ever existed, about his commitment to insurrectional forms. On the decision to close down the *Torchlight*, it is true that Bishop had been out of the island at the time, but there is no evidence to suggest that he opposed it. Indeed, in his commitment to a revolutionary media he made it clear on many occasions that he agreed fully with the *Torchlight* decision.[153] One argument is that his 1983 trip to the US was an indication of his growing moderation and was used by him to extend an olive branch to the Reagan Administration, but there is no evidence of this. The visit to the US was at least partly Coard's idea, all the minutes of the CC and PB show that the trip was supported both before and after by the leadership, Liam James, the Head of Security and an ex-OREL member, was in charge of arrangements for the trip and Bishop's speeches at Hunter College[154] and elsewhere retained their unswerving invective against US imperialism.

Differences did emerge in 1983 and did play a role in the accumulating crisis, but these differences were not at all ideological, but stemmed from the growing divergence of the two logics of leader and party. To understand this, we need to recall that in 1973, leadership had been shared by Whiteman and Bishop. On Coard's return in 1976, and even some time before this, a new tandem arose, with Coard in charge of organisation and tactics and Bishop with his charisma and pedigree in the revolution as the unquestioned popular leader. This new alignment was not met without resentment, and if there was any hostility in the CC towards Coard, it did not come from the fear of a competing Leninist/OREL trend, but out of jealousy that he, who had not been beaten in 1974, and who had been largely out of the island for the crucial formative years when 'mongoose' power was at its worst, was now being elevated to a position of supremacy. Thus, Radix from 1978, had accused Coard and, ironically from the perspective of later events, Louison, of trying to establish a power base within the party.[155] Initially this arrangement, despite the reservations from Radix and others, seemed to have worked, largely because of the excellent personal relationship which developed between Coard and Bishop. Maurice generally bowed to Bernard's tactical and ideological leadership, with Bernard in turn accepting his position of chief ideologue/tactician while ceding the kudos of popular and later national leadership to Maurice. This, by implication, meant that each in turn tended to suppress that side of his personality which would allow him to develop into territory already occupied by the other. The distorted view of a dour and closeted Coard and of a popular but politically naive Bishop both derive from a mistaken impression of their personalities, shaped in part by this delicate arrangement of power-sharing, which was unwritten, but real. Part of this arrangement extended into the area of protocol and Kirton recognised this when he noted:

> I worked with both of them and each used to tell me, if I
> submitted documents to one, then ensure that the other had a
> copy. I have no reason to believe on the basis of what I could
> see that there was any kind of tension at all between them.[156]

Beyond this delicate minuet, which was at the heart of the party, there
was a lesser, but nonetheless important degree of collective behaviour
among the top leaders of the revolution. This is best seen in the decision to
take power on 13 March, in which Bishop, despite being in the minority,
supported wholeheartedly the risky action in which all could have lost their
lives. But tension had been developing. After 1976, as Leader of the
Opposition, Bishop held an official position, and then after 1979 he was the
Prime Minister and unquestioned leader of the revolution. It had been the
party, with Coard as its main tactician, which had planned and executed the
1979 overthrow, but it was Bishop who was the focus of national and
international attention. Maurice became more independently prestigious,
while the party, still the engine of the top-down process, became, at least
publicly, more marginal. Before the revolution, it had been the 'Jewel
Boys', a loose term meaning the top leaders of the party, but after the
revolution, it was the Prime Minister or the PRG, with the NJM receding
into the background.

   A relevant example of how this new relationship developed, also indica-
tive of the nature of the Cuban influence on the revolution, surrounds the
question of military leadership. The revolutionary overthrow had been
guided by the Security and Defence Committee (SandD) of the party, but
after the revolution, the Cuban military personnel who assisted in developing the PRA, avoided dealing with the SandD committee and insisted that
there could only be one commander in chief of the armed forces, who of
course, was Bishop.[157] By adhering to the Castroite approach of the all-
powerful chief, the influential Cuban mission helped to undermine party
supremacy in the army as, at the same time it boosted Bishop's sense of
autonomy as the single leader.

   Ironically the party, in its own strategy of projecting Maurice, may have
contributed to this tension. At any public event, party members would lead
cheering sections, calling on Maurice to 'put on the heavy roller' on counter-revolution, or simply, 'M-A-U-R-I-C-E, MAURICE!' The possible psychological dimensions are not difficult to discern. Bishop was increasingly
the personalist leader, with his direct constituency not the party but the
'crowd'. For him, party decisions which impeded that relationship, must
have seemed increasingly uncomfortable or even irrelevant. For the Central
Committee, on the other hand – most of all, Bernard Coard – there must
have been a great resentment at the not-so-subtle loss of influence and the
shift in the delicate balance of forces among the 'guardians' at the top.

This was the background to Coard's resignation from the Central Committee and its two subordinate bodies, the Political Bureau and the Organising Committee in October 1982. He claimed that he was physically tired, that his overwhelming influence had intimidated other comrades and that the CC was 'slack' and in order not to have personality clashes with its Chairman, Bishop, he would rather resign.[158] There was substance in all these comments, but the last is most important. Somewhere between 1979 and 1982, that 'scrupulousness' of which Kirton speaks in the relationship between the two, had worn thin. Something more than the daily routine of meetings had brought this to a head. Layne asserts that there had been a sharp exchange between them as to whether senior officers should have been at a military meeting with the Commander-in-Chief or with Coard at an OC meeting.[159] Such an event, the climax of a deteriorating 'understanding', might help to explain the suddenness and adamancy of Coard's position. He was resigning not as Castro with hindsight suggests, as a well-calculated retreat to return in triumph a year later, but in infuriated protest about what he saw as Bishop undermining the unwritten law of scrupulous and chivalrous relationships between the guardians.

Yet his decision was both a reflection of an impasse and hastened the crisis. For the CC, under Bishop's chairmanship, chose this moment not to inform the people, nor even the other party comrades, of this resignation; not to call on them to find an avenue out of this crisis by broadening party democracy and instituting national democratic structures, but rather to *intensify Leninism*. Thus, out of the October 1982 CC meeting, the decision was taken that 'the party must be placed on a firm Leninist footing'.[160] Study was to be increased, membership requirements were to be tightened up, and punitive measures were to be instituted to deal with any breaches of party discipline, in order to overcome the 'objectively based backwardness and petty bourgeois nature of the society'.[161]

Ironically, this meeting led by Bishop, with Coard now no longer a member, had, by extreme voluntarism, placed the party on a collision course. The results became evident after the July 1983 plenary report of the CC. While noting that in March, the party had come dangerously close to losing its links with the masses, it berated the members, for their collective failure to transform along Leninist lines and again placed the blame on 'petty bourgeois attitudes'.[162] For the first time, the response of the burdened party members was to reject the leadership's decision. The Women's Committee threatened to resign *en bloc*; there was open revolt from party comrades who attacked the CC for criticising them but not itself; members then demanded that the CC meet again to review its decisions. The tail, at least within the party, had belatedly begun to wag the dog. Faced with this rebellion, when the CC reconvened on 26 August, attitudes had changed. James argued that the party was disintegrating; Unison Whiteman said that there was a breakdown of confidence in the CC; everyone saw the situation as serious, most notably Maurice Bishop who, in his summary, agreed with Owusu (James) that 'we are faced with the threat of disintegration'.[163]

In his otherwise penetrating analysis of the revolution, Gordon Lewis argues that in 1983, the ultra-left position 'led to a dismal diagnosis of the patient in order to carry out radical surgery'.[164] He is wrong on two counts. First, there was a crisis and a dismal diagnosis was therefore appropriate; second, the diagnosis was decisively not that of any faction, but of the entire leadership, led by Bishop himself. Radical surgery was required. But the wrong operation was carried out.

## *Surgery required; wrong operation*

On 16 September the CC reconvened to continue the evaluation of the crisis and to propose solutions. Liam 'Owusu' James led off by criticising Bishop's style of leadership of the party and called for a model of 'joint leadership' in the party, 'marrying the strengths of comrades Bishop and Coard'.[165] While at the earlier meeting there had been virtual unanimity on the recognition of crisis, this time there was division. Bishop was worried that the proposal expressed a lack of confidence in him and, prophetically, was concerned that the masses might interpret it as a sign of a power struggle within the revolution; Louison, at first unsure about it, was eventually firmly opposed. However, when the vote was taken, the clear majority was in favour: 9 supported the proposal, Louison was opposed and Bishop, Whiteman and Hudson Austin who had arrived at the meeting late, abstained.[166]

Despite the vote, Bishop had asked for time to consider its implications, and this was the background to the party general meeting on 25 September. Within the CC, some members were concerned that he was taking too long to accept the decision. His wavering was beginning to be interpreted as an example of the 'petty bourgeois trend' he and others had so consistently railed against. The meeting was an attempt to convince him otherwise, and as such, it was highly successful. At first, he expressed his deepest reservations, important for the historical record:

> the masses have their own conception and perception that may not be necessarily like ours who study the science. Our history shows that the masses build up a personality cult around a single individual.[167]

Then, following his remarks, member after member spoke from the floor, expressing faith and love for Maurice, but supporting the model of joint leadership. Bishop was deeply moved by what was obviously a genuine concern among the most senior members of the party – the people with whom he had fought against Gairy and spent four years together, building the revolution. He conceded to their wishes and the meeting, after some 16 hours of debate, ended in euphoria, with a symbolic embrace by the two leaders, and the singing of the 'Internationale'.[168]

This was a particularly important stage of the process. The CC had acted in what it thought was the best way to build the party and the movement. It had called back Bernard Coard, the ideologue, organiser and tactician, to re-establish on a more formal basis the *status quo ante*. If things were only like they were before, the presumption must have been, then the revolution could go forward. Joint leadership was not, as some have implied, a bolt out of the blue. It was simply the formal interpretation of Coard and Bishop's pre-1979 relationship. It was also perfectly in harmony with the project of revolution from above, because the cure to the ills of the moment was mistakenly seen to lie first and foremost in the nature of leadership, when what needed urgently to be addressed was the relationship of the entire leadership and party to the people as a whole.

An alternative scenario could have been to bring the economic and political problems being faced to the people in the form of a 1973-type people's convention, or even a budget or parish council debate, to openly thrash out the issues in all frankness and lay the basis for a deeper ongoing dialogue. This could have been the prelude to both party and national elections, which would have institutionalised leadership positions, spoken to the question of succession and served to further legitimate the PRG in Grenada and critically, in the Caribbean. Such a path was never really considered, although twice in the crisis, Bishop raised the question of how the people would perceive joint leadership, and in the days to come, Coard would raise for the first and last time, the need for 'popular control' over the party.[169] Had such a decision been taken in the early days, or even after his resignation in 1982, then a different outcome might have been possible. But the Central Committee and the party members were engaged in wishful thinking in their attempt to seek safe harbour in the old power relationship, when the new model, impelled by the history of Grenada, as Bishop succinctly put it, had crowned the single leader as the legitimate force.

It would be psychologically difficult for Maurice to climb down from a position of unquestioned leadership of party and people, legitimated as it was by the international community and popular acclaim at every turn, to a lesser position which events had passed by. Nor would the people accept this. Bishop was a genuine hero whose father had died sacrificially in the anti-Gairy struggle. Coard was a shady figure, whose fair-skinned Jamaican wife was seen as too pushy in the closed structures of Grenadian society and who had been the subject of ill-founded rumours dating back to his early differences with some party leaders. Although, as some would later argue, this was an internal party matter and did not concern Bishop's *state* leadership, such an argument is disingenuous. Such a decision could never be kept secret in Grenada, and Bishop was absolutely right that it would be interpreted as a power struggle and one which the party and Coard could never win. Bishop's decision on 25 September, then, was an honest response to the overwhelming and clearly non-conspiratorial wishes of the party ranks, but doubts must have remained in his mind and these were reopened in the following days as he left on a trip to Eastern Europe, returning to Grenada through Cuba.

## *The gridlock of events*

Bishop left the island on the 26 September for a scheduled trip to Hungary, leaving behind a mood of euphoria among the party comrades who had lined up individually to embrace him and Coard the day before. However, on his return on 8 October, he had again changed his mind. Louison and Whiteman had definitely worked to convince him to do so in Hungary[170] and it is highly unlikely that Castro – the exemplar of the *jefe maximo* – and the Cuban leadership who met with him while in Cuba, did not also encourage him in this direction. He naturally had a right to change his mind, but he did so with the knowledge that he would have almost the entire party opposed to him. Even at this delicate stage, the situation was not too far gone. Delegations could have met; differences been discussed; solutions sought. But what I call the 'gridlock of events', from which avenues of escape or resolution were increasingly limited, had begun to take over the process. Thus, from Cuba, Bishop's chief personal security man, Cletus St Paul, is alleged to have phoned his overall head in Grenada and physically threatened those opposed to the Prime Minister. Then, Coard and other members of the CC, fearing Cuban involvement behind St Paul's threat, instead of meeting Bishop on his arrival, virtually went underground. Days passed without any serious communication, further souring the atmosphere between both trends, strengthening the view among the party majority that Bishop had betrayed their pact of 25 September and building the view on Bishop's side that a conspiracy was at work.

Then, on 12 October, rumour hit the streets that Coard and his wife Phyllis were trying to kill Bishop, leading to the first physical clash, when a group in the suburban community of St Pauls tried to seize weapons from a militia station to protect their leader and one was shot. Damning to Bishop was the report from his number-two security man, Errol George, that it was he who had started the rumour.[171] Had Bishop, in the face of what he increasingly felt was a conspiracy, done what he thought was the only way to let people know what was happening? Or was the statement of the security officer a provocation, well-placed and timed? It is difficult to prove one way or the other, but its effect was devastating. When the party members reconvened on the 13 October to consider this latest event, the mood was the opposite of that when they had last met. George repeated his accusation, and when Bishop refused to deny the charges, the party members were up in arms against him. And then, the crucial decision in the eventual fall of the revolution was taken when the leadership decided to place the Prime Minister under house arrest. Up to this point, even with the damaging rumours on the street, the issue could theoretically still have been resolved internally, with some compromises on both sides. Once Bishop had been placed under house arrest, there was no returning to the old *status quo*. Either he, with his overwhelming popular support would triumph, or the party with its organisation and strategic hegemony in the military, would dominate. Whichever side won, the profile of the revolution could not be the same. A party victory could only mean rule by force because it did not have the legitimacy to rule without it. A Bishop victory, on the other hand, would have meant the absolute victory of the personality, a form closer to Gairyism but without the NJM as a counter-force for, however well-meaning Bishop was, it must be remembered that Gairy was equally a man of the people when he started his project in 1951.

A note on the question of majorities needs to be made here. On every important vote, from that for joint leadership, down to his appearance on 13 October to answer rumour-mongering, large majorities kept appearing against Bishop. Who were these people opposed on so many occasions to the popular leader? People like Chester Humphrey had been with the party from the beginning, had slipped out of the US while on a charge of exporting arms – presumably those used in the action on 13 March; John 'Chalkie' Ventour had been married weeks before and Maurice had been the best man at his wedding; Selwyn Strachan and Hudson Austin had been beaten and thrown into gaol alongside Bishop in 1973; Peter David, dropping his studies in Canada, had returned to help the revolution in whatever capacity and referred to Maurice as 'the chief'. These were his friends and closest people. Why oppose Maurice? Because on joint leadership they honestly felt that this was the best solution, while their subsequent response can only be understood as the rejection of a child who hero-worships his father and suddenly discovers that the father is less than perfect. Why did Bishop and his smaller group in turn, after the overseas trip, firmly oppose the party? Because by then, at least some honestly felt that there was a conspiracy at work. But what was at play was not a conspiracy, but two competing 'honesties' based on two logics of the revolution, in which the CC and the majority remained tied in to the older logic of party control, while Bishop increasingly responded to the logic of the paramount leader; both were premised on the deeper reality of revolution from above.

Much has been written about the rest elsewhere. House arrest, grievous a decision as it was, was not out of keeping with the perspective of paternalistic socialism, in which the guardians make all the decisions without reference to the people. Popular pro-Bishop demonstrations in the ensuing days, led to his release by a large crowd on 19 October. On his way to a huge mass meeting in the Market Square, a fateful decision was made to detour and occupy Fort Rupert, the main military installation overlooking St Georges, which was taken over by the crowd, and its garrison disarmed. A platoon of soldiers from Fort Frederick, the other fort in St Georges, then arrived to recapture Fort Rupert and, in the ensuing battle, the precise sequence of which, including who opened fire first, is open to dispute,[172] a number of people were killed. What is not in question, is that after this initial fire-fight, Bishop, Creft, Whiteman and others, were captured unharmed, put against a wall and shot, a brutal act which could find no justification in the previous crisis and which opened the door for the American-led invasion.

At each turning-point in the Grenada revolution, the leadership, almost instinctively, sought to solve problems and crises from above. In 1982, with Coard's resignation, the answer was to intensify Leninism. In July 1983, with increasing fear of foreign intervention and a demoralised population, this again was the first response. When revolt within the party threatened everything, the leadership at last recognised a deeper crisis, but the first answer was again to attempt to adjust the power structure, in order to put the ship back on course. This inability to escape from a deeply-entrenched cumulative and available ideological context of Leninism and hierarchy and not the chimera of conspiracy was the critical element in the *dénouement* of the revolution. If we retrace the historical path to the last of the major counter-revolutionary violence in 1980, a more popular and democratic course might have included: (a) the holding of general elections in 1980, open to the GNP, the GULP without Gairy and any other group openly engaged in violence; (b) the proposal, popular discussion and passage of a new multi-party constitution, linked to a popular system of parish and zonal councils in which no single party would have hegemonic control, and including regular consultations such as the national budget debate as central elements; (c) within the NJM itself, a return to an open tribune-like party, allowing wide membership, discussion and circulation of ideas including (d) an established system of elections in the party, in which any candidate could stand on joint or single tickets; (e) a statutory limitation on the length of tenure of the national leader, including, given the small island's limited human resources, the possibility of re-election after a term out of office. As an urgent programme, this was never on Coard's, Bishop's or the party's agenda. The fall of the revolution was essentially a crisis of democracy and the failure of the leadership to escape from a deeply-entrenched structure of hierarchy which it inherited. The lessons for the future of the Caribbean can easily be derived from this.

# Notes

1. See Gordon K. Lewis, *Grenada: The Jewel Despoiled* (Baltimore and London: The Johns Hopkins University Press, 1987.
2. Dov Zakheim, 'The Grenada Operation and Superpower Relations: A Perspective from the Pentagon', in Jiri Valenta and Herbert Ellison (eds), *Soviet/Cuban Strategy in the Third World After Grenada: Toward Preventing Future Grenadas* (Washington, DC: The Wilson Center, 1984), p. 21.
3. Otto Reich and Wayne Smith, 'Commentary on Grenada', in *Caribbean Review*, Vol. XIII, no. 3, Summer 1984, p. 4. A better example of the right-wing perspective is Gregory Sandiford and Richard Vigilante, *Grenada: The Untold Story* (Lanham, New York, London: Madison Books, 1984).
4. See Patrick Emmanuel, Farley Brathwaite and Eudine Barriteau, *Political Change and Public Opinion in Grenada: 1979–1984,* (Barbados: Institute of Social and Economic Research, 1986), pp. 23–4.
5. See Jiri and Virginia Valenta, 'Leninism in Grenada', in Valenta and Ellison (eds), 1984, pp. 32–3.
6. Fidel Castro, *Nothing Can Stop the Course of History*, Interview with Jeffrey M. Elliot and Mervyn Dymally (New York, London, Sidney: Pathfinder, 1986), p. 153. See also Hugh O'Shaughnessy, *Grenada: Revolution, Invasion and Aftermath*, (London: Sphere Books, London, 1984), p. 189 and Don Rojas, 'A Revolution Betrayed but not Destroyed', *Caribbean Perspective*, Vol. 2, no. 2, Spring 1984.
7. 'Interview with George Louison: New Jewel Leader Describes Revolution's Overthrow', *Intercontinental Press*, Vol. 22, no. 7, 16 April 1984, p. 208.
8. See Lewis, *Grenada: The Jewel Despoiled*, 1987.
9. See Lewis, 1987, p. 174 and Charles Mills, 'Getting Out of the Cave: Tension Between Democracy and Elitism in Marx's Theory of Cognitive Liberation', *Social and Economic Studies*, Vol. 39, no. 1, March 1990.
10. See Manning Marable, *African and Caribbean Politics: From Kwame Nkrumah to Maurice Bishop*, (London: Verso, 1987).
11. Lewis, 1987, p. 80.
12. See Jay R. Mandle, *Big Revolution, Small Country: The Rise and Fall of the Grenada Revolution*, (Maryland: The North-South Publishing Company, 1985), especially p. 54 passim, where he speaks about the paternalistic character of the revolution, Tony Thorndike, *Grenada: Politics, Economics and Society* (London: Frances Pinter, 1985) and Brian Meeks, *Social Formation and People's Revolution: A Grenadian Study*, PhD Thesis, University of the West Indies, Jamaica, 1988, especially Ch. 2, 'The Social Formation'. The weakness in Meeks's study is a tendency to rely on Althusserian theoretical constructs to drive home the point that the agents were operating within if not bound by, well-entrenched structures. This of course, occurred

180    *Caribbean Revolutions and Revolutionary Theory*

in a context of a deep concern with the absence of structures in earlier studies and its polemical bias might therefore be understood, if not excused.

13. See *A Note on Grenada Disturbances, February–March 1951*, Colonial Office Grenada Document, 1951.
14. See for example, Ken Post's study of the Jamaican social revolt of 1938, *Arise Ye Starvelings*, (The Hague, Boston, London: Martinus Nijhoff, 1978).
15. See Woodville Marshall, 'Notes on Peasant Development in the West Indies Since 1838', *Social and Economic Studies*, Vol. 17, no. 3, 1968, p. 255.
16. M. G. Smith, 'Structure and Crisis in Grenada', *The Plural Society in the British West Indies*, (Berkeley and Los Angeles: University of California Press, 1965), p. 269.
17. M. G. Smith, *Dark Puritan* (Kingston, 1963), p. 23.
18. M. G. Smith, *Stratification in Grenada*, (Berkeley and Los Angeles: University of California Press, 1965), pp. 237–8.
19. Gordon Lewis, *The Growth of the Modern West Indies* (New York, London: Modern Reader, 1968), p. 104.
20. Trevor Munroe, *The Politics of Constitutional Decolonisation, Jamaica, 1944-1962* (Jamaica: ISER, 1972), p. 14.
21. See *The West Indian Census, 1946, Vol. 11*, p. vii.
22. See Lewis, 1987, p. 7
23. Munroe, 1972, p.180.
24. See Jack Harewood, 'Population Growth in Grenada in the Twentieth Century', *Social and Economic Studies*, Vol. 15, no. 1, June 1966.
25. See, for example, W. Richard Jacobs, *Butler vs. The King: Riots and Sedition in 1937*, (Port of Spain: Key, 1976).
26. See M. G. Smith, 'Structure and Crisis In Grenada', 1965, pp. 282–3.
27. See *Note on Grenada Disturbances, February–March 1951*.
28. See Trevor Munroe, 1972, p. 33.
29. *Note on Grenada Disturbances*, p. 11.
30. See Pat Emmanuel, *Crown Colony Politics in Grenada, 1917–1951*, (Barbados: ISER, 1978).
31. See Archie Singham, *The Hero and the Crowd in a Colonial Polity* (New Haven: Yale University Press, 1968), p. 296.
32. See Lewis, 1987, p. 16.
33. Lewis, 1968, p. 158.
34. Singham, 1968, p. 277.
35. Ibid., 1968, p. 266.
36. See *Report of the Commission of Inquiry into the Control of Government Expenditure in Grenada, During 1961 and Subsequently*, (St Georges, Grenada: Government Printers,1962).
37. Singham, 1968, p. 212.
38. Ibid., p. 215.
39. Commission of Inquiry, 1962, para. 57.
40. See Pat Emmanuel, *General Elections in the Eastern Caribbean: A Handbook* (Barbados: ISER, 1979), p. 47.
41. See Ann Spackman, *Constitutional Development of the West Indies 1922–1968* (Caribbean Universities Press/Bowker, England, 1975), p. 382.
42. Three factors facilitated Gairy. In 1955 Hurricane Janet had destroyed the crops on many estates, forcing the planters into heavy debt to recover their losses. Then, falling nutmeg prices in the late fifties made it difficult for them to repay these debts. Finally, the growth of tourism in South St Georges was attracting labour from the land, increasing its average price and further

reducing the viability of most estates. See Bernard Coard, *The Role of the State in Agriculture* (Guyana: ISER UWI, IDS, May 1978, p. 7).

43. See Ibid., p. 2.
44. Ibid., p. 23.
45. See *Hansard*, 19 December 1969, p. 20.
46. See George Brizan, *The Nutmeg Industry, Grenada's Black Gold* (St George's, Grenada, 1977).
47. See *Abstract of Statistics, 1979* (St Georges, Grenada: Central Statistical Office) p. 126.
48. See Norma Abdullah, *The Labour Force in the Commonwealth Caribbean* (Trinidad: ISER, 1977), p. 20.
49. Grenada's balance of visible trade fell from EC$–18.79 million in 1969 to –35.86 million in 1971 and then to –27.97 million in 1973. See *Abstract, 1979*, p. 17. Net immigration was significantly positive for the first time in nine years in 1970. Between 1960 and 1970, there was an average outflow of 1000 persons while from 1971–72, there was an average inflow for those two years of 3100 persons. See *Abstract, 1979*, p. 17.
50. *Abstract, 1979*, p. 103.
51. See, for example, Brian Meeks, *The Development of the 1970 Revolution in Trinidad and Tobago*, MSC Thesis (unpublished), University of the West Indies, 1977, Ivor Oxaal, *Race and Revolutionary Consciousness*, (Cambridge Mass., London: Schenkman, 1971).
52. Brian Meeks, *Social Formation and People's Revolution: A Grenadian Study*, PhD thesis, University of the West Indies, 1988, p. 197.
53. See Eric Gairy, radio broadcast, 3 May 1970, in *Grenada: Commission of Inquiry into the Breakdown of Law and Order and Police Brutality* (Duffus Commission), 27 February 1975, (Kingston, Jamaica), p. 30.
54. See The Emergency Powers Act, Grenada Act No. 10 of 1970, pp. 34–5.
55. See W. Richard Jacobs and Ian Jacobs, *Grenada: The Route to Revolution,* (Havana: Cuadernos Casa, 1980), Ch. 8.
56. See Lewis, 1987, pp. 16–19.
57. See Emmanuel, 1979, p. 51.
58. See *Unfree and Unfair Elections – 1976*, People's Alliance Pamphlet, which examines the 1972 elections in detail.
59. Meeks, 1988, p. 201.
60. See Message from Lord Balniel to Hon. Herbert Blaize, Leader of the Grenada Opposition, 31 May 1973, *M.F. no. 7212*.
61. See Questions and Answers on NJM, *The New Jewel*, Vol. 2, no. 8, 3 March 1974, p. 6. It is of interest to note, though not damaging to the overall conclusion, that on closer examination only three of the five persons with tertiary education could be said to have come from a longstanding middle-class family. The parents of Coard, Radix and Bishop, were all in their own right middle-class, although Bishop's father had gone the route of a self-made man, working in the Aruban refineries and then building himself up as a businessman on his return. Whiteman's and Noel's family were definitely small landholders and they escaped the cycle of poverty by migrating to England and then doggedly pursuing their chosen careers. A rider then, would suggest that migration, as in Gairy's day, continued to be a critical avenue of escape from the suffocating structures of Grenadian society, and a weak middle meant that returning educated immigrants, still retaining the gloss of foreign experience, easily fitted into the structures of patronage and deference which have been suggested.

62. See Meeks, 1977, pp. 246–93.
63. Teddy Victor, Statement, NJM Coordinating Council Minutes, 21 July 1974, *M.F. no. 7213*.
64. For the early NJM's organisational structure, see How NJM is Organised, *M.F. no. 7213*. For the MAP positions on strategy and tactics for the anti-Gairy struggle, see MAP Position Paper No.1, 1972, *M.F. no. 8559*, and On Strategy and Tactics, October 1972, *M.F. no. 8559*.
65. Norman Girvan, *Keynote Address, 2nd Conference of Caribbean Graduate Students*, mimeo, Kingston, July, 1990.
66. See *The New Jewel*, Vol. 2 no.1, 15 March 1974.
67. See *The New Jewel*, Vol. 2 no. 44, 1974.
68. See *The New Jewel*, Vol .2 no. 44.
69. See *The New Jewel*, Vol. 2 no. 1, which gives a detailed listing of incidents between May and September 1973.
70. Dee Duffus Commission, 1975.
71. See Duffus Commission, 1975.
72. See *The New Jewel*, Vol. 1, nos 37 and 38, December 1973.
73. See Duffus Commission, 1975.
74. See Alister Hughes' verbatim recording of the events in the Duffus Commission, 1975, pp. 208–214.
75. See Chris Holness, 'The Present Political Situation in Grenada', *Socialism!*, Vol. 2, no. 1, Kingston, January 1975.
76. The Workers Liberation League (WLL) was the pre-party organisation which eventually became the Workers Party of Jamaica (WPJ) in 1978 with Trevor Munroe as its General Secretary.
77. Chris Holness, 1975.
78. See Marable, 1987, p. 235.
79. This insight comes from a discussion with Chester Humphrey who was an original member of the NJM and an early member of the Bureau with responsibility for Caribbean and Pan African affairs.
80. See Maurice Bishop, Some proposals for the Regeneration and Reactivation of the Movement, April 1975, MF no. 7994.
81. See Lewis, 1987, pp. 29–30.
82. See The New Agreement out of Bureau Meeting, 12 and 18 April *M.F.* 1975, *no. 7994*.
83. Bernard Coard, Fighting Membership of NJM, 22–3 June 1974, *M.F. no. 7994*.
84. See *The New Jewel*, Vol. 2, no. 8, 3 March 1974.
85. *Informal Interview with Chester Humphrey, 1990.* Humphrey and Jim Wardally had jumped bail in the US where it is alleged that they were involved in the export of weapons, purportedly for the 13 March overthrow. After the 1983 invasion, the US government tried to extradite Humphrey to face these charges, but in the face of popular opposition, the Government, at first hesitant, refused to send him. Now, Humphrey is President of Grenada's largest union, the Technical and Allied Workers' Union (TAWU) and an independent Senator representing labour.
86. *Interview with Nazim Burke, 1984.*
87. See Emmanuel, 1979, pp. 19 and 47.
88. See, for example, Jenny Pearce, *Under the Eagle: US Intervention in Central America and the Caribbean* (London: Latin American Bureau, 1982).
89. Although this was only one factor, there are credible charges of CIA-inspired

destabilisation contributing to the 1980 defeat of Manley's party, the PNP by the pro-American opposition, the Jamaica Labour Party (JLP), led by Edward Seaga. See, for example, Michael Kaufman, *Jamaica Under Manley: Dilemmas of Socialism and Democracy,* (London: Zed, 1983).

90.  See Howard Wiarda, 'Aftermath of Grenada: The Impact of the US Action on Revolutionary Prospects in Central America', in Valenta and Ellison (eds), 1984, p. 11.

91.  See Anthony Maingot, 'Grenada and the Caribbean Basin: Mutual Linkages and Influences', in Valenta and Ellison (eds), 1984, p. 35.

92.  See *Free West Indian,* Vol. 1, no. 23, March 1980, p. 14.

93.  Although some of this information is in the public domain, details on the vote, the precise size of the force and the amount of weapons comes from an unpublished document by Ewart Layne, Lieutenant Colonel in the disbanded People's Revolutionary Army (PRA) and at present one of the prisoners awaiting results of the appeal motion in the Maurice Bishop murder trial. See Ewart Layne, *Cuba–Grenada Relations and the October Tragedy,* St Georges (handwritten) 1990.

94.  Maurice Bishop, 'Line of March for the Party', in *Grenada Documents: An Overview and Selection* (Washington: US Departments of State and Defence, 1984), pp. 1–19.

95.  Merle Hodge and Chris Searle (eds), *Is Freedom We Making* (Barbados: PRG, 1982), p. 81.

96.  Mandle, 1985, pp. 53–4.

97.  See Lewis, 1987, p. 33.

98.  See, in particular, Chris Searle, *Grenada Morning: A Memoir of the 'Revo',* (London: Karia, 1989).

99.  Cited in Chris Searle, *Grenada: The Struggle Against Destabilization,* (London: Writers and Readers, 1983), p. 102.

100.  See Mike Morrissey, 'Country Preferences of Schoolchildren in Seven Caribbean Territories', in *Caribbean Quarterly,* Vol. 29, nos 3 and 4, September–December 1983, p. 7.

101.  See 'Grenada Chamber Gives its Nod', *Guardian,* 20 March 1979.

102.  See *The Washington Post,* 6 July 1979.

103.  See *The New Jewel,* 4 May 1980.

104.  See *Free West Indian,* Special Edition, 25 June 1980.

105.  See Pearce, 1982, p. 174.

106.  See *Report on the National Economy for 1981 and the Prospects for 1982,* presented by Bernard Coard, 29 January, 1982, St Georges, 1982, p. 64.

107.  See especially, Claremont Kirton, *Public Policy and Private Capital in the Transition to Socialism: Grenada, 1979–1983,* mimeo, 1985.

108.  See Emmanuel *et al.,* 1986, p. 123.

109.  See *Free West Indian,* Vol. 2, no. 29, 18 July 1981.

110.  Searle and Hodge, 1981, see especially p. 41.

111.  *Interview with Claremont Kirton,* 1986.

112.  *Interview with Bernard Bourne.*

113.  See Rosa Luxemburg, *The Russian Revolution and Leninism or Marxism?* (Ann Arbor: Michigan University Press, 1970).

114.  It is true that in June 1983 a Constitutional Commission had been set up which would draft a new constitution for public debate. But it is also fair to conclude that the direction that the PRG was moving in was that of single-party elections along a Cuban-type model. This had been the policy of the

party as far back as 1973 when it had been influenced by the Jamesian approach and Selwyn Strachan confirmed this in a July 1983 interview, when he indicated that there would be nominations in the electoral process for party members and 'people from the communities' – clearly excluding opposition parties. See *Free West Indian*, 9 July 1983.

115. See Grenada Documents, 1984, pp. 1–20.
116. Minutes of Extraordinary Meeting of Central Committee of NJM, 12–15 October 1982 in Grenada Documents, 1984, p. 105–1.
117. See *NJM Membership List as of July 1983*, private collection.
118. See Meeks, 1988, p. 332.
119. See Letter to Political Bureau NJM from Phyllis Coard Chairperson, Women's Committee, re Problems Affecting Women Party Members, 11 May 1982, *Grenada Documents*, 1984, p. 79–1.
120. See for example, Lewis, 1987, and Anthony Payne, Paul Sutton and Tony Thorndike, *Grenada: Revolution and Invasion* (London and Sydney: Croom Helm, 1984).
121. See Reich and Smith, 1984, p. 4. Frederick Pryor's study, while largely critical of the economy, is more balanced and recognises that there was significant improvement in most macro-economic indicators, but not to the extent suggested by the PRG. See Frederick Pryor, *Revolutionary Grenada: A Study in Political Economy* (New York, Westport, London, Praeger, 1986).
122. See Manifesto of the New Jewel Movement in *Independence for Grenada, Myth or Reality?*, Institute of International Relations, St Augustine, 1974.
123. See Maurice Bishop, 'Line of March for the Party', Grenada Documents, 1984, pp. 1–10.
124. See this debate in Lewis, 1987, p. 31.
125. See Mandle, 1984, pp. 23–33.
126. Clive Thomas, *The Next Time Around: Radical Options and Caribbean Economy*, mimeo, First Conference of Caribbean Economists, Kingston,1987.
127. See *World Bank Economic Memorandum on Grenada*, Washington DC, 1982.
128. See Meeks, 1988, pp. 412–19.
129. See Meeks, 1988, pp. 365–7.
130. See *World Bank, Economic Memorandum on Grenada*, 1982, p. 3.
131. See Pryor, 1986, p. 46; Meeks, 1988, p. 398.
132. See for 1978 under Gairy, *Grenada, Estimates and Expenditure for the Year 1978*, St Georges, 1978, for 1983, see *Report on the National Economy for 1982 and the Budget Plan for 1983 and Beyond*, St Georges, 1983.
133. See Economic Bureau Meeting, 22 April 1983, *M.F. no. 2293*.
134. See TAWU Report, June 1983, *M.F. no. 3290*.
135. Central Committee Report on First Plenary Session 13–19 July, 1982, in Grenada Documents, 1984, p. 110–12
136. See, for example, O'Shaughnessy, 1984, p. 104, Fidel Castro, 1986, p.153; Lewis, 1987, p. 80.
137. See Louison, 1984, p. 208; Marable, 1987, p. 255; Lewis, 1987, pp. 42–3.
138. See for example, Marable, 1987, p. 255.
139. See O'Shaughnessy, p. 189.
140. See Marable, pp. 250–1.
141. National Security Report, *M.F. no. 4841*.
142. Minutes of the Organizing Committee (OC) Meeting, 14 April 1983, *M.F. no. 2301*.

143. Workers Committee Report on Socialism classes, 4 July–19 August 1983, *M.F. no. 2032.*
144. See Layne, 1990.
145. Meeks, 1988, pp. 460–1. Louison's comments in Louison, 1984, p. 209.
146. Cited in *Free West Indian,* 19 March 1989.
147. EPICA, *Grenada: The Peaceful Revolution,* Washington DC, 1982, p. 122.
148. I am thankful to Nazim Burke and Chester Humphrey for early information on OREL, which I have taken on their word, but which also corresponds with my own reading of the group's documents and those from the NJM.
149. Castro, 1986, p. 213.
150. The implications of Leninism, which constricted party size, together with the realities of underdevelopment, which simply limited the pool of available talent, is captured in Ewart Layne's totally unrealistic and voluntarist listing of his tasks in 1983. In addition to being responsible for the overall running of the PRA and commander of the first military region, he was on a weekly basis the tutor for six political classes, study guide for applicant members to the party, liaison for the NJM party support group of workers on the airport construction site, Chairman of the Board of Directors of the Grenada Farms Corporation (the umbrella body which had taken over Gairy's state farms), Chairman of the Board of Directors of Grenada Agro-Industries Limited, and a member of the Political Bureau and of the Central Committee. He also, as a leader of the revolution, had from time to time to address Parish Councils and other meetings of a political nature. See Layne, 1990.
151. Louison, Interview, St Georges, 1984.
152. See Layne, 1990.
153. See, for example, Maurice Bishop, 'Freedom of the Press and Imperialist Destabilization', *Maurice Bishop Speaks: The Grenada Revolution, 1979–1983* (New York: Pathfinder, 1983), p. 157 passim.
154. 'Maurice Bishop Speaks to US Working People', Bishop, 1983, p. 287 passim.
155. See Interview with Chester Humphrey.
156. Interview with Claremont Kirton.
157. See Layne, 1990.
158. See Minutes of Extraordinary Meeting of CC, NJM, 12–15 October 1982, Grenada Documents, 1984, p. 105–1.
159. See Layne, 1990.
160. 12–15 October CC Minutes.
161. 12–15 October CC minutes.
162. Central Committee Report on First Plenary Session, 13–19 July 1983, Grenada Documents, 1984, p. 110–16.
163. Minutes of Emergency Meeting of NJM CC, 26 August 1983, Grenada Documents, p. 111–1.
164. Lewis, 1987, p. 44.
165. Extraordinary meeting of CC NJM, 14–16 September, 1983, Grenada Documents, 1984, pp. 112–14.
166. NJM CC Minutes, 14–16 September, Grenada Documents, pp. 112–32.
167. Minutes of Extraordinary General Meeting of Full Members, 25 September 1983, Grenada Documents, 1984, pp. 113–15.
168. See Paul Seabury and Walter McDougal (eds), *The Grenada Papers* (San Francisco, ICS, 1984), p. 314.
169. At an OC meeting on 19 September, Coard, newly returned to the body, suggested that there was a need to find 'creative ways to involve the masses

in the selection and promotion of party comrades', Minutes of OC, 26 September 1983, *M.F. no. 2018.*

170.   This is the position taken by a senior party member Nazim Burke, who was a member of the mission. *Interview with Nazim Burke.*

171.   See Errol George's statement, 12 October 1983, *M.F. no. 2646.*

172.   See Tony Gifford, *The Grenada Murder Trial: No Case for Hanging,* Committee for Human Rights in Grenada, London, 1987.

# Conclusion: Post-colonial revolutions from the middle

And in any case, how many of those who made the great social revolutions of the world foresaw the actual results of their endeavours?

Eric Hobsbawm

What then can be rescued of the image and meaning of revolution from the Caribbean experience? First, it seems fair to agree with Dunn[1] that revolutions are highly complex events located in a particular time and place, each in turn influenced and transformed by the preceding accumulation of revolutionary experiences and as such, need desperately to be de-linked from a teleological notion of history. Revolutions, like life in all its multiple dimensions, are like multi-level chess games, with incalculable options and choices at any single moment. There is no deterministic explanation which can account for Fidel Castro's chance survival of the *Granma* landing; or Fonseca's death two years before the triumph of the Nicaraguan Revolution; or Maurice Bishop's decision to march on the fort, instead of meeting with the throngs waiting in the market square; nor to explain adequately the 'gridlock of events' in Grenada, with purposeful and chance occurrences piling one on top of the other, until a traffic-jam of consequences forces history in a particular direction; nor is there an explanation which can say with certainty how these revolutions would have unfolded if these events had gone differently. Much of the study of revolution and indeed, life, is a matter of chance and cannot be reduced to simple formulae.[2]

Yet, while rejecting a positivist approach which would postulate 'necessary and sufficient' conditions for revolutionary situations and outcomes, there are nonetheless, 'resonances' running through all three examples, which are shared to a degree, with other revolutions in other societies and times. An abandonment of determinism cannot mean an abandonment of a search for commonalities, discrepancies and counter-examples. With some trepidation then, we might suggest if not a taxonomy, then perhaps a definition and ordering of the mid-to-late twentieth-century Caribbean Revolution. Located in the constellation of revolutionary movements, it can be described as a post-colonial revolution from the 'middle'. In this, it is fairly easily differentiated from Skocpol's 'social revolution' which is initiated as the result of sharp, often military competition between 'great states'. The attempt by the more backward among these to modernise and compete and the resultant crisis which this generates in the state and in the society as a whole, is the sequence of events leading to revolutionary situation. For the small, post-colonial states, as Farhi suggested in her study of Nicaragua and Iran, crisis is not generated by war, or, strictly speaking 'inter-state competition', but by a complex of factors which can crudely be reduced to their subordinate and tenuous position in the world economy and system of nation-states. It is not coincidental, as Halliday convincingly posits, that between 1974 and 1980, in the most important 'wave' of this century, some fourteen revolutions occurred in the Third World,[3] including two of our Caribbean trio. It is at the conjuncture of a window opened up by the bi-polar competition between great states, coupled with a favourable regional balance among lesser states – the permissive world context – and an eco-nomic crisis – usually generated by the cyclical recurrence of recession in the world economy, that Third World, post-colonial revolutions occur. But here, a further distinction is required, because these revolutions are not in the French, Russian or Chinese sense, 'accompanied by class-based revolts from below': they are led by the middle, guided by a middle-class concep-tion of ideological 'correctness' and consolidated – if this stage is reached – with the reincorporation of the popular classes under the hegemony of the middle. This was certainly reflective of the Cuban and Grenadian experi-ences, but the Nicaraguan revolution provides an apparent counter-exam-ple. Nicaragua can best be described as a 'subverted' revolution, in which the middle-class revolutionaries lost hegemony and control, as they in turn, under popular pressure, were partially transformed in their perception of the necessity for middle-class hegemony.[4]

But if there are clear distinctions between the great, social revolution and the post-colonial revolution from the middle, it also needs to be differenti-ated from the classic type of 'revolution from above'. Ellen Trimberger's study of the Turkish Revolution, the Meiji Restoration in Japan, Peru and Egypt, suggested five typical characteristics for revolution from above, viz:

1. The takeover of political power and the initiation of political change is led by the highest military and civil bureaucrats of the old regime.
2. There is little or no mass participation in the revolutionary takeover or the initiation of change.
3. The extra-legal takeover and the initiation of change is accompanied by very little violence, counter-revolution, etc.
4. The initiation of change is undertaken in a pragmatic, step-by-step manner, using the existing bureaucratic apparatus for radical aims.
5. Nonetheless, military bureaucrats who lead a revolution from above,

destroy the political and economic base of the aristocracy or upper class.[5]

Most notably, the revolution from the middle *does not involve* existing bureaucrats in leading positions in the state apparatus, but disenchanted, young, *potential* state-builders, whose avenue to power has been blocked by previous events. In this, it is important to note that all three successful overthrows were possible after unsuccessful rehearsals: in Cuba, the 1933 overthrow of Machado; in Nicaragua, Sandino's undefeated but ultimately unsuccessful war against US-backed neo-colonialism; and in Grenada, the upsurge of 1951, which brought Eric Gairy to prominence.

In all three examples, these tests to the survival of the state – themselves initiated by a round of economic recession and external political conjuncture – could not spark off a process of revolution from above, because of the absence of an entrenched military/civilian bureaucracy, autonomous, self-conscious and willing to dynamically initiate change. At the same time, we should note the weakness of the traditional oligarchy, whose state of decline is one of the accelerators of crisis in the first instance, the relative weakness of the dependent national bourgeoisie, and from 'below', the corresponding organisational and political weaknesses of workers and peasants, who, play a role in the revolt, but are unable to define an independent project.

The result, in this 'vacuum of leadership', is the emergence of the quixotic leader, the Bonaparte who, from his relatively humble background, or lowly military position, is able to appeal to the revolting masses, but at the same time, as the Governor said of Gairy in 1951, was willing to 'play'[6] by the rules of the game. These rules were based on the recognition by the hegemonic power that the old ruling bloc of compromises and alliances at the top was no longer viable and, in a world rapidly moving into a bi-polar frame of reference, adherence to the international positions of the dominant power was the most important criterion for the admissibility of a post-colonial regime. Thus, from the State Department's, and in Grenada's case, the Colonial Office's, perspective, the appropriate slogan might well have been, borrowing Castro's later remark, 'within the boundaries of the Monroe Doctrine and anti-communism, anything: Outside, nothing'.

Here, however, the parallel with Marx's notion of Bonapartism begins to break down, because if that phenomenon was the product of a fairly developed nineteenth-century capitalist society,[7] Caribbean Bonapartism emerges in the context of weak and dependent capitalist relations. If Bonaparte 'in the last instance' came down on the side of the capitalist class, the Caribbean Bonapartes saw themselves in their own right, as autonomous accumulators of power and wealth. In the context of a fractured ruling bloc in which they had been given *carte blanche* to rule from above, Somoza, Batista and Gairy used the state to make economic and political incursions firstly against their competitors 'up above' and inevitably against their initial supporters 'down below'. Land was seized from the oligarchy; traditional areas of the economy controlled by the bourgeoisie were encroached upon and both these strata were increasingly marginalised from their already tenuous positions in the state. Both these groups resisted the monopolistic tendencies of the ruler, as did the popular forces, but it was from another excluded group, the intellectual middle, that surprisingly, the greatest resistance emerged.

In locating the Caribbean intellectual middle, we should differentiate it from Nun's[8] usage of the term, which identifies the middle as a stratum frustrated by the oligarchy from becoming bourgeois. The middle in our context is not in the first instance concerned with economic accumulation, unlike its 'Bonapartist' oppressors, but is a state-building middle. Either themselves from intellectual or lower middle-class backgrounds, or if more wealthy, as in Castro's case, out of the mainstream of the local oligarchy, they are usually trained at university in law or the humanities. In the confines of relatively backward societies, more so in Grenada and Nicaragua than Cuba, this tiny group of persons possesses a virtual monopoly on new ideas and on independent thought.

While Régis Debray's[9] identification of this group is by no means novel, his focus on the high intellectuals in French society and their inflated, indeed, exclusive role in opinion-formation, is an important point of reference. Debray's study traces the growth of intellectual dominance through the university system in the nineteenth century, then through the printing press and consolidating in the modern electronic 'mediocracy'. The suggestion here is that while Debray's thesis refers to an advanced 'post-industrial' society, in an ironic sense, the small size and limited intellectual field in the Caribbean, compensates for its technological backwardness, endowing the intellectuals with influence at least commensurate to the French *haut intellectuel*.[10]

With no deep tradition of property relations; with limited alternative avenues for promotion in the weak, attenuated private sector; with, in the Cuban case at least, a tradition of promotion through the vehicle of the state and in the other cases, the recognition that this was the natural avenue for the fulfilment of ambitions; then the state-building middle becomes a dangerous force, a 'loose cannon on the deck' when, in this matrix, its natural avenues are frustrated. The existence of such a configuration, with young, ambitious, frustrated elements from the middle, is not, historically speaking, a peculiar event. Trimberger identifies for example, the 'Loyalists' in Japan after Perry's 1853 intervention, and the 'Young Turks' in Turkey of the 1870s, who

> were led by intellectuals with relatively high status, with practical experience in civil or military bureaucratic offices, and

with some Western training. They were all led to revolt against high bureaucratic reformers because of frustrated personal ambition.[11]

In the end, these middle, bureaucratic revolts failed because, as she suggests, their programmes were unclear, they had ineffective organisations and all failed to develop independent, popular, power bases.[12] While there are clearly many differences between the young intellectuals of Ottoman Turkey and Tokugawa Japan and the Caribbean experience, not the least of which is the latter's location within the bureaucracy, it is important that Trimberger, generally a structuralist, should point to questions of strategy and tactics, i.e. questions of *agency* for this early example of middle-class failure. For it is our contention that as the stratum most open to ideas and expression – the 'chattering classes' – and least tied to a purely economic base with its influence on the determination of social consciousness, the intellectual middle is uniquely placed to respond to the cumulative and available ideological context. This in part accounts for the later successes, building, as it were, on the earlier examples of failure. In this, though, the Caribbean contingent is closer to Debray's 'middle intellectual', receiving fragments of political thought some time after its eclipse in the domain of the 'high intellectuals' in the metropole. Thus, the cumulative and available ideological context is seldom a fully developed ideational system, but constructed in bits and pieces from metropolitan diffusion and local experience. And, it is not so much received as a critical analysis, but more often than not, as manifest truth.

In the mid-to-late twentieth century, the cumulative and available ideological context provided the frustrated, state-building middle with a workable strategy for the seizure and consolidation of power, under the rubrics of 'nationalism' and 'Marxism–Leninism' and including the following elements:

1. The view that small states, even 'micro' states like Grenada could attain genuine independence via the route of revolution and, ultimately, through 'socialist orientation', achieve socialism.
2. That the balance or 'correlation' of forces in the world had changed and that revolutions, once victorious, would receive assistance from the prestigious and increasingly powerful socialist world, allowing them to survive the machinations of imperialism.
3. That in order to seize and retain power, the Leninist prescription of a tightly-organised vanguard of selectively chosen fighters was the only effective tool to ensure victory, and beyond that, the consolidation of revolutionary power.
4. That 'bourgeois democracy' and its trappings, including bourgeois notions of 'rights' and 'justice' should be discarded in the post-

revolutionary state and substituted for by 'proletarian' forms of participatory democracy and economic rights.

5. That the Marxian notion of historical materialism was 'true' and therefore revolution and socialism were inevitable.

It is fair to say that from my own perspective in Kingston in the late seventies, such an approach did not seem particularly far-fetched. In every case of revolution, with the notable exception of Iran, Leninist parties and Leninist tactics were proving eminently successful. Havana, at the 11th World Festival of Youth and Students in 1978 was not only a showcase for the unity, solidarity and prosperity of the Cuban people, but a victory parade for the growing wave of revolutionary states. The Soviet Union had proved in the Cuban case that it would provide lavish assistance to the 'newly free' states; and, where the Soviets were parsimonious, as the case of Grenada illustrated, the Cubans were more than willing to step in and fill the gap.

But while Leninist strategies proved highly effective for the seizure of power, the chosen post-revolution strategy of socialist orientation, or in the Cuban case, even more rapid transition of state ownership and control, proved to be, in a word, unworkable. What was perceived in Brezhnevian doctrine to be a changed correlation of forces,[13] was nothing more than a temporary window of possibility. The Soviet Union was never able to provide an 'economic umbrella' of trade and aid for all the proliferating revolutionary states,[14] beyond one or two showcase examples, which even in the case of Cuba, retained the main structural distortions in its economy. Nor, in the far more credible arena of military protection, as the experiences of Nicaragua, Mozambique and above all Afghanistan, so evidently illustrated, was the Soviet Union able to protect revolutionary states against the tactic of 'low-intensity conflict',[15] initiated by an aggressive and invigorated United States under Ronald Reagan's leadership.

And, as the eighties lengthened, it became increasingly clear that the Soviet Union itself, bled white by its military competition with the Americans and foreign economic commitments which its creaking, over-centralised system could not support, would have to withdraw on the best available terms from the Cold War. Under Gorbachev, and particularly after his 1988 election as President, the USSR distanced itself from the ideological position of the Brezhnev years that revolutionary movements in the Third World were progressive and should necessarily be supported, and severely reduced its commitment to this region, at the same time seeking compromise and working together with the United States to reduce tension in a number of conflict areas, including South Asia, Southern Africa and Central America. Writing in 1989 before the fall of the Berlin Wall, Fred Halliday's position was that these developments, together with the talks and agreements on strategic and nuclear weapons signalled the end of the Cold War, but not the end of Third World crises nor the end of Soviet/US competition.[16] In defence of the first proposition, he advanced the view, which has been implicit throughout this study, that Third World crises and revolutions have their own internal dynamic, although they operate on, and are influenced by, an international field; for the second proposition, however, he suggested that the underlying cause of conflict was the competition between two substantially different socioeconomic systems which were irreconcilable and would therefore continue. From the perspective of the nineties, with an Eastern bloc no longer in existence, with the Soviet Confederation heading, albeit chaotically, toward a market economy and with the Communist Party out of office, this view would seem to require serious revision. The US leadership in the military force against Iraq and the willingness of the Soviets to comply with US resolutions in the Security Council supporting war, all point to the end, not just of the Cold War, but of bipolarity.

Socialist orientation as a guide to development was therefore, from its inception, fatally flawed, as were other elements in the ideological context which merit mention. The vanguard, effective tool as it was for overthrow, as the Grenada example demonstrated, was damaging to the efficient organisation of the post-revolutionary state. Equally, the absence in the Marxist frame and its Leninist and Stalinist interpretations, of an adequate discussion of democracy, of the philosophical basis for 'rights' and of an alternative ethics,[17] indirectly facilitated the authoritarian profile of leadership, particularly in Cuba and Grenada, as it was the break from orthodoxy, assisted by less entrenched currents of thought, which played a role in the FSLN's devolution of centralised power. Yet, in a period when the baby is being thrown out with the bath water, it is important to offer the *caveat*, as Lukes does, that Marxism

> offers a conception, a way of interpreting the concept of free-
> dom, and of the constraints upon or obstacles to it, that is far
> deeper and richer than negative and classical liberal views. As
> an account of the sources of unfreedom and as a vision of
> emancipation . . . it cannot be ignored by those who profess
> to take liberty seriously, which must include those who take
> socialism seriously.[18]

If then, we have focused on the middle and the importance of its received ideas as critical, if not necessary and sufficient elements in the making of revolution, this points all the more clearly to areas of our loose framework which require further thought and research. The permissive world context for one, has been introduced as a 'fact', but its nature, outside of a descriptive frame, has been insufficiently explained. Halliday, without Wallerstein's ideological baggage, has pointed nonetheless, to the fairly regular recurrence of revolutionary waves, going back as far as 1848. In the twentieth century, an early wave can be identified among countries that had 'avoided outright colonisation, but were subjected to partial modernisation by capital',[19] including Persia, Egypt, Russia, the Ottoman Empire and Mexico. In the post-Second World War period, a first wave (1944–54) saw revolutions in Albania, Yugoslavia, China, Korea, Vietnam and Bolivia and unsuccessful attempts in the Philippines, Iran, Malaya and Guatemala. A second postwar wave saw Iraq, North Yemen, Cuba, the Congo and Algeria have successful revolutions between 1958 and 1962 and then a long break occurs until between 1974 and 1980, fourteen revolutions, as previously mentioned, took place.

This study has argued that these openings are the result of temporary, recurring warps, which open up to the deeper rhythms of inter-statal competition and economic crises, but Wallerstein does present a powerful neo-Marxist *explanandum*, in his notion of dialectically unravelling crises heading inexorably towards world revolution. Further study of these waves is obviously necessary and germane to the very essence of the state-centred arguments explored here. But in addition, many other histories can and need to be written on the phenomenon of Caribbean revolution. If it remains our assertion that it is the crisis in the *statal classes* which precipitates the revolutionary situation, then it is the character of the entry of the forces from below, which mediates its eventual outcome. A 'Thompsonian' social history of those forces who fought alongside the Sandinistas, who sacrificed and continue sacrificing for the Cuban revolution and who stood up briefly but bravely against the American invasion of Grenada is glaringly absent.

The collapse of socialism in Eastern Europe, as Saddam Hussein's rapid entry into Kuwait so graphically illustrated, has not signalled the end of history. Crises will continue in the Third World, in which in some instances, middle-class elites, excluded from power, will seek to form alliances, adopt strategy from the available ideological context and attempt to construct revolutionary projects. Revolution, as the experience of the NICs of South East Asia has demonstrated, is not the only avenue to modernisation and development and, further, the end of the Cold War has laid to rest a particular conception of revolution based on assistance from socialist states. But revolution, by its very act, is an opening up of the historical options, loosening the constraints which inhibit change, and, like 'wormholes' in history, might shorten the route to a better society.

But even if John Dunn's less sanguine notion of revolution as being essentially a metaphor for power and direction in a world of uncertainty is correct, then future revolutionary movements, if and when they emerge, might learn from a new ideological context, which, taking its major lessons from the experiences we have examined, might try to: encourage the emergence of popular activity from below; allow the free and unfettered exchange of ideas; encourage a non-oligarchical market, limiting the power and scope of entrenched wealth based on privilege and tradition; allow all parties equal access to promulgate their views, with, critically, equal access to electoral resources; discuss and ratify a popular constitution and constantly return to the people to discuss and ratify important laws; and place limits on the power and authority of individuals and executives, in order to curtail the re-emergence of authoritarian government.

If determinism needs to be laid to rest, it might yet be a source of optimism to propose, as Callinicos and Anderson do, coming ironically, from a Marxist field, that over the past 1500 years, the balance in the relative roles played by structural conditions and conscious human agency in resolving organic societal crises, has shifted from the former to the latter.[20] This advances the hope that even if there is no map for the road ahead, gradually, via a process of groping from one historical conjuncture to the next, the possibility of a better polity, of humble people playing a greater role in social life, an increasing freedom to be involved in politics and 'from politics',[21] may yet be on the open-ended agenda of human history.

## Notes

1.   John Dunn, *Modern Revolutions: An Introduction to the Analysis of a Political Phenomenon*, Second Edition (Cambridge: Cambridge University Press, 1989), pp. 231–3.
2.   For the classic argument against crude positivism in the social sciences and particularly in the study of revolutionary phenomena, see Alasdair MacIntyre, 'Ideology, Social Science and Revolution', *Comparative Politics*, Vol. 5, no. 3, April 1973.
3.   See Fred Halliday, *Cold War, Third World: An Essay on Soviet-US Relations*, (London, Sydney: Hutchinson Radius, 1990), p. 29.
4.   This 'partial transformation' is brought home in an interview by Humberto Ortega who, controversially, has been retained by the Chamorro Government as head of the armed forces. In it, he upholds the view that the revolution still continues, but also supports the institutionalisation of multi-party elections and the constitutionality of the new government. In the final count, however, he bows to popular initiative over the purely constitutional government. His answer to the question 'Would you let Chamorro be overthrown?' is instructive: *Ortega*: 'As a soldier, I obey the law. As a revolutionary, I believe that the law has to be applied justly. We're not going to let anyone create chaos or try to overthrow the government. At the same time, if the government's actions are so drastic that they provoke people to take to the streets, we have to tell the leaders of the government that we can't save them', 'Juggling Past and Present, Humberto Ortega Insists his Sandinista Connection is no Obstacle to Stability', *Time*, 22 October 1990.
5.   See Ellen Kay Trimberger, *Revolution From Above: Military Bureaucrats and Development in Japan, Turkey, Egypt, Peru*, (New Brunswick, New Jersey: Transaction, 1978), p. 3.

194 Caribbean Revolutions and Revolutionary Theory

6.   See *A Note on Grenada Disturbances, February–March 1951*, Colonial Office, Grenada Documents, 1951.
7.   See Trimberger, 1978, p. 5.
8.   See Jose Nun, 'The Middle Class Military Coup Revisited', in Abraham Lowenthal and Samuel Fitch (eds), *Armies and Politics in Latin America*, Revised Edition (New York, London: Holmes and Meier, 1986).
9.   See Régis Debray, *Teachers, Writers, Celebrities: The Intellectuals of Modern France*, (London: Verso, 1981).
10.   Payne's recent analysis of the elevated role of intellectuals from the University of the West Indies in politics and thought in their respective territories supports this proposal. See Anthony Payne, *Governments, Intellectuals and International Relations: The Politics of the University of the West Indies, 1968–1984*, University of Warwick Occasional Papers in Caribbean Studies No. 7, 1990.
11.   Trimberger, 1978, p. 78.
12.   See ibid., 1978, pp. 83–92.
13.   See Halliday, 1990, p.100.
14.   See ibid., 1990, p. 110.
15.   See ibid., 1990, p. 103.
16.   See ibid., 1990, p. 163.
17.   See especially, Steven Lukes, *Marxism and Morality* (Oxford, New York: Oxford University Press, 1985).
18.   Lukes, 1985, p. 149.
19.   Halliday, 1990, p. 29.
20.   See Alex Callinicos, *Making History*, (Cambridge: Polity, 1989), p. 229 and Perry Anderson, *Arguments Within English Marxism*, (London: Verso, 1980).
21.   See Hannah Arendt, *On Revolution*, (Harmondsworth: Pelican, 1987) (first published, 1963) p. 279.

# Select bibliography

## *Reports and official documents*

*Grenada: Commission of Inquiry into the Breakdown of Law and Order*, (Duffus Commission) Kingston, 27 February, 1975.

*Report of the Commission of Inquiry into the Control of Government Expenditure in Grenada During 1961 and Subsequently*, (1962). St George's Government Printers.

Central Statistical Office (1979). *Abstract of Statistics*, St George's.

Colonial Office Report (1951). *A Note on Grenada Disturbances: February–March, 1951*, St George's.

World Bank (1982). *Economic Memorandum on Grenada*, Washington, DC.

## *NJM documents taken from Grenada in 1983*

These documents are mainly from those taken by the US forces after the October 1983 invasion. They are to be found in the National Archives in Washington, DC. The code at the end is from the filing system used in the National Archives and indicates the particular microfiche on which the document can be found.

Bernard Coard: Fighting Membership of NJM, 22–3 June 1974, *MF no. 7994*.

Economic Bureau Meeting, 22 April 1983, *MF no. 2293*.

Errol George's Statement, 12 October 1983, *MF no. 2646*.

How NJM is Organized, *MF no. 7213*.

MAP Position Paper No. 1, 1972, *MF no. 8559*.

Maurice Bishop: Some Proposals for the Regeneration and Reactivation of the Movement, April 1975, *MF no. 7994*.

Message from Lord Balniel to Hon. Herbert Blaize, *MF no. 7212*.

Minutes of the Organizing Committee (OC) Meeting, 14 April 1983, *MF no. 2301*.

Minutes of OC, 26 September 1983, *MF no. 2018*.

National Security Report, *MF no. 4841*.

On Strategy and Tactics, *MF no. 8559*.

TAWU Report, June 1983, *MF no. 3290*.

Teddy Victor Statement, NJM Coordinating Council Minutes, 21 July 1974, *MF no. 7213*.

The New Agreement out of Bureau Meeting, 12 and 18 April 1975, *MF no. 7994*.

Unfree and Unfair Elections, 1976, *People's Alliance Pamphlet, 1976*.

*Workers' Committee Report on Socialism Classes, 4 July–19 August 1983, MF no. 2032.*

# Newspapers and news services

Free West Indian
Latin American Weekly Report
Latin American Weekly Review
Latin American Regional Reports: Mexico and Central America
Latin American Regional Reports: Caribbean Report
The New Jewel
The New York Times
The Los Angeles Times
The Trinidad Guardian
The Miami Herald
The Independent
The Wall Street Journal
Time

# Books, theses and articles

Abdullah, Norma (1977). *The Labour Force in the Commonwealth Caribbean*, ISER, Trinidad.

Abel, Christopher and Torents, Nissa (eds). *José Martí: Revolutionary Democrat*, London: Athlone Press.

Althusser, Louis (1970). *For Marx*, New York: Vintage.

Anderson, Perry (1980). *Arguments Within English Marxism*, London: Verso.

Arendt, Hannah (1963). *On Revolution*, London: Faber and Faber.

Aya, Rod (1979). 'Theories of Revolution Reconsidered', *Theory and Society*, Vol. 8, no. 1.

Azicri, Max (1988). *Cuba: Politics, Economics and Society*, London, New York: Frances Pinter.

Berger, Peter and Michael Hsin-Huang Hsiao (1988). *In Search of an East Asian Development Model*, New Brunswick, New Jersey: Transaction Books.

Bermann, Karl (1986). *Under the Big Stick: Nicaragua and the United States Since 1848*, New York: South End Press.

Bishop, Maurice (1983). *Maurice Bishop Speaks: The Grenada Revolution 1979–1983*, New York, London, Sydney: Pathfinder.

_____ (1984). *Line of March for the Party, Grenada Documents: An Overview and Selection*, US Departments of State and Defense, Washington, DC.

Black, George (1981). *Triumph of the People: The Sandinista Revolution in Nicaragua*, London: Zed Press.

Blasier, Cole and Mesa-Lago, Carmelo (1979). *Cuba in the World*, Pittsburgh: Pittsburgh University Press.

Blomstrum, Magnus and Bjorn Hettne (1984). *Development Theory in Transition*, London, Zed Press.

Bonsal, Philip (1971). *Cuba, Castro and the United States*, Pittsburgh: University of Pittsburgh Press.

Brinton, Crane (1953). *The Anatomy of Revolution*, London: Jonathan Cape.

Brizan, George (n.d.). *The Nutmeg Industry: Grenada's Black Gold*, St George's.

Burbach, Roger and Orlando Nunez (1987). *Fire in the Americas: Forging a Revolutionary Agenda*, London: Verso.

Callinicos, Alex (1989). *Making History*, Cambridge: Polity.

Calvert, Peter (ed.) (1988). *The Central American Security System: North–South and East–West*, Cambridge: Cambridge University Press.

Castro, Fidel (1986). *Nothing Can Stop the Course of History*, Interview with Jeffrey M. Elliott and Mervyn Dymally, New York, London, Sydney: Pathfinder.

\_\_\_\_ (1989). *In Defense of Socialism: The Thirtieth Anniversary of the Cuban Revolution*, New York, London, Sydney, Toronto: Pathfinder.

Chaliand, Gerard (1977). *Revolution in the Third World*, Brighton: Harvester Press.

Christian, Shirley (1986). *Nicaragua: Revolution in the Family*, New York: Vintage.

Close, David (1988). *Nicaragua: Politics, Economics and Society*, London: Frances Pinter.

\_\_\_\_ and Carl Bridge (eds) (1985). *Revolution: A History of the Idea*, Sydney: Croom Helm.

Coard, Bernard (1982). *Report on the National Economy for 1981 and the Prospects for 1982*, St Georges.

\_\_\_\_ (1983). *Report on the National Economy for 1982 and the Budget Plan for 1983 and Beyond*, St George's.

\_\_\_\_ (1978). 'The Role of the State in Agriculture', mimeo, ISER, University of the West Indies, IDS, Guyana, May.

Cohan, A.S. (1975). *Theories of Revolution*, London: Nelson.

Colburn, Forrest (1986). *Post Revolutionary Nicaragua: State, Class and the Dilemmas of Agrarian Policy*, Berkeley: University of California.

Conroy, Michael (1990). *The Political Economy of the 1990 Nicaraguan Elections* (draft), Texas.

Corragio, José Luis (1986). *Nicaragua: Revolution and Democracy*, London: Allen and Unwin.

Craig, Susan (ed.) (1982). *Contemporary Caribbean: A Sociological Reader*, Trinidad.

Debray, Regis (1967). *Revolution in the Revolution: Armed Struggle and Political Struggle in Latin America*, New York: Monthly Review.

\_\_\_\_ (1981). *Teachers, Writers, Celebrities: The Intellectuals of Modern France*, London: Verso.

Domínguez, Jorge (1989). *To Make a World Safe for Revolution: Cuba's Foreign Policy*, Cambridge, Mass., London: Harvard University Press.

\_\_\_\_ (ed.) (1982). *Cuba: Internal and International Affairs*, Beverley Hills, London, New Delhi: Sage.

\_\_\_\_ (1978). *Cuba: Order and Revolution*, Cambridge Mass., London: Harvard University Press.

Draper, Theodore (1965). *Castroism: Theory and Practice*, New York, Washington, London: Frederick A. Praeger.

Dumont, René (1974). *Is Cuba Socialist?* London: André Deutsch.

Dunkerley, James (1988). *Power in the Isthmus: A political history of modern Central America*, London: Verso.

Dunn, John (1989). *Modern Revolutions: An Introduction to the Analysis of a Political Phenomenon*, Cambridge: Cambridge University Press.

\_\_\_\_ (1984). *The Politics of Socialism: An Essay in Political Theory*, Cambridge: Cambridge University Press.

Eisenstadt, S. N. (1978). *Revolution and the Transformation of Societies*, New York: The Free Press.

Elsasser, Nan and Nelson Valdés (1989). 'Dancing with Fidel: Santería Gods in Cuba', *Arete*, Vol. 1, no. 6.

Emmanuel, Pat (1978). *Crown Colony Politics in Grenada: 1917–1951*, Barbados: ISER.

_____ (1979). *General Elections in the Eastern Caribbean: A Handbook*, Barbados: ISER.

_____, Farley Braithwaite and Eudine Barriteau (1986). *Political Change and Public Opinion in Grenada: 1979–1984*, Barbados: Institute of Social and Economic Research.

EPICA (1982). *Grenada: The Peaceful Revolution*, Washington, DC.

Fagen, R. R. (1969). *The Transformation of Political Culture in Cuba*: Stanford: Stanford University Press.

_____ , Carmen Diana Deere and José Corragio, (eds) (1986). *Transition and Development: Problems of Third World Socialism*, New York: Monthly Review.

Farhi, Faridah (1988). 'State Disintegration and Urban-Based Revolutionary Crisis: A Comparative Analysis of Iran and Nicaragua', *Comparative Political Studies*, Vol. 21, no. 2, July.

Ferguson, James (1990). *Grenada: Revolution in Reverse*, London: Latin American Bureau.

Feuer, Lewis S. (1969). *Marx and Engels: Basic Writings on Politics and Philosophy*, New York: Fontana.

Franqui, Carlos (1980). *Diary of the Cuban Revolution*, New York: Viking.

_____ (1988). *Vida, Aventuras, Desastres de un Hombre Llamado Castro*, Barcelona: Planeta.

Fukuyama, Francis (1989). 'The End of History?' *The National Interest*, Summer.

Gifford, Tony (1987). *The Grenada Murder Trial: No Case for Hanging*, London: Committee for Human Rights in Grenada.

Gillespie, Richard (ed.) (1990). *Cuba After Thirty Years: Rectification and Revolution*, London: Frank Cass.

Gilmore, William, C. (1984). *The Grenada Intervention: Analysis and Documentation*, London, New York: Mansell.

Goldfrank, Walter (1979). 'Theories of Revolution and Revolution Without Theory', *Theory and Society*, Vol. 7, nos 1 & 2.

Goldenberg, Boris (1965). *The Cuban Revolution and Latin America*, London: Allen & Unwin.

Goldstone, Jack (1979). 'Theories of Revolution: The Third Generation', *World Politics*, No. 32.

González, Eduardo and Ronfeldt David (1986). *Castro, Cuba and the World*, Santa Monica, CA.: Rand Corporation.

González, Edward (1974). *Cuba under Castro: the limits of charisma*, Boston: Houghton Mifflin.

Graham, Hugh D., and Ted Gurr (1969). *Violence in America*, New York: Signet.

Gramsci, Antonio (1970). *Selections from the Prison Notebooks*, New York: International.

_____ (1977). *Selections from Political Writings*, 1910–1920, New York: International.

Guerra y Sánchez, Ramiro (1964). *Sugar and Society in the Caribbean: An Economic History of Cuban Agriculture*, New Haven, London: Yale University Press.

Guevara, Ernesto (1969). *Reminiscences of the Cuban Revolutionary War*, Harmondsworth: Pelican.

Gunn, Gillian (1990). 'Will Castro Fall?', *Foreign Policy*, No. 79, Summer.

Gurr, Ted (1971). *Why Men Rebel*, Princeton: Princeton University Press.

Habel, Janette (1991). *Cuba: The Revolution in peril*, preface by F. Maspero, London: Verso.

Halebsky, S. and J. Kirk (eds) (1985). *Cuba: Twenty Five Years of Revolution: 1959–1984*, New York: Praeger.

Halliday, Fred (1990). *Cold War, Third World: An Essay On Soviet–US Relations*, London, Sydney: Hutchinson-Radius.

Harewood, Jack (1966). 'Population Growth in Grenada in the Twentieth Century', *Social and Economic Studies*, Vol. 15, no. 1, June.

Harris, Richard and Carlos Villas (eds) (1986). *Nicaragua: A Revolution Under Siege*, London: Zed Press.

Hennessy, Alistair (ed.) (1992). *Intellectuals in the 20th Century Caribbean Vol. II, Hispanic and Francophone*, London: Macmillan.

____ and Lambie, George (eds) (1992). *The Fractured Blockade: Western European–Cuban Relations since 1959*, London: Macmillan.

Hermassi, Elbaki (1976). 'Toward a Comparative Study of Revolutions', *Comparative Studies in Society and History*, Vol. 18, no. 2, April.

Hobsbawm, Eric (1970). 'From Social History to the History of Society', *Daedalus*, Vol. 100, no. 1, Winter.

Hodge, Merle and Chris Searle (eds) (1982). *Is Freedom We Making?* Barbados.

Hodges, Donald, C. (1986). *Intellectual Foundations of the Nicaraguan Revolution*, Austin: University of Texas Press.

Holness, Chris (1975). 'The Present Political Situation in Grenada', *Socialism!*, Vol. 2, no. 1, January.

Horowitz, David (1974). *The Rise and Fall of Project Camelot*, Cambridge, Mass.

Horowitz, I. L. (ed.) (1981). *Cuban Communism*, New Brunswick: Transaction Books, 5th edn.

Huberman, L., and Sweezy, Paul M. (1988). *Regis Debray and the Latin American Revolution*, New York: Monthly Review.

Huntington, Samuel (1984). 'Will More Countries Become Democratic?' *Political Science Quarterly*, Vol. 99, no. 2, Summer.

Institute of International Relations (1974). *Independence for Grenada: Myth or Reality?* St Augustine, Trinidad.

Inter-American Commission on Human Rights (1978). *Report on the Human Rights Situation in Nicaragua*, General Secretary, Washington, DC: OAS.

Jacobs, W. Richard (1976). *Butler, vs the King: Riots and Sedition in 1937*, Port of Spain: Key.

____ and Ian Jacobs (1980). *Grenada: The Route to Revolution*, Havana: Cuadernos Casa.

Johnson, Chalmers (1968). *Revolutionary Change*, London: University of London.

Karol, K.S. (1970). *Guerrillas in Power: The Course of the Cuban Revolution*, New York: Hill and Wang.

Kaufman, Michael (1983). *Jamaica Under Manley: Dilemmas of Socialism and Democracy*, London: Zed Press.

Kirton, Claremont (1985). *Public Policy and Private Capital in the Transition to Socialism: Grenada, 1979–1983*, mimeo.

Krejci, Jaroslav (1983). *Great Revolutions Compared: The Search for a Theory*, Brighton: Wheatsheaf.

Knight, Alan (1991). 'Social Revolution: A Latin American Perspective', *Bulletin of Latin American Research*.

LaFeber, Walter (1984). *Inevitable Revolutions: The United States in Central America*, New York, London: Norton.

Landau, Saul (1989). 'Notes on the Cuban revolution', *The Socialist Register*, London.

Layne, Ewart (1990). *Cuba–Grenada Relations and the October Tragedy* (handwritten), St Georges.

Lebon, G. (1913). *The Psychology of Revolution*, New York: Putnam.

Lehmann, David (1990). *Democracy and Development in Latin America*, Cambridge: Polity.

Leogrande, William (1979). 'The Revolution in Nicaragua: Another Cuba?' *Foreign Affairs*, Fall.

Levine, Barry (ed.) (1983). *The New Cuban Presence in the Caribbean*, Boulder: Westview Press.

Lewis, David E. (1984). *Reform and Revolution in Grenada: 1950–1981*, Havana, Casa de las Americas.

Lewis, Gordon K. (1968). *The Growth of the Modern West Indies*, New York, London: Modern Reader.

Liss, Sheldon, B. (1987). *Roots of Revolution: Radical Thought in Cuba*, Lincoln and London: University of Nebraska Press.

Louison, George (1984). 'Interview with George Louison: New Jewel Leader Describes Revolution's Overthrow', *Intercontinental Press*, Vol. 22, no. 7, 16 April.

Lowenthal, Abraham and Samuel Fitch (eds) (1986). *Armies and Politics in Latin America*, New York, London: Holmes and Meier.

Lukes, Steven (1985). *Marxism and Morality*, Oxford, New York: Oxford University Press.

Luxemburg, Rosa (1970). *The Russian Revolution and Leninism or Marxism?*, Ann Arbor, Michigan.

MacGaffey, Wyatt Barnett, Clifford R. (1962). *Cuba: Its People: Its Society: Its Culture*, New Haven: HRAF Press.

MacIntyre, Alasdair, 'Ideology, Social Science and Revolution', Comparative Politics, Vol. 5, no. 3, April 1973.

Mandle, Jay R. (1985). *Big Revolution, Small Country: The Rise and Fall of the Grenada Revolution*, Maryland: The North South Publishing Company.

Marable, Manning (1987). *African and Caribbean Politics: From Kwame Nkrumah to Maurice Bishop*, London: Verso.

Marchetti, Peter (1982). 'Church and Revolution in Nicaragua: An Interview with Peter Marchetti', *Monthly Review*, Vol. 34, no. 2 July/August.

Marshall, Woodville (1968). 'Notes on Peasant Development in the West Indies Since 1838', *Social and Economic Studies*, Vol. 17, no. 3.

Marx, Karl and F. Engels (1975). *Marx Engels: Selected Correspondence*, Moscow: Progress.

Medvedev, Roy (1976). *Let History Judge: The origins and consequences of Stalinism*, London: Spokesman Books for the Bertrand Russell Foundation.

Meeks, Brian (1977). *The Development of the 1970 Revolution in Trinidad and Tobago*, MSC Thesis, UWI, Jamaica.

———— (1988). *Social Formation and People's Revolution: A Grenadian Study*, PhD Thesis, UWI, Jamaica.

Mesa-Lago, Carmelo (1978). *Cuba in the 1970s: Pragmatism and Institutionalization*, Albuquerque: University of New Mexico Press.

———— (1981). *The Economy of Socialist Cuba: A Two-Decade Appraisal*, Albuquerque: University of New Mexico Press.

Mills, Charles (1990). 'Getting Out of the Cave: Tension Between Democracy and

Elitism in Marx's Theory of Cognitive Liberation', *Social and Economic Studies*, Vol. 39, no. 1, March.

Moore, Barrington (1987). *Social Origins of Dictatorship and Democracy*, Harmondsworth: Penguin.

Moore, Carlos (1988). *Castro, the Blacks and Africa*, Berkeley: University of California Press.

Morley, Morris H. (1987). *Imperial State: The United States and Revolution and Cuba, 1952–1986*, Cambridge: Cambridge University Press.

Morrissey, Mike (1983). 'Country Preferences of Schoolchildren in Seven Caribbean Territories', *Caribbean Quarterly*, Vol. 29, nos 3 and 4, September–December.

Munroe, Trevor (1972). The Politics of Constitutional Decolonisation: Jamaica, 1944–1962, Jamaica: ISER.

O'Connor, James (1964). 'On Cuban Political Economy', *Political Science Quarterly*, Vol. 79.

O'Kane, Thish and Elia Kuant (1990). *Nicaragua: Political Parties and Elections 1990*, Working Paper, Managua: CRIES.

O'Shaughnessy, Hugh (1984). *Grenada: Revolution, Invasion and Aftermath*, London: Sphere.

Ortega, Humberto (1981). *Nicaragua: The Strategy of Victory: Interview by Marta Harnecker with Humberto Ortega, Sandinistas Speak*, London: Zed Press.

Oxaal, Ivor (1971). *Race and Revolutionary Consciousness*, Cambridge, Mass., London: Schenkman.

Paige, Jeffrey (1975). *Agrarian Revolution: Social Movements and Export Agriculture in the Underdeveloped World*, New York: Free Press.

Palma, Gabriel (1978). 'Dependency: A Formal Theory of Underdevelopment or a Methodology for the Understanding of Concrete Situations of Underdevelopment?', *World Development*, Vol. 6, nos 7 and 8.

Pastor, Robert (1987). *Condemned to Repetition: The United States and Nicaragua*, Princeton: Princeton University Press.

Payne, Anthony (1990). *Governments, Intellectuals and International Relations: The Politics of the University of the West Indies, 1968–1984*, University of Warwick, Occasional Papers in Caribbean Studies, No. 7.

_____ , Sutton, Paul, and Thorndike, Tony (1984). *Grenada: Revolution and Invasion*, London and Sydney: Croom Helm.

Pearce, Jenny (1981). *Under the Eagle: US Intervention in Central America and the Caribbean*, London: Latin American Bureau.

Pérez, Louis A. (1988). *Cuba: Between Reform and Revolution*, New York: Oxford University Press.

Petras, James (1981). 'Nicaragua: The Transition to a New Society', *Latin American Perspectives*, No. 29, Spring.

Pettee, George (1913). *The Process of Revolution*, New York: Harper and Brothers.

Post, Ken (1978). *Arise Ye Starvelings*, The Hague, Boston, London: Martinus Nijhoff.

Poulantzas, Nicos (1978). *Social Classes and Political Power*, London: Verso.

Pryor, Frederick (1986). *Revolutionary Grenada: A Study in Political Economy*, New York, Westport, London: Praeger.

Reich, Otto and Wayne Smith (1984). 'Commentary on Grenada', *Caribbean Review*, Vol. 13, no. 3, Summer.

Rojas, Don (1984). 'A Revolution Betrayed But Not Destroyed', *Caribbean Perspectives*, Vol. 2, no. 2, Spring.

Rossett, Peter and John Vandermeer (eds) (1983). *The Nicaragua Reader*, New York: Grove.

_____ (eds) (1986). *Nicaragua: Unfinished Revolution: the New Nicaragua Reader*, New York: Grove.

Salert, Barbara (1976). *Revolutions and Revolutionaries: Four Theories*, New York: Elsevier.

Sandiford, Gregory and Richard Vigilante (1984). *Grenada: The Untold Story*, Lanham, New York, London: Madison Books.

Sartre, Jean-Paul (1961). *Sartre on Cuba*, reprinted Westport: Greenwood Press.

Saunders, Richard M. (1985). 'Military Force in the Foreign Policy of the Eisenhower Presidency', *Political Science Quarterly*, Spring.

Scheer, Robert and Zeitlin, Maurice (1964). *Cuba: An American Tragedy*, Harmondsworth: Penguin Books.

Seabury, Paul and Walter McDougal (eds) (1984). *The Grenada Papers*, San Francisco: ICS.

Searle, Chris (1989). Grenada Morning: A Memoir of the '*revo*', London: Karia Press.

_____ (1983). *Grenada: The Struggle Against Destabilisation*, London: Writers and Readers.

Seers, Dudley (ed.) (1964). *Cuba: The Economic and Social Revolution*, Chapel Hill: The University of North Carolina Press.

Shahabuddeen, M. (1986). *The Conquest of Grenada: Sovereignty in the Periphery*, Georgetown: University of Guyana.

Singham, Archie (1968). *The Hero and the Crowd in a Colonial Polity*, New Haven: Yale University Press.

Sklar, Holly (1988). *Washington's War on Nicaragua*, New York: South End Press.

Skocpol, Theda (1977). 'Wallerstein's World Capitalist System: a Theoretical and Historical Critique', *American Journal of Sociology*, Vol. 82, no. 5, March.

_____ (1973). 'A Critical Review of Barrington Moore's Social Origins of Dictatorship and Democracy', *Politics and Society*, Fall. '

_____ (1988). 'Rentier State and Shi'a Islam in the Iranian Revolution', *Theory and Society*, Vol. 11, May.

_____ (1979). *States and Social Revolutions*, Cambridge: Cambridge University Press.

_____ (1988). 'Social Revolutions and Mass Military Mobilization', *World Politics*, Vol. xi, no. 2, January.

Smelser, Neil (1961). *Theory of Collective Behaviour*, London: Routledge and Kegan Paul.

Smith, Michael, G. (1963). *Dark Puritan*, Kingston, Jamaica.

_____ (1965). *The Plural Society in the British West Indies*, Berkeley and Los Angeles: University of California Press.

_____ (1965). *Stratification in Grenada*, Berkeley and Los Angeles: University of California Press.

Smith, Robert, F. (ed.) (1966). *Background to Revolution: The Development of Modern Cuba*, New York: Knopf.

Spackman, Ann (1975). *Constitutional Development of the West Indies: 1922–1968*, Caribbean Universities Press/Bowker.

Spalding, Rose J. (ed.) (1987). *The Political Economy of Revolutionary Nicaragua*, Boston, Mass., London: Allen and Unwin.

Stubbs, Jean (1990). *Cuba: The Test of Time*, London: Latin American Bureau.

Szulc, Tad (1986). *Fidel: A Critical Portrait*, New York: Avon.

Taylor, Stan (1984). *Social Science and Revolutions*, London: Macmillan.

Thomas, Clive Y. (1986). *The Rise of the Authoritarian State in Peripheral Societies*, New York: Monthly Review.

_____ (1987). *The Next Time Around: Radical Options and Caribbean Economy*, mimeo, First Conference of Caribbean Economists, Kingston, Jamaica.

Thomas, Hugh (1971). *Cuba, or the Pursuit of Freedom*, London: Eyre and Spottiswoode.

Thorndike, Tony (1985). *Grenada: Politics, Economics and Society*, London: Frances Pinter.

Tilly, Charles (1978). *From Mobilization to Revolution*, New York, Addison-Wesley.

Trimberger, Ellen Kay (1978). *Revolution from Above: Military Bureaucrats and Development in Japan, Turkey, Egypt, Peru*, New Brunswick, New Jersey: Transaction.

Unger, Roberto, M. (1987). *False Necessity: Anti-Necessitarian Theory in the Service of Radical Democracy*, Cambridge: Cambridge University Press.

United States Senate (1976). Select Committee on Intelligence Activities: Covert Action, Washington, DC: US Government Printing Office.

Verdes, Leroux, Jeanne (1987). *La lune et le caudillo: le rêve des intellectuals et le régime Cubain (1959–71)*, Paris: L'Arpenteur.

Valenta, Jiri and Esperanza Durán (eds) (1987). *Conflict in Nicaragua: A Multi-Dimensional Perspective*, Boston, Mass., London: Allen and Unwin.

Valenta, Jiri and Herbert Ellison (eds) (1984). *Soviet Cuban Strategy in the Third World After Grenada: Toward Preventing Future Grenadas*, Washington, DC: Wilson Centre.

Vilas, Carlos (1986). *The Sandinista Revolution: National Liberation and Social Transformation in Central America*, New York: Monthly Review.

Wallerstein, Immanuel (1984). *The Politics of the World Economy*, Cambridge: Cambridge University Press.

_____ , Terrence Hopkins and Giovanni Arrighi (1989). *Antisystemic Movements*, London: Verso.

Walton, John (1984). *Reluctant Rebels: Comparative Studies of Revolution and Underdevelopment*, New York: Columbia.

Weber, Henri (1981). *Nicaragua: The Sandinist Revolution*, London: NLB.

West, W. Gordon (1986). *Vigilancia Revolucionaria: A Nicaraguan Policing Resolution to the Contradiction Between Public and Private*, mimeo.

Wolf, Eric (1971). *Peasant Wars of the Twentieth Century*, London: Faber and Faber.

Wright-Mills, C. (1960). *Listen Yankee, The Revolution in Cuba*, New York: Ballantine Books.

# Index